PAUL

AS A PROBLEM IN HISTORY
AND CULTURE

PAUL

AS A PROBLEM IN HISTORY AND CULTURE

The Apostle and His Critics through the Centuries

PATRICK GRAY

BakerAcademic

a division of Baker Publishing Group
Grand Rapids, Michigan

Published by Baker Academic
a division of Baker Publishing Group
P.O. Box 6287, Grand Rapids, MI 49516-6287
www.bakeracademic.com

Printed in the United States of America

Library of Congress Cataloging-in-Publication Data

Names: Gray, Patrick, 1970–
Title: Paul as a problem in history and culture : the apostle and his critics through the centuries / Patrick Gray.
Description: Grand Rapids, MI : Baker Academic, 2016. | Includes bibliographical references and index.
Identifiers: LCCN 2015037190 | ISBN 9780801048838 (cloth)
Subjects: LCSH: Paul, the Apostle, Saint.
Classification: LCC BS2506.3 .G73 2016 | DDC 225.9/2—dc23 LC record available at http://lccn .loc.gov/2015037190

16 17 18 19 20 21 22   7 6 5 4 3 2 1

Contents

Part 2: Anti-Pauline Contexts, Subtexts, and Pretexts

ACKNOWLEDGMENTS

A number of friends and colleagues have contributed (knowingly or unknowingly) to the writing of this book. For their encouragement in this project and for reading drafts, making suggestions, feigning interest, answering queries, and supplying sources, I want to thank James Ernest, Dave Mason, Mark Muesse, John Murray, Tim Huebner, Dan Ullucci, John Kaltner, Steven McKenzie, Courtney Collins, Steve St. John, David Vishanoff, Brent Johnson, Larry Wright, and Abbey Judd. Wells Turner and the rest of the staff at Baker also provided valuable guidance as I prepared the manuscript for publication. To Rhodes College I owe a debt of gratitude, not only for the support provided by the administration but also for the opportunity to teach the outstanding students who come here. Finally, I am thankful for Alex, Lily, Joseph, and Dominic, for their love and encouragement.

ABBREVIATIONS

General

BCE	before the Common Era	NT	New Testament
CE	Common Era	OT	Old Testament

Old Testament

Gen.	Genesis	Song of Sol.	Song of Solomon
Exod.	Exodus	Isa.	Isaiah
Lev.	Leviticus	Jer.	Jeremiah
Num.	Numbers	Lam.	Lamentations
Deut.	Deuteronomy	Ezek.	Ezekiel
Josh.	Joshua	Dan.	Daniel
Judg.	Judges	Hosea	Hosea
Ruth	Ruth	Joel	Joel
1–2 Sam.	1–2 Samuel	Amos	Amos
1–2 Kings	1–2 Kings	Obad.	Obadiah
1–2 Chron.	1–2 Chronicles	Jon.	Jonah
Ezra	Ezra	Mic.	Micah
Neh.	Nehemiah	Nah.	Nahum
Esther	Esther	Hab.	Habakkuk
Job	Job	Zeph.	Zephaniah
Ps(s).	Psalm(s)	Hag.	Haggai
Prov.	Proverbs	Zech.	Zechariah
Eccles.	Ecclesiastes	Mal.	Malachi

New Testament

Matt.	Matthew	Luke	Luke
Mark	Mark	John	John

Acts	Acts	Titus	Titus
Rom.	Romans	Philem.	Philemon
1–2 Cor.	1–2 Corinthians	Heb.	Hebrews
Gal.	Galatians	James	James
Eph.	Ephesians	1–2 Pet.	1–2 Peter
Phil.	Philippians	1–3 John	1–3 John
Col.	Colossians	Jude	Jude
1–2 Thess.	1–2 Thessalonians	Rev.	Revelation
1–2 Tim.	1–2 Timothy		

Other Ancient Sources

b.	Babylonian Talmud
C. Galil.	Julian, *Contra Galilaeos*
Hist. eccl.	Eusebius, *Historia ecclesiastica*
Hom.	*Pseudo-Clementine Homilies*
Rec.	*Pseudo-Clementine Recognitions*

INTRODUCTION

A Thorn in the Flesh

Hollywood is normally the last place one looks for penetrating analysis of complicated social, religious, or cultural questions. While its moving pictures may be worth thousands of words, film is primarily a visual medium and as such has a limited capacity for argument or explanation. It excels in creating impressions, moods, and emotions. Yet like the proverbial stopped clock that still gives the correct time twice a day, Hollywood occasionally cuts right to the heart of the matter, rendering in a compelling fashion the very impressions, moods, and emotions evoked by a complex issue.

One such instance is found in the 1988 film *The Last Temptation of Christ*, directed by Martin Scorsese. Mel Gibson's *The Passion of the Christ* generated considerable debate before and after its release in 2004, but the controversy that swirled around Scorsese's production was just as great. Debate about *The Passion of the Christ* focused on negative portrayals of Jewish characters. With *The Last Temptation of Christ*, the matter was much more primal: sex. During a dream sequence Jesus imagines living an ordinary life and growing old rather than dying on the cross. One scene in the dream depicts Jesus consummating his marriage to Mary Magdalene. After Mary dies, he marries Mary of Bethany, commits adultery with her sister Martha, and fathers children by both women. Audiences were none too pleased, and widespread protests accompanied the theatrical release. One could perhaps contemplate the offending scenes as an imaginative exploration of the doctrine of the incarnation—what does it mean that, in Jesus, God became a human being, and what, exactly, is entailed by the biblical claim that Jesus "in every respect has

1

been tested as we are, yet without sin" (Heb. 4:15)?—but the graphic image of Jesus engaged in sexual intercourse crossed a line with many viewers in the United States and overseas.[1]

Largely overlooked in the commotion was a different scene, one equally provocative, one could argue, as the scene with Mary Magdalene. Near the conclusion, Jesus visits a village where he hears a man preaching to a small crowd gathered in the street. The man is Paul of Tarsus. Jesus confronts him when he is finished and claims that Paul's "gospel" about the death and resurrection of Jesus is a fiction. Paul continues the conversation when Jesus says that "the world can't be saved by lies." Paul disagrees, insisting that the "Jesus" he preaches is much more powerful than the real thing: "I make [the truth] out of longing and faith. . . . If it's necessary to crucify you to save the world, then I'll crucify you! And I'll resurrect you, too, whether you like it or not."

Like the rest of the film, the scene is adapted from the novel of the same name by Nikos Kazantzakis, first published in Greek in 1955. In the novel, the clash with Jesus and the negative portrait of Paul are even more pronounced. Shortly after marrying Jesus, Mary Magdalene is killed by a mob led by a preconversion Saul, described as a squat, fat, bald hunchback with crooked legs. "Shut your shameless mouth!" Paul tells Jesus when he denies being the Son of God. Jesus calls him "son of Satan" when he says that, facts be damned, he will not stop proclaiming Jesus as the Messiah. "What is 'truth' [after all]?" Paul asks, echoing the infamous question of Pontius Pilate (John 18:38). He laughs at Jesus's objections:

> Shout all you want. I'm not afraid of you. I don't even need you any more. The wheel you set in motion has gathered momentum: who can control it now? . . . Joseph the Carpenter of Nazareth did not beget you; I begot you—I, Paul the scribe from Tarsus in Cilicia. . . . I have no need of your permission. Why do you stick your nose in my affairs?[2]

As Jesus weeps in despair, Paul bids him farewell and says, more cheerfully, "It's been a delight meeting you. I've freed myself, and that's just what I wanted: to get rid of you. Well, I did get rid of you and now I'm free; I'm my own boss." Scenes such as this one no doubt help to explain why the novel was condemned by the Greek Orthodox Church and placed on the Index of

---

1. For discussion of the film's portrayal of Jesus, see Baugh, *Imaging the Divine*, 51–71. The controversy surrounding the film is discussed by Baugh in "Martin Scorsese's *The Last Temptation of Christ*"; see also Lindlof, *Hollywood under Siege*.

2. Kazantzakis, *Last Temptation of Christ*, 477–78. The image of Jesus setting the wheel of history in motion only to lose control of it may be borrowed from Schweitzer, *Quest of the Historical Jesus*, 370–71.

Forbidden Books by the Vatican in 1954—even before it was published in Greek the following year.[3]

Life imitates art. In this instance, it works in the opposite direction, with the art of Kazantzakis and Scorsese imitating a particular slice of life. The scene dramatizes a long-standing argument about Paul's legacy that continues to the present day. The question that has roiled a wide range of thinkers can be put very succinctly: Who founded Christianity, Jesus or Paul? To most observers the answer seems obvious. Who else but *Christ* could have founded *Christianity*? During the nineteenth century, an increasing number of historians and theologians begin to credit Paul with a formative role in the course of Christian history even more profound than that of Jesus. In the meantime, not only scholars but popular authors and public figures as well have taken part in the debate, consistently lamenting the degree to which Christian theology amounts to little more than "a series of footnotes to St. Paul."[4] Hazel Motes, the backwoods preacher in Flannery O'Connor's *Wise Blood*, starts the "Church without Christ" for others like him who are alienated from traditional Christianity. Undaunted by the difficulty in imagining it, prospective members of the Church without Paul are by no means in short supply in the modern world.

The list of those who have weighed in on the matter is long and illustrious, including philosophers, poets, professors, playwrights, psychologists, and politicians. In his 1854 diary Søren Kierkegaard writes that the Protestantism of his day is "completely untenable" because it is "a revolution brought about by proclaiming 'the Apostle' (Paul) at the expense of the Master (Christ)."[5] George Bernard Shaw remarks with characteristic aplomb, "No sooner had Jesus knocked over the dragon of superstition than Paul boldly set it on its legs again. . . . He does nothing that Jesus would have done, and says nothing that Jesus would have said."[6] Shaw's friend H. G. Wells is no less displeased with Paul because he "imposed upon or substituted another doctrine for . . . the plain and profoundly revolutionary teachings of Jesus."[7] According to Alfred North Whitehead, the man who "did more than anybody else to distort and subvert Christ's teaching" was the same man about whom Robert Frost has a character in his blank verse dialogue *A Masque of Mercy* announce,

3. See Antonakes, "Christ, Kazantzakis, and Controversy in Greece."

4. Meeks, "Christian Proteus," 689, quoting Sydney E. Ahlstrom.

5. Rohde, *Diary of Søren Kierkegaard*, 172.

6. G. B. Shaw, "Prospects of Christianity," xcix–c. "There is not one word of Pauline Christianity in the characteristic utterances of Jesus" (ibid., c).

7. Wells, *Outline of History*, 952. "What Jesus preached was a new birth of the human soul; what Paul preached was the ancient religion of priest and altar and the propitiatory bloodshed" (511).

"Paul: he's in the Bible too. He is the fellow who theologized Christ almost out of Christianity. Look out for him."[8] Carl Jung is "frankly disappoint[ed] to see how Paul hardly ever allows the real Jesus of Nazareth to get a word in."[9] Friedrich Nietzsche likewise asserts that there would be no Christianity without Paul, who embodies "the opposite type to that of the life of the 'bringer of glad tidings.'"[10]

What is there to commend the idea that Paul is the true founder of Christianity? He is perhaps the earliest figure whose writings the church saw fit to preserve for posterity, earlier even than the Gospels. He was not only a man of ideas but also a man of action, founding a number of communities in leading Roman cities. It is easy to take this for granted—starting churches is what missionaries do, after all. But if he had simply delivered the good news to individuals without forming them into groups, the new religion might not have had any staying power. A movement that is fundamentally social in nature, moreover, is very different from one that consists of "the feelings, acts, and experiences of individual men in their solitude," in William James's famous definition of religion.[11] Furthermore, these communities were composed largely of gentiles, a demographic fact of immense theological significance for the development of a movement honoring the memory of a man who once told a non-Jewish woman that he was sent "only to the lost sheep of the house of Israel" (Matt. 15:24). By any reckoning Paul was the most influential champion of gentile inclusion. Finally, any number of signal Christian doctrines can be traced to Paul's writings. Sin, salvation, faith, the end times, the Holy Spirit, the church—the church's views on these and many other concepts would be unrecognizable without the Pauline stamp they bear.

While the notion that Paul founded Christianity should not be rejected out of hand as patently ridiculous, neither is it as self-evident as its proponents seem to think. Paul may be the earliest Christian writer, but he indicates that the movement was already up and running by the time he stopped persecuting it and became a member. He claims to be handing on traditions that he has received from others, not introducing novel teachings. Furthermore, as the ardently pro-Paul author of the Acts of the Apostles indicates, he is not the first follower of Jesus to reach out to non-Jews. And it should not count for nothing that very few Christians—and even then, only very recently—have ever thought of Paul as the founder of their faith. That title is reserved for

8. Whitehead, *Dialogues*, 307; Frost, *Masque of Mercy*, 8. Whitehead adds: "It would be impossible to imagine anything more un-Christlike than Christian theology."

9. Jung, "Psychological Approach to the Dogma of the Trinity," 153.

10. Nietzsche, *Antichrist*, 617 (§42).

11. James, *Varieties of Religious Experience*, 31.

Jesus. It may not be found in Scripture or in any of the historic creeds, but most Christians of most times and places reserve that title for Jesus.

Who deserves the title? Answering this question is not as straightforward as it may seem. It may be the case that key terms in the debate, such as "founder" and "Christianity," are not defined with sufficient clarity to yield a single correct answer. But this observation is hardly satisfying. Semantics are only one variable in a more complicated equation. There is something other than purely objective historical investigation going on in the various attempts to solve it. When it is said that Paul is the founder of Christianity, much more is implied than that a particular name belongs in a particular box on an organizational flowchart. Neither is giving the title to Jesus free of historical and theological presuppositions. Because Jesus is the default choice, however, it is clear that Paul's "advocates" are trying to say something more. Indeed, they are saying more, and usually more than they realize. To call them Paul's advocates, of course, is a bit misleading since they are certainly not his defenders. Almost without exception, to refer to Paul as the founder of Christianity is to pay him a backhanded compliment.

This is just one of many ways to register one's protest against the outsized impact Paul has had on the church and, through the church, the rest of the world. Criticism of Paul is almost as old as Christianity itself, but it can be found with increasing frequency over the past two centuries. The sources from which it issues can be surprising. According to Adolf Hitler, "The decisive falsification of Jesus's doctrine was the work of St. Paul," who "used his doctrine to mobilize the criminal underworld and thus organize a proto-Bolshevism."[12] David Ben-Gurion, the first prime minister of the State of Israel, comments that while "Jesus probably differed little from many other Jews of his generation," it was Paul's "anti-Jewish emphasis" that "gave Christianity a new direction."[13] According to Sayyid Qutb, who deeply influenced Osama bin Laden and has been called "the philosopher of Islamic terror," Paul's preaching "infected" Christianity from the beginning because it was "adulterated by the residues of Roman mythology and Greek philosophy."[14] And when Mahatma Gandhi explains, "I draw a great distinction between the Sermon on the Mount and the Letters of Paul," he leaves little doubt as to which one he prefers.[15] Who would have guessed that a loathing for Paul is the one tune that this unlikely quartet would sing in harmony?

12. Trevor-Roper, *Hitler's Secret Conversations*, 63, 117–18.
13. Ben-Gurion, *Israel*, xviii.
14. Qutb, *Islam*, 37–38.
15. Gandhi, "Discussion on Fellowship," 461–64 (quote on 464). He adds, "They are a graft on Christ's teaching, his own gloss apart from Christ's own experience" (464).

Consider the tone in addition to the substance of the accusations directed his way. Prolific poet and translator Stephen Mitchell calls Paul "the greatest and yet the most misleading of the earliest Christian writers." Although there are things he admires about the apostle,

> in a spiritual sense, he was very unripe. The narrow-minded, fire-breathing, self-tormenting Saul was still alive and kicking inside him. He didn't understand Jesus at all. He wasn't even *interested* in Jesus. . . . We can feel in the writings of Paul the Christian some of the same egotism, superstition, and intolerance that marred the character of Saul the Pharisee.[16]

No less ambivalent is the Lebanese author Kahlil Gibran, the best-selling poet of the twentieth century and posthumous favorite of the 1960s counterculture. Gibran describes Paul as "a strange man" whose soul is "not the soul of a free man." Jesus "taught man how to break the chains of his bondage that he might be free from his yesterdays," but Paul "is forging chains for the man of tomorrow. He would strike with his own hammer upon the anvil in the name of one whom he does not know."[17] In *The Fire Next Time*, James Baldwin says that "the real architect of the Christian church was not the disreputable, sun-baked Hebrew who gave it his name but the mercilessly fanatical and self-righteous St. Paul," who, "with a most unusual and stunning exactness, described himself as a 'wretched man.'"[18] Such comments reveal a personal animus that is difficult to ignore.

Perhaps the unkindest cut of all, at least from a modern perspective, is to say that Paul takes himself and everything else too seriously. John Knox tries to put it gently:

> We look in vain for any sign of humor in Paul's letters. He would have been both happier and wiser if he could sometimes have laughed at and with himself and at and with others; perhaps he did, but surely not often enough, since in that case at least an occasional chuckle would have found its way into his letters.[19]

Artistic renderings of the apostle reinforce this impression: Paul does not know how to smile.

16. Mitchell, *Gospel according to Jesus*, 41–42, emphasis original.
17. Gibran, *Jesus the Son of Man*, 61–62.
18. Baldwin, *Fire Next Time*, 32, 58.
19. Knox, *Chapters in the Life of Paul*, 87. Jakob Jónsson (*Humour and Irony*, 223–42) identifies a number of humorous elements in Paul's letters. It would likely do little to change Knox's mind since the most common are sarcasm and mockery of beliefs he does not share—not the most endearing of traits.

Maybe Paul should be excused for being a killjoy because it is not his fault. Tantalized by his enigmatic reference to a "thorn in the flesh" in 2 Cor. 12:7, scholars have speculated that Paul was afflicted by migraines, epilepsy, a speech impediment, rival teachers, demonic possession, persecution by Satan, repressed homosexual urges, frustrated heterosexual desires, astigmatism, bipolar disorder, the evil eye, a nagging wife, psychic trauma, chronic fatigue, unrequited love, earaches, hearing loss, persistent hiccups, gangrene, arthritis, Maltese fever, sciatica, gout, malaria, ringworm, low self-esteem, depression, and leprosy—and this is only a partial list.[20] With so many hardships, one supposes, it is no wonder he was so unpleasant. Browsing through these theories, based for the most part on the thinnest slivers of evidence, one occasionally senses a measure of schadenfreude that is poorly concealed.

Whatever it was, Paul famously lamented this "thorn in the flesh" as something that disturbed and distressed him and would not go away. As one of the most significant figures in the history of Western civilization, Paul has influenced and inspired countless individuals and institutions. He has also proven to be a thorn in the side of many others. This book is about Paul and those who regard him as a problem, indeed, the most nettlesome problem of the past two thousand years. Everyone loves Jesus, it seems, but Paul is another matter. As often as not, his contributions are treated as unfortunate detours from the way, the truth, and the life of Jesus. Who is the true founder of Christianity, and would a world without Paul look radically different? Given the multitude of variables involved, a resolution to this perennial debate will for the foreseeable future continue to elude those who take part in it. The approach taken here is neither to join the chorus of Paul's critics nor to mount a full-fledged defense but, rather, to report on the participants and to take note of the attitudes and assumptions at work. Since those who hate him—not entirely unlike those who love him—do so for radically different and even diametrically opposed reasons, it may be that the controversy divulges less about Paul than about his detractors and their contexts.

Determining what constitutes anti-Paulinism can admittedly be a bit arbitrary. Part of the difficulty has to do, in the first place, with identifying the proper object of criticism. Does Acts supply reliable information, or should it be treated with extreme skepticism? Is "Paul" to be found in all thirteen letters attributed to him in the NT or only in the seven undisputed letters (Romans, 1–2 Corinthians, Galatians, Philippians, 1 Thessalonians, and Philemon)? Quite apart from his deeds, it is no less of a challenge to limit one's focus to

20. Mullins, "Paul's Thorn in the Flesh"; Hisey and Beck, "Paul's 'Thorn in the Flesh'"; Leary, "'Thorn in the Flesh'"; and Jegher-Bucher, "Pfahl im Fleisch."

his words. J. W. C. Wand learned this lesson when he wrote *What St. Paul Said* (1952) and later deemed it necessary to write a follow-up, *What St. Paul Really Said* (1968), a title subsequently borrowed by N. T. Wright for his own contribution to the topic (1997). Sensing that the matter was not as simple as listening to "what Paul said" and that someone had to cut this Gordian knot, Gary Wills followed these works with his own—*What Paul Meant* (2006).

The guiding principle in the following pages is to err on the side of inclusivity if only because Paul's critics do not always discriminate between "the real Paul" and, for lack of a better word, "the ersatz Paul." Sorting out genuine anti-Paulinism from would-be anti-Paulinism on such a basis, moreover, would be to beg the question. That is to say, discovering "the real Paul" is a very difficult task about which very smart people disagree mightily. Accordingly, I will approach criticism of Paul as a wide-ranging, multifarious phenomenon and pay close attention to how this criticism is expressed in his critics' own words. How they say it can convey as much as what they say. While it may be difficult to formulate a precise definition of anti-Paulinism, most people know it when they see it.

That Jerome in preparing the Vulgate rendered Paul's "thorn" into Latin as *stimulus* seems all too fitting in light of his nearly unparalleled capacity to provoke. (Daniel Kirk takes a more diplomatic tack, stating that Paul is "a challenging and theologically generative partner along the way of following Jesus.")[21] Intellectual histories often attend primarily to scholarly responses to such provocations, even though scholars have a limited influence on the general public, much to the chagrin of many scholars. "Popular" interpretations produced by those with no special training in biblical studies deserve a place in any worthy survey of this history. In any event, the distinction between scholarly and popular interpretations of Paul should not be drawn too sharply. A number of intellectuals have held enormous sway in worldly affairs for good and ill, if only from the grave. And no matter how thick the walls, those inside the academy are never entirely insulated from the winds that blow outside. An exhaustive history of the ways in which Paul has been interpreted—be it sympathetically, suspiciously, reverently, blasphemously, politically, artistically, or any other way—is obviously beyond the scope of any single volume.[22] The present volume makes no such attempt at comprehensiveness. Its focus will instead be on a narrower segment of this vast body

21. Kirk, *Jesus Have I Loved, but Paul?*, 3.
22. Surveys include Schweitzer, *Paul and His Interpreters*; Bultmann, "Zur Geschichte der Paulus-Forschung"; Ellis, *Paul and His Recent Interpreters*; Wiles, *Divine Apostle*; Merk, "Paulus-Forschung, 1936–1985"; Furnish, "Pauline Studies"; Hafemann, "Paul and His Interpreters"; Seesengood, *Paul*; and Westerholm, *Blackwell Companion to Paul*, 299–604.

of material—those writers who take a dim view of Paul—though even this niche turns out not to be so narrow after all.

The following chapters are divided between two parts. Part 1 ("Anti-Paulinism through the Centuries") provides a roughly chronological survey of the ways in which Paul has bewitched, bothered, and bewildered people over the centuries, both inside and outside the traditional precincts of the church. Chapter 1 ("The First Hundred Years") looks back to the NT and the earliest evidence for negative perceptions of Paul. As it turns out, his own letters provide the clearest indication that he faced opposition, and his defensiveness concerning his status as an apostle suggests that doubts about his relationship with Jesus are present from the outset of his ministry. Chapter 2 ("The Premodern Era") traces the trajectory of this criticism as it develops among Jewish and non-Jewish observers and takes a new form with the rise of Islam in the medieval period. Paul assumes a large role in the Reformation and its aftermath, and the different attitudes toward his writings that emerge alongside new approaches to the study of early Christianity in the early modern period are discussed in chapter 3 ("The Enlightenment and Beyond"). Chapter 4 ("The Nineteenth Century") treats this increasingly hostile narrative against the Enlightenment backdrop of shifting theological convictions and trends in the academic discipline of biblical studies. Chapter 5 ("Yesterday and Today") follows the procession of notable participants in this ongoing argument into the twentieth century and up to the present, sampling opinions on offer not only inside the academy but in popular discourse as well.

Part 2 ("Anti-Pauline Contexts, Subtexts, and Pretexts") expands on a number of particular topics and themes that arise at various points in the history of anti-Paulinism detailed in part 1. Paul continues to have a complicated relationship with Jews and Muslims. The legacy of anti-Semitism has led many scholars to reevaluate Paul, who frequently receives the blame for centuries of hostility that culminate with the Holocaust. Postwar treatments of this question and of Paul's role in the "parting of the ways" between Judaism and Christianity, along with contemporary Muslim expressions of anti-Paulinism, are the subject of chapter 6 ("In the Tents of Shem"). Chapter 7 ("Jesus versus Paul") considers the rhetorical parallels between comparisons of Jesus and Paul and the contrast between "religion" and "spirituality." Many critics implicitly rely on hypothetical arguments about what a world without Paul might look like. Chapter 8 ("A World without Paul?") thus attempts to situate criticism of Paul and claims about his role in the origins of Christianity within the context of counterfactual history, an approach to understanding the past that is as controversial inside the academy as it is popular in the wider culture. Chapter 9 ("Not by Paul Alone") examines other figures who have been nominated for the title of founder and the critical issues their candidacies raise. Whether the arguments and anxieties about the respective roles of Jesus and Paul are unique to Christianity or shared with other major world religions and figures such as Muhammad, Confucius, and Moses is the subject of chapter 10 ("From Jesus to Paul").

PART 1

Anti-Paulinism through the Centuries

1

THE FIRST HUNDRED YEARS

The Problem of Paul in the New Testament

Criticism of Paul shoots up during the Enlightenment and reaches full bloom in the centuries following it. The view of Paul as the betrayer of the movement started by Jesus is one species of this broader ideological genus. Less appreciated is the lengthy germination process preceding its recent flourishing. Buds and sprouts of varying robustness and tenacity appear sporadically, sometimes being weeded out and sometimes going dormant until a more hospitable season. Later anti-Paulinism derives from a surprisingly ancient stock, the seeds of which can be found as early as the first century. This chapter will survey the diverse forms this hardy perennial takes in the earliest surviving evidence: the NT. On the surface and lurking just underneath, the NT itself reveals a remarkable amount of material indicating that Paul was not universally admired. His teachings, his manner of life, and his personality are all called into question implicitly or explicitly in a wide range of texts. From the outset, Paul evokes strong reactions from everyone he encounters.

The Acts of the Apostles

The author of the Acts of the Apostles is writing some time later than the figure he portrays as one of the heroes of his narrative.[1] Although his historical

---

1. Acts has been dated as early as the mid-60s and as late as ca. 130; see Fitzmyer, *Acts of the Apostles*, 51–55.

reliability has been called into question, much of his testimony accords with the testimony of Paul's own letters and parallels many of the criticisms made in later centuries. The apostle Paul becomes a problem, it seems, even before he becomes the apostle Paul. Christians surely viewed him with fear and trembling, if not hatred and disgust, when he was persecuting them, though no contemporaneous record of this opinion survives.[2] One suspects that trepidation about this former persecutor may have lingered among Christians, if only for a short while (Acts 9:21, 26). No sooner does he join the Christians than he is targeted for harassment, receiving death threats from Jews and Hellenists alike (9:23, 29; 13:50; 14:2, 19). His general attitude toward the law of Moses and, in particular, his liberal stance on the necessity of circumcision is what irks his Jewish critics most.[3] (To his likely surprise and chagrin, in Acts 16:3 Timothy learns that Paul's position on the latter is not hard and fast.) He is a pest and a rabble-rouser, apt to disturb the peace in ways that cause trouble for the Jews (24:5). Hints that Paul does not always get along well with others may also be detected (15:39). Many gentiles have a more favorable impression of Paul, but much more typical is the response of the Roman procurator Festus: "You are out of your mind" (26:24). The Greek philosophers with whom he debates in Athens scoff at the same thing, that is, his bizarre insistence on the resurrection of Jesus (17:18–20, 32; cf. 24:20–21; 25:18–19). Demetrius and his fellow silversmiths in Ephesus have more philistine complaints: Paul's preaching has turned so many people away from idol worship that the silversmiths' profit margin has shrunk (19:23–27).

The Pauline Letters

The letters complement this picture on several points. They may even provide the names of some of Paul's earliest critics.[4] Repeated references to the

---

2. All references to his infamous past appear in the Pauline literature or in Acts (Acts 7:58; 8:3; 9:1–5, 13–14; 22:4–5; 26:9–11; 1 Cor. 15:9; Gal. 1:13, 23; Phil. 3:6; 1 Tim. 1:12–15). In a collection of legends from late antiquity, Paul appears at the head of the party that arrests Jesus before his crucifixion; see Piovanelli, "Exploring the Ethiopic *Book of the Cock*."

3. Acts 15:1–2, 5; 18:12–13; 21:27–28; 25:7–8. Jewish resistance is elsewhere attributed to jealousy of Paul's missionary success (13:45; 17:5). Medieval readers tend to exaggerate Jewish opposition to Paul, as Seesengood notes (*Paul*, 140–41), but it is hardly the case that they invent it out of whole cloth.

4. Hymenaeus and Alexander (1 Tim. 1:20), and possibly Phygelus and Hermogenes (2 Tim. 1:15). Alexander in 1 Timothy may be the same person as Alexander the coppersmith who does Paul "great harm" and "strongly opposed [his] message" in 2 Tim. 4:14–15. Hymenaeus is mentioned again, with Philetus, in 2 Tim. 2:17–18 as espousing a problematic understanding of the resurrection. Even scholars who regard the Pastoral Epistles as inauthentic

opposition he encounters, whether violent or not, and the defensive tone he frequently adopts suggest that Paul was a polarizing figure from an early period.[5] In adopting the slogan "Christ crucified," Paul is fully aware that his central message will meet with disapproval from virtually every conceivable direction (1 Cor. 1:23). It is "a stumbling block to Jews and foolishness to Gentiles." Information from the letters can be divided into two categories: evidence of (1) personal attacks on Paul's character, missionary modus operandi, or personality; and evidence of (2) theological or ideological criticism of his teaching.[6]

1. Nowhere is the ad hominem nature of first-century anti-Paulinism more evident than in 2 Corinthians. That Paul and his Corinthian correspondents have a fraught relationship is clear from numerous comments (2:1–3; 7:5). With access to only one side of the conversation, it is still possible to learn a great deal about the negative impression Paul created among many of his contemporaries. He could come across as indecisive and lacking in gravitas (1:17; 11:16; cf. 1 Cor. 2:2–5). Given his remarks in 2 Cor. 10:1, it appears that he cuts a much less imposing figure in person than in his letters. "His letters are weighty and strong," they say, "but his bodily presence is weak, and his speech contemptible" (10:10). He mentions his lack of training as a public speaker, a shortcoming that may have been accentuated through comparison with other teachers who arrived in Corinth during his absence (11:5–6). The Corinthians, perhaps underwhelmed by his lackluster rhetorical performance, want proof that Christ is speaking in Paul (13:3; cf. 1 Cor. 7:40). For this reason, his boasting is perplexing and perturbing to some members of the community (2 Cor. 10:8). Paul's response—more boasting (1:12; 10:15; 11:10, 16–18, 21, 30; 12:1, 5–6, 9)—may not have endeared him to everyone in Corinth.[7]

Also apparent are questions about Paul's integrity and the legitimacy of his ministry. Itinerant preachers customarily presented letters of recommendation upon arriving at a new locale, and Paul addresses murmurs about his failure to conform to this practice (2 Cor. 3:1; cf. Acts 28:21). He rejects the insinuation that he has somehow overstepped his authority in his dealings with the Corinthians (2 Cor. 10:14). His insistence in 1:12 that he always has spoken with frankness and sincerity and his explicit remarks in 12:16 indicate that

---

often concede that these names may belong to real opponents of Paul during his lifetime, if only added for the sake of biographical verisimilitude; see Dibelius and Conzelmann, *Pastoral Epistles*, 127.

5. E.g., 1 Cor. 4:4–5; 16:9; 2 Cor. 4:8–11; 6:4–5; 11:23–25; 12:10; Gal. 6:17.

6. It is important to keep in mind that not all of Paul's erstwhile "opponents"—those whom he attacks in his letters—would have necessarily seen themselves as such. On the methodological issues involved, see Sumney, "Studying Paul's Opponents."

7. On Paul's boasting in its ancient context, see Forbes, "Comparison, Self-Praise, and Irony."

someone has accused him of duplicity.[8] Intimations that Paul was accused of being dishonest or disingenuous are likewise found in his declarations that he is telling the truth and not lying (Rom. 9:1; 2 Cor. 11:31; Gal. 1:20; 1 Tim. 2:7). These criticisms may have originated with a small group of opponents in Corinth or with the opponents to whom he refers, perhaps sarcastically, as "super-apostles" (*hyperlian apostoloi*: 2 Cor. 11:5; 12:11).[9] The vehemence of Paul's rejoinders, however, bespeaks a fear on his part that they are gaining traction in the larger congregation.

Perhaps the strangest element for many readers to encounter is the suspicion of Paul's refusal to accept financial support from his converts, a policy he adopts in his dealings with the Thessalonians as well (2 Cor. 11:7–8; 12:13; cf. 1 Thess. 2:9; 2 Thess. 3:7–9). This criticism is related to the collection he is taking up for the poor in Jerusalem, which is drawing blame (2 Cor. 8:20–21). When he brings the matter up in 2 Cor. 12:16, the picture comes into clearer focus in a way that resonates with many modern readers: they may believe that the "collection" is a scam designed to line his pockets. To those who are maligning him, he emphatically replies, "We have wronged no one, we have corrupted no one, we have taken advantage of no one" (2 Cor. 7:2).

Many of these themes are already found in Paul's earlier correspondence with the Corinthians. He acknowledges that he is held in disrepute and that, by the world's standards, he looks like a fool (1 Cor. 4:9–10). Furthermore, his decision not to ask for financial support, defended at length in 1 Cor. 9, raised the eyebrows of many Corinthians. Ancient city dwellers looked askance at wandering teachers, who might support themselves in various ways, each of which carried its own special stigma.[10] One might beg like the Cynics, whose lifestyle nauseated the average Greek citizen. Sophists had better personal hygiene, but their custom of taking a fee for their lectures gave them a bad reputation similar to that often borne by lawyers today. Having the support of a wealthy patron provided more stability but ran the risk of damaging one's reputation for frankness and sincerity, since lapdogs are careful not to bite the hand that feeds them. Members of the upper classes, finally, might have turned up their noses at his policy of earning his living by manual labor (Acts 18:3; 2 Cor. 11:27; 1 Thess. 2:9; 2 Thess. 3:8).[11] Some of the Corinthians may have

8. Paul highlights his frankness to deflect criticism here, but this frankness could create problems at other times (Gal. 4:16).

9. Many attempts have been made to identify and describe the views of Paul's opponents in 2 Corinthians. For a survey, see C. K. Barrett, "Paul's Opponents in II Corinthians."

10. See Stambaugh and Balch, *New Testament in Its Social Environment*, 144–45.

11. On whether Paul himself was proud or ashamed of his labor, see Still, "Did Paul Loathe Manual Labor?"

turned Paul's otherwise laudable practice against him, seeing it as evidence of a bad conscience over his claims to be an apostle.[12] At the very least, the well-known phenomenon of people valuing something in accordance with how much they have paid for it may be at work, to Paul's detriment.

2. Theological or ideological criticism of Paul is implicit in other letters. In 2 Thess. 2:1–3, for example, there is the suggestion that someone is contradicting Paul's teachings on the second coming of Christ. This may be the result of an innocent misunderstanding of Paul's remarks in 1 Thessalonians or a more deliberate act of deception, in which someone has forged a letter in Paul's name. Many scholars regard 2 Thessalonians as pseudonymous in large part because of perceived inconsistencies between 1 and 2 Thessalonians on the question of the second coming. If the eschatological scenarios laid out in the two letters are in fact incompatible and the author of 2 Thessalonians is writing to "correct" Paul, then the pseudonymous author is himself a critic of Pauline teaching, albeit a critic anxious to be seen as faithful to the apostle's legacy.[13]

Due to the rhetorical character of 2 Thessalonians and the other letters, it can be difficult to be absolutely certain that Paul is dealing with actual and not merely hypothetical disagreements with his teachings. In Romans, Paul regularly employs the diatribe, a discursive style widespread in Greco-Roman philosophical schools where the aim is to persuade an audience by anticipating any objections to the speaker's position on a given subject. It simulates the back-and-forth exchange between opponents in a debate, with the speaker voicing ("some might say . . .") and then responding to the questions and faulty conclusions of an imaginary interlocutor.

The tone Paul adopts, however, indicates that his letter to Rome is no mere classroom exercise. Romans suggests that Paul and his teachings have been called into question on various grounds: because he downplays the status of Israel as God's chosen people and the value of circumcision as the sign of the covenant (Rom. 3:1–2); because his reading of Scripture allows unfaithful Israelites to "nullify the faithfulness of God" (3:3); because he implies, inadvertently, that God is unjust in showing wrath toward sinners (3:5); because his theology limits the God of Israel to the level of a tribal deity (3:29); and because he seeks to overturn the law or impugn its integrity by making it responsible for sin (3:31; 7:7, 13). Without naming names, Paul says in 3:8

---

12. Conzelmann, *I Corinthians*, 154.

13. Arguments for and against the Pauline authorship of 2 Thessalonians are summarized by Malherbe, *Letters to the Thessalonians*, 349–74. On the assumption that the two letters are irreconcilable on this point, it is perhaps difficult to take 2 Thess. 2:1–3 as nothing more than a friendly amendment since it implies that Paul was wrong on a matter of great import.

that "some people" are slandering him by attributing to him an ends-justify-the-means theology of salvation ("Let us do evil so that good may come"). This last comment is related to the criticism of his teaching on divine grace that he rebuts in 6:1–2, 15: "Should we continue in sin in order that grace may abound?"[14] Here, as elsewhere, Paul's staunch reply is "By no means!" He similarly rejects the notion that he is either insinuating on the one hand that God's choosing of Jacob over Esau is unjust (9:14) or, on the other hand, that God has once and for all repudiated his people Israel in making salvation available to gentiles (11:1, 11). The palpable angst he expresses in 9:1–5 illustrates how badly these criticisms stung him.

If in Romans one hears a wounded outcry from a man accused of indifference to or outright apostasy from Israel, in Galatians the tone is considerably more combative. Opposing teachers with "a different gospel" starkly at odds with Paul's preaching provoke him to declare in Gal. 1:9, "If anyone proclaims to you a gospel contrary to what you received, let that one be accursed!" Based on Paul's vigorous response, it appears that they were arguing for the necessity of circumcision—for gentile as well as for Jewish believers—for membership in the people of God (5:10–12; 6:12–13, 15). "False brothers" (2:4) from Jerusalem have infiltrated the community and are maligning the particular brand of "freedom" that constitutes the core of the gospel Paul has shared with the Galatians. These are Christians from a Jewish background who share Paul's belief in Jesus as the Messiah but disagree with the Pauline corollary, namely, that gentiles are not obliged to observe "works of the law" such as circumcision, kashrut laws, and special Jewish feasts.[15] In this context, then, in Gal. 1:10 ("Am I now seeking human approval, or God's approval? Or am I trying to please people?") Paul is not reacting to personal jibes to the effect that he is a mealy-mouthed flatterer. His remonstrance cuts to the heart of the matter prompting him to write in the first place. To wit, Paul flatly rejects the notion that, in relativizing the importance of circumcision, he is watering down the pure gospel in order to appeal to gentiles.[16]

Judging by the defense he mounts in Galatians, 2 Corinthians (11:22; 12:12), and Philippians (3:4–6), Paul routinely faced skepticism about his Jewishness, his relationship to the Jerusalem church, and by extension his apostolic

14. See Canales, "Paul's Accusers."

15. The identity and views of those opposed to Paul's ministry in Galatia are the subject of a vast secondary literature; cf. Jewett, "Agitators and the Galatian Congregation"; Ellis, "Paul and His Opponents"; and W. Russell, "Who Were Paul's Opponents in Galatia?"

16. Dunn, *Epistle to the Galatians*, 49–50. Less certain is the suggestion made by Hans Dieter Betz (*Galatians*, 55n108) that Paul may be denying charges that he used "magic and religious quackery" akin to sorcery in an attempt to "persuade God" by means of spells or bribery.

credentials.[17] In targeting his status as an apostle, the "super-apostles" of 2 Corinthians were directly or indirectly raising the question of his fidelity to Jesus. He worries that his followers are too quick to embrace "another Jesus" than the one he has proclaimed to them and feels compelled to remind them that he too is a "minister of Christ" (2 Cor. 11:4, 23). Doubts about Paul's bona fides on this point lead them to "desire proof that Christ is speaking" in him (13:3).

Such concerns are present also in 1 Corinthians, where they have yet to reach the crisis stage seen later in his correspondence.[18] The most graphic yet enigmatic allusion occurs in 1 Cor. 15:8, where Paul compares himself to a miscarriage or an aborted fetus (ektrōma, "one untimely born"). Some scholars speculate that he was called a monster due to some physical deformity or mocked as a dwarf or a midget for being short of stature.[19] Others agree that the expression is a nod to negative attitudes toward Paul but see it as proceeding from something more than pettiness or mean-spirited joking. Calling Paul an "abortion" may have originated as a term of abuse to parody his claim to be called from the womb, like one of the prophets, such as Isaiah or Jeremiah (Isa. 49:1, 5; Jer. 1:5).[20] Since an aborted fetus is cast aside as unwanted, it may be more straightforward to see reflected in Paul's choice of words a sense that he has been singled out as lacking the same authority as the other apostles.[21]

The following verse supports this last interpretation. When Paul continues, "For I am the least of the apostles, unfit to be called an apostle," any critic present for the reading of Paul's letter to the congregation would be sorely tempted to interject a loud "Amen!" Luther, Calvin, and many other commentators infer from 1 Cor. 15:9 that Paul had been criticized on these grounds. On what basis might Paul's contemporaries have doubted his qualifications? The answer lies in the definition of the office of apostle that was current in Corinth, if not in every locale where Paul ministered. An apostle is an envoy.

17. Gerd Lüdemann (*Opposition to Paul*, 35–115) attempts to reconstruct this view of Paul as it appears during his lifetime.

18. See, e.g., the discussion of his policy of self-support, where in response to his own rhetorical question (1 Cor. 9:1: "Am I not an apostle?") he states, "If I am not an apostle to others, at least I am to you; for you are the seal of my apostleship in the Lord" (9:2).

19. Robertson and Plummer, *First Epistle of St. Paul to the Corinthians*, 339; for Paul as a dwarf, see Boman, "'Paulus abortivus,'" 50. Markus Schaefer suggests that the use of the term is a way of referring to Paul's stubbornness, though the way the abortion simile would communicate this meaning is far from clear ("Paulus, 'Fehlgeburt' oder 'unvernünftiges Kind'?," 216–17).

20. Nickelsburg, "Ἔκτρωμα," 202–5.

21. Matthew W. Mitchell ("Reexamining the 'Aborted Apostle,'" 483–84) is unsure whether the language originates with Paul or with his critics.

God or Christ sends a representative to reveal a message or accomplish a task, and the one sent is an apostle. Apostleship comes to acquire a special meaning at an early stage, referring to those who had once been disciples of Jesus and witnesses to the resurrection (Matt. 10:1–2; 28:16–20; Mark 3:14; Acts 1:21–26).[22] Luke testifies to this understanding when he has Peter say, "So one of the men who have accompanied us during all the time that the Lord Jesus went in and out among us, beginning from the baptism of John until the day when he was taken up from us—one of these must become a witness with us to his resurrection" (Acts 1:21–22). All "apostles" in this sense were Jesus's "disciples," but not all disciples qualified as apostles. It is surprising to find this in Acts, since the author is so obviously sympathetic to Paul, and yet this job description would seem to exclude Paul from the apostolate. Elsewhere Paul appears to minimize the importance of having walked with the Lord even as he stresses the continuity of his message with that of the Twelve (1 Cor. 15:3–4; cf. 2 Cor. 5:16). By laying claim to the title, Paul thus found himself embroiled in an acrimonious debate about the nature of apostleship.

Controversies about apostleship mark a point of intersection between personal and theological critiques of Paul in the first century. Message and messenger are not quite inseparable, but the one undeniably complements the other. Credible witnesses willing and able to proclaim the good news of Jesus's life, death, and resurrection are important because of the early Christian conviction that the events denoted by the phrase "the gospel" did not occur in some misty realm of myth, long ago and far away. And no matter how worthy the messenger, apostleship becomes null and void without a valid message to proclaim. Criticism of one therefore assumes or implies criticism of the other. This facet of Pauline opposition fits comfortably within its Jewish and Greco-Roman context, in which it was standard practice to disparage the teachings of a rival philosophical school by disparaging the character of its teachers. One could argue in the opposite direction as well, suggesting that debased morals would result from false teachings. Since Paul uses this strategy, it would not be surprising if his opponents had returned the favor.[23]

---

22. The NT does not present a uniform concept of apostleship, and it is not clear how early "the apostles" became a term reserved for the Twelve. On the uses of the term in the NT, see C. K. Barrett, "Apostles"; Schnackenburg, "Apostles"; and Agnew, "Origin of the NT Apostle-Concept."

23. Karris, "Polemic of the Pastoral Epistles." In Philippians, Paul turns this trope on its head: far from allowing his opponents to shame him and embarrass his followers for having a teacher who spends so much time in jail, Paul says that his incarceration "has really served to advance the gospel" (Phil. 1:12 RSV).

Other Canonical Texts

Outside Acts and the Pauline writings there is little evidence of animus toward Paul in the pages of the NT. The author of 2 Peter (3:15–16) states that Paul's letters are on occasion "hard to understand," leading "the ignorant and unstable [to] twist [them] to their own destruction." Nothing in this remark necessarily means that these readers are intending to slander Paul.[24] With "friends" who so badly mangle his teachings, the author of 2 Peter might ask, who needs enemies?

It may be that the most significant of Paul's early critics are those who never mention him by name. When the author of the Letter of James declares that "a man is justified by works and not by faith alone" because "faith apart from works is dead" (2:24, 26 RSV), many scholars argue that he is taking aim at radical or distorted forms of Paulinism or even at Paul himself, who writes that "a man is justified by faith apart from works of law" (Rom. 3:28 RSV). Some believe that James (or someone writing in his name) misunderstands Paul's position, while others believe that James understands him all too well but rejects the revolutionary implications of his argument. Still others hold that they are not addressing each other at all but, rather, are independently adding their voices to a debate taking place within first-century Judaism. Since the Reformation, few subjects have occupied NT scholars as much as this question.[25]

Although he does not speculate about any personal animus toward Paul on the part of James, Martin Luther lays down the basic lines of this approach when he declares James to be "in direct opposition to St. Paul and all the rest of the Bible" in ascribing justification to works.[26] This interpretation sees James as representing the position that Paul regularly attempts to counter in his letters, namely, that his emphasis on grace is a recipe for moral laxity. Whether James belongs to the chorus singing this tune is uncertain, but it was obviously in the air. This line of attack will appear in the following century in what is often labeled Jewish Christianity and in later centuries as well.[27]

Other scholars interpret the putative anti-Paulinism of James 2 differently. K. J. Coker, for example, believes that it has less to do with a theological faith/works binary than with the politics of identity, with James criticizing Paul for

---

24. It is possible that these readers are willfully misunderstanding Paul with a view to casting aspersions on his teachings about the second coming and divine judgment. If so, Paul makes their task easier by the occasional obscurity of his prose.

25. The body of secondary literature devoted to the issue is immense; see Penner, "Epistle of James," 288–92; M. M. Mitchell, "Letter of James"; and Allison, "James 2:14–26."

26. Luther's comments appear in the preface to James in his 1522 German translation of the NT; see Dillenberger, *Martin Luther*, 35.

27. Lüdemann, *Opposition to Paul*, 35–115.

not taking seriously the brutal effects of empire on the oppressed.[28] Martin
Hengel looks beyond this key passage and detects indirect polemic aimed at
Paul's theology and personal behavior in several other passages.[29] The worldli-
ness that is condemned in James (1:27; 4:4, 13) is ostensibly associated with
urbane travelers immersed in commercial pursuits but is in reality pointed at
Paul and his grand missionary strategy anchored in the major metropolitan
areas of the Roman world, which made him beholden to well-to-do friends
and acquaintances and compromised his dedication to helping the needy.
Paul's pride in his missionary successes is likewise behind the condemnation
of boasting in James 4:16. In defending himself, Paul often swears oaths
"with God as [his] witness," in violation of the prohibition against swearing
that James (5:12) draws from the Sermon on the Mount (Matt. 5:34–37).
According to this reading, James (5:13–16) goes so far as to taunt Paul for
the "thorn in the flesh" that remained with him even after Paul prayed three
times for relief. This suffering—the result of unconfessed sin—could have
been ended if only Paul had been willing to submit himself to the authority
of the elders (including James?) for prayer and anointing. James's closing
admonition (5:19–20) to bring back the sinner who wanders from the truth
is thus no general exhortation but a pointed reference to the apostle whose
deficient understanding of faith and its relation to works is rejected earlier in
the letter. Hengel concedes that his hypothesis is elaborate and surmises that
James carried out his polemical purpose so subtly that its true import could
be grasped only by the parties directly affected by the first-century dispute
between these rival teachers, at least until Hengel himself connected the dots.
Unlike many other writers, neither Hengel nor Coker appears to be project-
ing a personal hostility toward Paul onto James, though Coker's reliance
on postcolonial theory suggests that his reconstruction of the hypothetical
argument between James and Paul—which "provides fertile ground for the
church and the academy to re-conceptualize the effects of colonialism on the
biblical authors as well as modern readers"—may be unduly influenced by
twentieth-century categories and concerns.[30]

While James is the primary focus of scholars who find critics of Paul among
the canonical authors, the Letter of Jude and the Gospel of Matthew have

28. Coker, "Nativism in James 2:14–26." According to Coker, "Paul represents everything
that James stands against" in that he espouses a "hybrid" model of resistance characterized by
blurring the boundaries between colonizer and colonized (46). James argues for a purer form
of piety set in opposition to surrounding cultural norms and rejects Pauline "hybridity" as a
form of assimilation and compromise.

29. Hengel, "Jakobusbrief."

30. Coker, "Nativism in James 2:14–26," 48.

attracted attention as well. Jude inveighs against "ungodly persons who pervert the grace of our God into licentiousness" (v. 4 RSV). Gerhard Sellin sees this as an allusion to Paul and his excessive emphasis on grace that encourages a libertine approach to morality.[31] The author of Jude identifies himself as the brother of James—no coincidence, according to some scholars, given the common concerns about the undesirable implications of Paul's antinomianism expressed in their letters. Matthew has been called to testify against Paul along similar lines. Jesus states in the Sermon on the Mount that he has not come "to abolish the law or the prophets" but to fulfill them (Matt. 5:17), a declaration that S. G. F. Brandon and others interpret as a veiled criticism of Paul's law-free gospel.[32] When Matthew has Jesus conclude that whoever breaks one of the least of the commandments "will be called least in the kingdom of heaven" (5:19), in this view, he is taking a jab at Paul's self-identification as "the least of the apostles" (1 Cor. 15:9; cf. Eph. 3:8). The elevation of Peter in Matt. 16:17–19 is similarly seen as serving an anti-Pauline function, standing in the same tradition as Paul's antagonists in Galatia who urge gentiles to observe Torah in its entirety.

That James is a critic of Paul is more plausible than the notion that Matthew and Jude have him in mind. Already in his own letters Paul confronts egregious misunderstandings of the nature of divine grace (Rom. 3:8; 6:15; Gal. 5:13)—an indication that he and the author of Jude may be on the same side of this debate in early Christianity. The case for Matthew's anti-Paulinism may likewise be too clever by half, especially when Brandon supports it with the peculiar theory that the unnamed "enemy" in the parable of the tares (Matt. 13:24–30) is none other than Paul.[33] Speculative theories about the compatibility of various canonical texts are uncommon, naturally, until a collection of texts is recognized as canonical, a process that commences as early as the middle of the second century. When questions about Paul and his relationship to other strands of early Christianity are taken up in earnest during and after the Reformation, historical judgments and theological concerns often run in parallel lines.

---

31. Sellin, "Häretiker des Judasbriefes." Bart Ehrman sees Jude's criticism of the opponents' denigration of angels in v. 8 as corroborating evidence that the author has Paul in mind (*Forgery and Counterforgery*, 302–5).

32. Brandon, *Fall of Jerusalem*, 231–37; Sim, "Matthew's Anti-Paulinism." Sim also sees anti-Pauline polemic in the ending of Matthew's Gospel ("Matthew, Paul and the Origin and Nature of the Gentile Mission").

33. For a critical assessment of Brandon's reading, see W. D. Davies, *Setting of the Sermon on the Mount*, 317–41.

It is uncertain whether Paul was as significant during his lifetime as he came to be in later centuries. That he made enemies is beyond dispute, even if scholars at times project the theological debates of later eras onto the texts under consideration. The list of complaints lodged against him—that he is domineering, dishonest, and too quick to set aside the requirements of Torah—will sound familiar to modern observers, who are not unique in linking their theological criticisms with personal attacks. Fair or not, however, at least Paul's earliest critics were his contemporaries and not engaged in amateur psychoanalysis across cultures and at a remove of nearly two thousand years.

No one in this period faults Paul for founding a new religion contrary to the wishes of the master he claims to serve. Judaism and the messianic sect that will become Christianity do not arrive at a definitive parting of the ways during his lifetime, which no doubt helps to explain the different emphases in first-century evaluations of the apostle and those of the present day. To the extent that Paul is compelled to defend his status as an apostle, however, it would appear that concerns about his continuity with Jesus are present in a nascent form. These concerns come into sharper relief as soon as the second century.

2

THE PREMODERN ERA

The Early Church, Late Antiquity, and the Middle Ages

De mortuis nihil nisi bonum.[1] By the time the last book of the NT is written, Paul has left the scene. Over succeeding decades and centuries, his admirers are many, but so are those who wantonly violate the admonition to speak no ill of the dead. Praise and blame are based on interpretations of Acts and the letters and on various legends and lingering rumors, since no one with a living memory is around to settle disputes about what he was like or what he taught. From the end of the first century until the dawn of the Reformation, criticism of Paul issues from four sources: Christians, Jews, pagans, and Muslims.[2]

Christians

By the time of Irenaeus late in the second century, Paul becomes "the Apostle"—indeed, "the Divine Apostle" (Clement of Alexandria, *Stromateis* 2.20); as such, he is criticized only rarely by Christians writing in the patristic and

1. Of the dead [say] nothing unless good.
2. These categories are, of course, far from perfect—see, most recently, Christopher Jones, *Between Pagan and Christian*—but they provide an adequate scheme for organizing the material. Here, "Christian" includes anyone self-identifying as a devotee of Jesus, whatever heresiologists like Irenaeus and Epiphanius may have thought, and "pagan" refers to anyone other than Christians, Jews, and Muslims, without the pejorative connotations the label often bears.

medieval periods.[3] In the search for anti-Paulinism, the second-century *Acts of Paul and Thecla* produces a false start with its physical description of Paul as short, bald, hook-nosed, and bowlegged, with eyebrows that meet in the middle. It is tempting for modern readers to see this as an unflattering portrait, given that it diverges from Western notions of beauty on almost every point. Read in the light of the principles of ancient physiognomy, however, Paul's physical appearance in this text is probably meant to express extremely positive qualities of character and personality.[4] Apart from such aesthetic concerns, the permissive view of women's participation in ministry reflected in this document made many Christians nervous about Paul, but this was held to be a distortion of the historical record, and thus the wariness of writers like Tertullian does not reflect any rebuke of Paul.

Second- and third-century gnostic texts that quote or allude to Paul—such as the *Gospel of Truth*, Ptolemy's *Letter to Flora*, and the *Interpretation of Knowledge*—generally do so in an approving manner. Marcion esteems Paul above all other authorities, whether or not he understands him.[5] His ten-letter Pauline corpus, the *Apostolikon*, however, does not include the Pastoral Epistles, which Tertullian says Marcion rejected (*Adversus Marcionem* 5.21). Clement of Alexandria refers to other heretics who reject 1–2 Timothy (*Stromateis* 2.11). Neither Clement nor Tertullian gives a clear indication of the basis for this rejection, and some scholars speculate that Marcion does not so much reject them as he is ignorant of their existence.[6] According to Jerome, Tatian accepted the Letter to Titus but rejected several others, possibly because they conflicted with his own extreme asceticism.[7] Tatian was a leader of the Encratites, whom Origen mentions as a sect that repudiates Paul's writings and the Acts of the Apostles on the same grounds (*Contra Celsum* 5.65). Eusebius includes the Severians and the Cerinthians in this category as well (*Hist. eccl.* 4.29.1–5; some scholars would categorize these

---

3. General surveys of Paul and his reception in the premodern period include Dassmann, *Stachel im Fleisch*; Lindemann, *Paulus im ältesten Christentum*; Légasse, *L'antipaulinisme sectaire*; Meeks and Fitzgerald, *Writings of St. Paul*, 169–351; Pervo, *Making of Paul*; Seesengood, *Paul*, 74–147; Cartwright, *Companion to St. Paul*.

4. Omerzu, "Portrayal of Paul's Outer Appearance." According to Roland Bainton, when asked what he thought Paul looked like, Martin Luther joked, "I think he was a scrawny shrimp like Melanchthon" (*Here I Stand*, 81).

5. Adolf von Harnack famously quipped that "Marcion was the only Gentile Christian who understood Paul, and even he misunderstood him" (*Outlines*, 1:89).

6. John Knox, e.g., argues that Marcion does not know of the Pastorals, which are actually written in response to Marcion's influence (*Marcion and the New Testament*, 73–76).

7. Jerome, Prologue to *Commentarium in Titum* (Patrologia Latina 26:555). See also Pervo, *Making of Paul*, 197, who notes that Tatian is the earliest writer to question the authorship of the Pastorals on the grounds that they contradict teachings found in other letters.

groups as Jewish-Christian). Beyond this, gentile Christian writers in this period appear to say only good things about Paul, or they say nothing at all.[8]

One criticism of Paul reflected in Christian writings of the fourth century has to do with the purported inconsistency of his teachings. Pagans naturally voiced this opinion in their writings against Christianity. The painstaking care with which John Chrysostom, in *De laudibus sancti Pauli apostoli*, addresses the charge may indicate that it has gained some purchase within the church, though there is little clear evidence that gentile Christians in his day are condemning Paul for inconsistency.[9] The same is true when it comes to accusations that he is a hypocrite, a shameless flatterer, a coward, or a chameleon. Whatever the basis for such claims and whatever their source, Christian authors are inclined to mount a defense, even turning his supposed contradictions into proof of his adaptability and rhetorical cunning.

Apocryphal correspondence between Paul and the Roman Stoic Seneca produced in the fourth century exhibits this tendency.[10] "Seneca" heaps praises on "Paul" yet feels it necessary to remark, however delicately, on the quality of his prose. "I wish that refinement of language might not be lacking to the majesty of your theme," he says in Letter 7, promising in Letter 9 to send a book on elegance of expression. Because his writings are often "allegorical and enigmatic," Seneca advises Paul in Letter 13 to embellish his words "with a certain amount of refinement . . . and comply with the pure Latin style, giving a good appearance to your noble utterances." At the same time, Seneca acknowledges that "the gods are accustomed to speak through the mouths of the innocent and not through those who pride themselves on their learning" (7). Augustine (*Confessions* 3.5.9) admits that he was similarly put off by the inferior literary stylings of biblical authors like Paul in the Old Latin translation, though the postconversion Augustine blames his intellectual pride rather than Paul. Origen as well says that anyone who can tell good Greek diction can see the marked difference between the apostle and the eloquent author of the Letter to the Hebrews (Eusebius, *Hist. eccl.* 6.25.11–12).

A rare and relatively mild instance of criticism is seen at the beginning of the fifth century in Jerome's interpretation of the dispute between Peter and Paul at Antioch in his commentary on Galatians.[11] Paul says in Gal. 2:11–14

---

8. The silence of writers in this period who say little about Paul may signal assent or ambivalence; cf. Padovese, "L'antipaulinisme chrétien," 415–21. Christopher W. Skinner suggests that veiled criticism of Paul is to be found in the Coptic *Gospel of Thomas*; see "*Gospel of Thomas*'s Rejection."

9. M. M. Mitchell, "'Variable and Many-Sorted Man'"; Reis, "Flip-Flop?"

10. Translated in J. K. Elliott, *Apocryphal New Testament*, 547–53.

11. Myers, "Law, Lies and Letter Writing."

that he called Peter out for hypocrisy because he had refrained from eating with gentiles for fear of offending "the circumcision party" (Gal. 2:12 RSV). Jerome has doubts that any such confrontation took place as described since it would have been hypocritical of Paul, who "to the Jews . . . became as a Jew, in order to win Jews" (1 Cor. 9:20). Instead, Paul would have initiated a public dispute only by prior consent with Peter in private. This famous dispute was thus, according to Jerome, an event staged for the sake of the unity of the church at Antioch, where Peter pretends to keep kosher and Paul pretends to rebuke Peter, thereby demonstrating his solidarity with the gentiles. In a testy exchange, Jerome (*Epistulae* 75.4) says that he borrowed the idea from Origen and John Chrysostom, but Augustine (*Epistulae* 28) is having none of it, replying that Jerome has made Paul into a liar. The disagreement between the two church fathers fades, but this is not the last time the Antioch incident will come up in attacks on Paul.

Jewish-Christian writers provide the primary locus for Christian criticism of Paul in antiquity.[12] This position is based in large part on the conviction that Mosaic law is a binding expression of God's will and that Paul had gone too far in relaxing its requirements to draw in gentile proselytes. Patristic sources identify a number of such groups. The Elchasaites, according to Hippolytus, trace their origins to an early second-century prophet, Elchasai, and require circumcision, observe the Sabbath, pray facing Jerusalem, and honor Christ (*Refutatio omnium haeresium* 9.8–12). Eusebius says that they use the OT and the Gospels but reject Paul (*Hist. eccl.* 6.38). He also describes the Ebionites as a sect that observes Jewish law and denies that faith in Christ alone is sufficient for salvation (*Hist. eccl.* 3.27.1–6), echoing as well the earlier report of Irenaeus (*Adversus haereses* 1.26.2) that they reject Paul's letters and regard him as an apostate from the law.[13] The Ebionites, whose name is derived from a Hebrew term meaning "the poor," may also have claimed to represent the original community of Jesus's followers (Epiphanius, *Panarion* 30).[14] Are these the same poor in Jerusalem for whom Paul was gathering a collection (Acts 11:29–30; Rom. 15:26; 2 Cor. 8–9; Gal. 2:10)? Those who regard Paul as the founder of Christianity often answer this question in the affirmative and say that the offering was

---

12. On the range of religious orientations covered by the term "Jewish Christianity," see Brown, "Not Jewish Christianity and Gentile Christianity"; and Jackson-McCabe, "What's in a Name?" Jewish Christianity in the early period tends to oppose Pauline views, but there existed groups in this category that appear to have been defined by factors other than opposition to Paul; see Donahue, "Jewish Christianity."

13. Irenaeus also argues that the Ebionites ought to accept the letters if they make use of Luke-Acts, which gives a positive evaluation of Paul (*Adversus haereses* 3.15.1).

14. Keck, "Poor among the Saints"; Luomanen, "Ebionites and Nazarenes."

declined.[15] Epiphanius (*Panarion* 30.16.6–9) further credits the Ebionites with circulating a document called the *Ascents of James*.[16] This document alleges that Paul's parents were both Greek and thus he was not Jewish by birth. Only when he falls in love with the high priest's daughter does he become a proselyte to Judaism and undergo circumcision. When he is denied her hand in marriage, the jilted lover flies into a rage and begins to denigrate key elements of Jewish custom such as circumcision, the Sabbath, and the law.

The *Ascents of James* may have been used by the author of the most substantive example of Jewish-Christian literature written in opposition to Paul, the collection known as the *Pseudo-Clementines*. This material is attributed to Clement of Rome at the end of the first century but most likely was written in the third or fourth century. It includes a prefatory letter from Peter to James (*Epistula Petri*), a series of *Homilies* delivered by Clement and sent to James, and a collection of narratives (*Recognitions*) about Clement's conversion and travels with Peter. Although Paul is not named in this literature, most scholars believe that he is "the enemy" attacked under the guise of Simon Magus.[17]

Peter urges James in the *Epistula Petri* not to share his written sermons with any gentiles unless they have been thoroughly examined and found worthy. This will ensure that they adhere to a strict monotheism and moral code and are not led astray by the ambiguities found in the Scriptures. Schism will be the result if James does not follow this policy. Indeed, gentiles have already begun to reject Peter's proclamation for the lawless teaching of "the enemy." Concerns seen elsewhere about Paul distorting or abandoning Torah via strained exegesis and his outreach to non-Jews fit with the author's warnings here, which are supported with reference to a saying of Jesus about the law (Matt. 5:18 RSV: "Till heaven and earth pass away, not an iota, not a dot, will pass from the law until all is accomplished").

In the Clementine *Homilies*, the vitriol directed at Paul (most scholars are agreed that in these texts "Simon Magus" stands for Paul) is even more palpable. God works with pairs, says Peter, and these pairs follow a predictable pattern: Peter follows Simon/Paul, who first went to the gentiles, just as light follows darkness, knowledge follows ignorance, and healing follows disease. This order of affairs was foretold by Jesus, who said that a false gospel had to be spread by a certain deceiver before the true gospel would set things

---

15. E.g., Lüdemann, *Opposition to Paul*, 59–62.

16. Bauckham, "Origin of the Ebionites," 164–71.

17. Lüdemann, *Opposition to Paul*, 169–94; Meeks and Fitzgerald, *Writings of St. Paul*, 230–34; Wehnert, "Antipaulinismus in den Pseudoklementinen." Markus Bockmuehl (*Remembered Peter*, 102–13), however, has raised serious objections to the equation of Simon Magus and Paul.

right (*Hom.* 2.17.3–4). This deceiver, Simon/Paul, comes from Satan, who promised to send out apostles to sow error in the Lord's name (11.35.3–6). Jesus had Simon/Paul in mind when he warned his disciples about wolves in sheep's clothing (Matt. 7:15). Simon/Paul tells Peter that Peter is the one who has been deceived by his own senses and that the privileged access to Jesus's true teachings that he presumes to have is illusory, anticipating Peter's charge that it is ludicrous to trust in visions of the sort that Simon/Paul claims to have experienced (*Hom.* 17.13). The historical Paul could be sensitive to this charge (Gal. 1:11–12), and it is intriguing to see Simon/Paul take its underlying message and turn it back on Peter when he accuses him of deviating from the teachings of Jesus (*Hom.* 17.4–5; *Rec.* 2.27–28, 47; the force of this argument is somewhat diminished, however, when he adds that Jesus's teachings are themselves internally inconsistent).

Much of the material in the *Homilies* is recycled in the *Recognitions*. Simon/Paul is boastful, a lover of glory, and well versed in Greek literature, which serves him well in proselytizing the polytheistic gentiles (*Rec.* 2.7; *Hom.* 3.4). He is portrayed as a magician with amazing powers by which he seduces the crowds. He has the ability to fly, resist flames, walk through mountains, make statues walk, melt iron, become invisible, turn stones into bread, change his physical appearance (including metamorphosis into a sheep or goat), and cause young boys to grow beards (*Rec.* 2.9; 3.47; *Hom.* 2.32). But he is unable to best Peter in public debate as the apostle follows him from one city to the next in order to correct his false teachings.

Peter's duels with Simon are preceded in the *Recognitions* (1.27–71) by an anti-Pauline account, not found in the *Homilies*, in which James debates with the Jewish sects in Jerusalem—Sadducees, Samaritans, Pharisees, scribes, and disciples of John the Baptist—for seven days. So persuasively does he speak that they are about to be baptized when an "enemy" incites a riot, throws James down the temple steps, and, in terms of missionary objectives, snatches defeat from the jaws of victory (1.70). James is left for dead, and the window of opportunity closes for bringing about the conversion of his fellow Jews. That the enemy had been commissioned by the chief priest to travel to Damascus and persecute followers of Jesus confirms that he is to be identified with Paul, whose fault it is that Christianity strays so far from its Jewish origins.[18] This will remain a common theme even after Jewish forms of Christianity effectively disappear.

18. Lüdemann, *Opposition to Paul*, 183–84. A marginal note in the manuscript strengthens this suspicion. It should be noted, however, that the appearance of "the enemy" and Simon Magus in the same document raises questions as to whether both figures should be read as stand-ins for Paul.

Jews

While Christian criticism of Paul virtually disappears in late antiquity, it continues in non-Christian Jewish circles. Second-century Christian texts report that (non-Christian) Jews rejected Pauline teachings such as the resurrection and divinity of Jesus and the atoning significance of his death on the cross, though he is nowhere named as the target (Justin, *Dialogue with Trypho* 94–96; *Gospel of Peter* 8.28–30). The same is true of passages from the Mishnah, the Talmud, and later rabbinic writings, which have been scrutinized as possible covert allusions to the apostle.[19] Elisha ben Abuyah, the paradigmatic apostate of rabbinic tradition, has been put forward as the alias of Paul on the basis of parallels in reports of their mystical experiences.[20] Even more reminiscent is the description of the man in the Mishnah who "profanes the Hallowed Things and despises the set feasts and puts his fellow to shame publicly and makes void the covenant of Abraham our father, and discloses meanings in the Law which are not according to the *Halakah*, even though a knowledge of the Law and good works are his."[21] "That pupil" who repeatedly scoffs at Rabbi Gamaliel, shows "impudence in matters of learning," "interprets Torah in a perverse manner," and subsequently turns away is identified as Paul by some scholars (*b. Šabbat* 30b).[22] The *Nishmat Kol Ḥay*, an ancient liturgical prayer recited on the Sabbath and at Passover, has also been read as an anti-Pauline composition—written, according to medieval Jewish traditions, by the apostle Peter.[23]

Jewish writers in the medieval period continue to deprecate teachings closely associated with Paul, as when Nachmanides (d. 1270) finds fault with those preoccupied with the details of the messiah's coming because they are not fundamental principles and knowledge of them does not promote fear and love of God (*Melakhim* 12.2). But they also begin to single out Paul by name. Many criticisms replicate those leveled by Jewish Christians in the second century. In ninth- and tenth-century Iraq, Dawud ibn Marwan al-Muqammis and Jacob Kirkisani take issue with Pauline innovations for which no precedent

19. Hirschberg, "Allusions," 82–86; Langton, *Apostle Paul in the Jewish Imagination*, 25. Hirschberg notes that heretics (*minim*) in the Talmud echo Pauline teachings and that, in antiquity, these would have included ideas from the Letter to the Hebrews.

20. Wise, "Paul and the Mystics," 55–56, connecting the references to visions in 2 Cor. 12:1–6 to *b. Berakot* 57b and discussing the humiliations suffered by Paul in his dealings with the Jerusalem authorities. Elisha ben Abuyah is the protagonist of Milton Steinberg's classic 1939 novel, *As a Driven Leaf*.

21. *'Abot* 3.12, trans. Danby.

22. See Klausner, *From Jesus to Paul*, 309–12 (quotes on 310–11), who accepts the authenticity of the claim in Acts that Paul was a student of Gamaliel.

23. Légasse, "La legende juive des Apôtres," 115–17; Bekkum, "Poetical Qualities."

could be found either in Torah or in the teachings of Jesus.[24] The twelfth century saw several Jewish writers enter the literary fray in response to Christianity and Islam as well, especially in Spain, where the *reconquista* was in full swing. The culprit held responsible for many of these errors is not Jesus, but Paul.[25] Popular works such as the *Book of Nestor the Priest*, in which Paul's teachings about Jesus are blamed for promoting belief in two gods, were sometimes read in this setting by Muslims, whose antipathy matched that of Jewish scholars.[26] Recurring elements in this Jewish critique are the claims that Christians distort the meaning of the Scriptures and make spurious claims about the messianic and divine status of Jesus, who never intended to found a new religion. Karaite authors like Judah Hadassi who did not recognize the binding authority of the Mishnah and Talmud nevertheless agreed with the rabbis on these counts.

Although the attention of most thirteenth- and fourteenth-century polemical literature is focused on Jesus and the Gospels, Paul continues to appear. In the Ashkenazi *Niẓẓaḥon Vetus* (*Old Book of Polemic*), Paul's writings "in their own book of errors" are cited as the cause of the Christians' rejection of circumcision and Sabbath observance, even though by doing this they "contradict the Torah of Paul's teacher Jesus" (§§42, 158; Matt. 5:18 is quoted, as in other texts that emphasize Paul's antinomian tendencies).[27] Writing some time after his forced but temporary conversion to Christianity, the Catalan philosopher Profiat Duran sees the medieval church as having departed from the simple origins it had with Jesus, as did his contemporaries John Wycliffe and Jan Hus, but pushes the moment of its deviation all the way back to "the deceiver" Paul. Jesus and his immediate disciples, "those who err" or "the mistaken ones," were indeed misguided and ignorant of the law but never intended for later generations to treat Jesus as divine or to subscribe to such notions as original sin or transubstantiation.[28]

24. Al-Muqammis's work is lost but is quoted by Jacob Kirkisani. For their comments on Paul, see Chiesa and Lockwood, *Ya'cūb al-Qirqisānī on Jewish Sects and Christianity*, 61–62, 137–39.

25. Lasker, "Jewish-Christian Debate in Transition"; Langton, *Apostle Paul in the Jewish Imagination*, 26–27. Other twelfth-century writers who make this charge about Jesus's followers, though without naming Paul specifically, include Abraham bar Ḥiyya, Judah ha-Levi, Abraham ibn Daud, and Maimonides; see Lasker, "Anti-Paulinism, Judaism," 285.

26. This text draws on an even earlier work written in Judeo-Arabic titled *Account of the Disputation of the Priest*; see Lasker, "*Qissat Mujadalat al-Usquf.*"

27. Berger, *Jewish-Christian Debate*, 70, 173. The same claim is made by the contemporary commentator Ibn Kammūna; see Perlmann, *Ibn Kammūna's Examination*, 83.

28. Talmage, "Polemical Writings of Profiat Duran"; see also Ochs, *Matthaeus adversus Christianos*, 257–85.

Last but certainly not least in terms of its longevity and influence is the *Sepher Toledot Yeshu* ("Book of the Generations of Jesus").[29] Over one hundred medieval manuscripts of this collection of legends exist, in several different versions and in several different languages. The earliest manuscript dates to the eleventh century, but the stories it contains go back several centuries. It tells of Jesus's scandalous birth, his feats of sorcery, his death, and the efforts of his followers to perpetuate his legacy as the messiah by stealing his body. Paul makes a cameo near the end of the story. Many Israelites remain devoted to Jesus despite the efforts of the Jewish sages to halt the movement. The sages hatch a plan that involves recruiting Simeon Kepha to pose as a disciple of Jesus. Simeon teaches the Israelite followers of Jesus to abandon Jewish feasts, dietary laws, and circumcision. In the final line, it is said that the true aim of Simeon—"or Paul, as he was known to the Nazarenes"—was to bring about an amicable divorce and thereby to put an end to intra-Jewish strife.[30] This criticism of Paul thus takes the form of a cynical compliment. Such a writing gave Jewish scholars a venue for poking fun at their Christian neighbors that was less perilous than the formal disputations in which they were often compelled to participate. Church authorities' attempts to suppress the *Toledot Yeshu* did not succeed in diminishing its popularity among Jews or its use by Muslim polemicists.

Pagans

No non-Jewish criticism of Paul from the first century has survived. In fact, no mention whatsoever of Paul or of Christianity appears in non-Jewish sources until early in the second century. Pliny the Younger (*Epistulae* 10.96), Tacitus (*Annales* 15.44), and Suetonius (*Nero* 16.2) first mention Christianity but make no reference to Paul. Tacitus and Suetonius discuss the Christians as Nero's scapegoats for the great fire of Rome in 64, at which time Paul is martyred according to early church tradition reported by Eusebius (*Hist. eccl.* 2.25.5). Clement of Rome (*1 Clement* 5.5–7) and Ignatius of Antioch (*To the Ephesians* 12) make earlier mention of his martyrdom but do not mention the method—beheading. Decapitation is the sincerest form of criticism. Paul's success as "apostle to the gentiles" obscures the fact that most gentiles, like most of the Jews to whom he preached, had little use for his message.

29. Translated in M. Goldstein, *Jesus in the Jewish Tradition*, 148–54.
30. Rashi, the greatest of the medieval commentators on the Talmud, similarly mentions Paul along with John and Peter as Jews who intentionally introduce the Latin language into Christian literature in order to create confusion and thereby to facilitate the exit of Jesus's followers from the people of Israel (see his commentary on *b. ʿAbodah Zarah* 10a).

Tacitus and Suetonius speak of Christianity in the same terms. Suetonius calls the Christians "a class of men given over to a new and mischievous superstition," and Tacitus calls their faith a "pernicious superstition" breaking out after being temporarily checked by the death of Jesus.[31] "Superstition" (Greek: *deisidaimonia*; Latin: *superstitio*) is the standard slur in the first-century Mediterranean for denigrating defective religiosity (Theophrastus, *Characteres* 16; Horace, *Satirae* 2.3.79). Roman writers routinely characterize foreign cults like that of the Jews as superstitious and, by extension, politically subversive.[32] The emotion of fear receives special emphasis when Greco-Roman writers apply the label (Plutarch, *De superstitione* 167C–F; Lucian, *Philopseudes* 37). One can only imagine what a cosmopolitan Greek like Plutarch or an adviser to the Roman emperor like Seneca would think were he to hear Paul tell the Philippians to work out their salvation "with fear and trembling" (Phil. 2:12).

And imagine is all that one can do since he does not show up in pagan sources until much later. Unreasonable though he may have been, it seems unlikely that Nero or some other imperial official would have executed Paul simply on account of strange customs or beliefs about the natural world. But disturbances of the peace seemed to follow him everywhere he went, and Rome had less patience with perceived rabble-rousers, especially foreign ones. Few pagan writers would have distinguished Christians from Jews during Paul's lifetime, and so Paul may have fallen victim to an indiscriminate xenophobic outburst. In the *Martyrdom of Paul*, a pious legend that originates as part of the second-century *Acts of Paul*, Paul acts and speaks in a way that would have raised the very sorts of suspicions associated with superstition by Romans. Nero becomes nervous when his cupbearer, who has been healed by Paul, says he will fight for Christ, the "king of the ages" who "destroys all kingdoms under heaven." When two other guards proclaim their solidarity, Nero issues an edict that all "soldiers of Christ" be executed. Paul is arrested and questioned by Nero: "What induced you to come secretly into the Roman Empire and to enlist soldiers in my territory?"[33] His answer fills the emperor with terror: They fight for a king who will come from heaven to judge the lawless and destroy the world with fire. Apocalyptic threats of this sort were regarded as a form of sedition. When it was coupled with the obstinacy of Christians in the face of death, many felt as though their suspicions were confirmed. Many Romans in the first few centuries would have judged Paul

31. Unless otherwise indicated, all quotations of classical authors are from the Loeb Classical Library editions.

32. E.g., Cicero, *De divinatione* 2.72.148; Cicero, *Pro Flacco* 67; Pliny the Elder, *Naturalis historia* 13.9.46; see also Janssen "'Superstitio.'"

33. J. K. Elliott, *Apocryphal New Testament*, 385–88 (quotes on 387).

guilty on these grounds until proven innocent. He may be seeking to preempt such accusations with his instructions to the Roman Christians to obey the governing authorities in Rom. 13:1–7.[34]

The earliest known literary attack on Christianity by a pagan author is written late in the second century by Celsus. Little is known about Celsus or his work, the *True Doctrine*, apart from what has been preserved in Origen's response, *Contra Celsum*, written in the middle of the third century.[35] Especially problematic for Celsus are Christian beliefs about the incarnation and the resurrection of the dead and the practice of honoring Jesus in a way that compromises Christian claims to monotheism (*Contra Celsum* 4.2; 8.14, 49). The latter issue is related to a line of attack that many later critics of Paul will pursue, namely, that Christianity cuts itself off from its roots when it departs from Judaism (2.1–11; 5.25). Celsus further parodies Christians' reliance on faith, their fetishization of the cross, and their proselytizing by and among the ignorant (1.9; 3.55; 6.34; he singles out fullers and leather workers for mockery but not tent makers). From these particular points of emphasis and from Origen's use of Paul to counter Celsus's arguments, one might infer that Paul was among Celsus's targets.[36] According to Origen (1.9), Celsus is even familiar with Christians who quote a rough paraphrase of 1 Cor. 1:25. But "for some unknown reason he forgot or did not think of saying anything about Paul, who after Jesus established the churches in Christ" (1.63). Paul may have been exempt since much of Celsus's attention is focused on portraying Jesus as a magician and Paul says so little about Jesus's miracles, but Origen suggests that the miraculous reversal seen in the apostle's life may have left Celsus speechless.[37]

Eusebius (*Hist. eccl.* 6.19) says that Origen's response was known to Porphyry, a Neoplatonist who late in the third century launched his own broadside entitled *Against the Christians*, a fifteen-volume tour de force that prompted rejoinders from Methodius, Apollinarius, Augustine, and others.[38] This work

---

34. Polycarp, Irenaeus, and Theophilus of Antioch quote Paul for this purpose; see Grant, *Greek Apologists*, 20.

35. See Wilken, *Christians as the Romans Saw Them*, 94–125. For a translation of Origen's text, see Chadwick, *Origen: Contra Celsum*.

36. Meeks and Fitzgerald (*Writings of St. Paul*, 265n2) list Pauline ideas addressed by Celsus.

37. Hierocles Sossianus, who persecuted Christians as governor of Bithynia early in the fourth century, also accuses Peter and Paul of wizardry, adding that they were "liars and devoid of education" as well (Eusebius, *Contra Hieroclem* 2; see Conybeare, *Treatise of Eusebius*); see Barnes, "Sossianus Hierocles." The unnamed "high priest of philosophy" who calls them "disseminators of deceit" according to Lactantius (*Divinarum institutionum* 5.2; see W. Fletcher, *Lactantius*) is also thought to be Hierocles.

38. Grant, "Porphyry among the Early Christians."

survives only in fragments, like that of Celsus, because the Council of Ephesus in 431 and Theodosius II in 448 issued decrees that it be burned.[39] The earliest critics of Christianity had rarely read the NT, but Porphyry displays an intimate familiarity with the Gospels and Paul's letters. In the few surviving fragments, Porphyry paints an unflattering picture of Paul.[40] He is boastful, divisive, intemperate, petty, and "malevolently impertinent" in his dealings with Peter, the prince of the apostles. "The whole world has been subjugated by Paul from the ocean up to the Red Sea," and he has used magical powers to gain financially from "rich little women" to whom he has introduced the faith.[41] Given his view that the NT authors habitually misinterpret the OT, it is hard to imagine that Paul would have been spared.[42]

Among the last gasps of pagan criticism of Paul in antiquity comes from Emperor Julian (361–363), not so affectionately known to posterity as "the Apostate." Reared as a Christian, he turned against the church and sought to undermine its influence when he ascended to the throne. He implicates Paul, who "surpassed all the magicians and charlatans of every place and every time," in many of the elements he finds abhorrent about Christianity in his polemical tract *Contra Galilaeos* (*Against the Galileans*).[43] Many of the arguments he marshals echo those of Celsus and Porphyry, whose works he likely read.

According to Julian, Paul cannot make up his mind whether God is the special God of Israel or the God of all nations, changing his views as an octopus changes its colors (*C. Galil.* 106B–E). To the extent that Paul emphasizes the continuity with Jewish tradition, Julian says that the Christian God is guilty of showing favoritism by abandoning the gentiles in their benighted state for ages and ages. (He accentuates this "scandal of particularity" by calling the Christians "Galileans," a reference to the backwater region where their supposedly universal faith originated.) But he holds it against him whenever Paul diverges from Jewish teaching, citing the proclamation of a new covenant and the disavowal of circumcision as two prime examples (319D–320C, 351A–C). For Paul to teach these things is pure presumption since Jesus never claims to

39. It is unclear whether Porphyry's work was intended to serve as intellectual justification for the persecutions of Christians initiated by Diocletian (Wilken, *Christians as the Romans Saw Them*, 134–35).

40. Berchman, *Porphyry*, 167–70; cf. Meeks and Fitzgerald, *Writings of St. Paul*, 265–66.

41. Berchman, *Porphyry*, 167–70.

42. Simmons, "Porphyry of Tyre's Biblical Criticism"; cf. Berchman, *Porphyry*, 58–59.

43. Julian, *C. Galil.* 100A; see W. Wright, *Julian*. Less than half of Julian's work has survived as part of a fifth-century response composed by Cyril of Alexandria; see N. Russell, *Cyril of Alexandria*, 190–203.

be "the end of the law" (Rom. 10:4).[44] And while Julian is favorably disposed toward syncretism, Paul's brand is not to his taste in that it combines the worst possible aspects of Judaism and pagan religion. It is an unholy alloy combining Jewish ethnocentrism with gentile libertinism (*C. Galil.* 238B–E). In addition to these theological charges, Julian pronounces Paul guilty by association with the dregs of society like the egregious Corinthian sinners whom he flatters by including them among the sanctified, foolishly believing that the waters of baptism could actually cleanse them of their vices (245A–D).

Julian wished to revive what he saw as a noble religious and philosophical tradition that was in danger of being lost, and the suppression of Christianity was an essential part of this program. His insistence that Christianity was in essence an apostasy from Judaism is based on a personal familiarity with the Gospels and the Letters of Paul. He respects the antiquity of Jewish traditions, but it would be naive to think that his attitudes toward Judaism and, even more so, his plan to rebuild the temple in Jerusalem were simply a function of magnanimity. It was calculated to subvert triumphalistic Christian claims to represent the true Israel.[45] He dies before he is able to accomplish his goals and is buried in Paul's hometown, Tarsus (Ammianus Marcellinus, *Res Gestae* 25.10.5).

That Cyril of Alexandria sees fit to write a rebuttal in *Contra Iulianum* around 440 CE suggests that Julian's arguments were taken quite seriously by Christian leaders and that pagan influences linger on several decades after his death. Julian's writings, along with those of Porphyry, may have been used by an anonymous opponent of Paul whose arguments are preserved in the *Apocriticus* of Macarius Magnes.[46] Macarius is thought to be the bishop of Magnesia who goes by that name early in the fifth century. Whoever he is,

---

44. Nor does Jesus claim to be divine, according to Julian. In his historical novel about Julian, Gore Vidal embellishes Paul's role in the "Galilean impiety" (*Julian*, 297–300). "It is the wonder of our age," says Vidal's Julian, "how this simple-minded provincial priest was so extraordinarily transformed into a god by Paul of Tarsus." Jesus never thought of himself as divine and never contradicted the law of Moses: "Only by continual reinterpretation and convenient 'revelations' have the Galileans been able to change this reformer-rabbi's career into a parody of one of our own gods." He was simply "a reforming Jewish priest . . . with no interest in proselytizing outside the small world of the Jews." By Julian's day, when "the horde of bishops got through with Jesus," little of his original message was left (300). Julian himself does not go quite so far, however, blaming the author of the Gospel of John instead of Paul for deifying Jesus (*C. Galil.* 327B–C).

45. Wilken, *Christians as the Romans Saw Them*, 184–96.

46. Crafer, *Apocriticus of Macarius Magnes*, xvi–xxviii; Barnes, "Porphyry *Against the Christians*." Quotations here are taken from Hoffmann, *Porphyry's "Against the Christians."* Hoffmann believes these fragments are the work of Porphyry, but Barnes believes they come from a later writer who may be familiar with Porphyry.

the anonymous pagan provides the most thorough non-Christian assault on Paul—his thinking and his character—from the ancient world.

Like Porphyry, this critic is working with a firsthand knowledge of writings by and about Paul, quoting or alluding to Acts, Romans, 1 Corinthians, Galatians, 1 Thessalonians, and 1 Timothy (*Apocriticus* 3.30–36; 4.1–2). His most frequent rebuke is that Paul is a liar and a hypocrite. Mental illness—of the sort seen in having Timothy circumcised in spite of his assertion that the procedure is pointless—might be grounds for mitigating Paul's guilt, but one looks in vain for any leniency here. By becoming "all things to all people," he indulges the basest tendencies of his gullible hearers. In trying to be both a Roman and a Jew, he ends up hopelessly confused and "nullifies the usefulness of each [tradition] for he limits their worthwhile distinctions with his flattery" (3.31). On top of these character flaws, Paul's writings are theologically suspect. To the eschatological notion expressed in 1 Cor. 7:31 (RSV) that "the form of this world is passing away," one hears the Panglossian objection that, if this is true, God has not created the best of all possible worlds (4.1). Likewise, Paul apparently believes that the Creator intervenes willy-nilly to alter the laws of physics in claiming that the faithful will be able to fly up and meet Christ in the sky at his second coming (1 Thess. 4:15–17). He adds, sardonically, that Paul was wrong about the schedule for Jesus's second coming by three hundred years and counting (4.2). Is Paul a knave or a fool? Both, it seems.

The most original complaint, if not entirely fair because it takes an off-hand remark out of context, is that Paul cares too little about the welfare of animals (*Apocriticus* 3.32). This observation is made about the defense of the apostolic prerogative to accept payment by quoting Deut. 25:4 ("You shall not muzzle an ox when it is treading out the grain") in 1 Cor. 9:9–10 (RSV) and then adding, "Is it for oxen that God is concerned? Does he not speak entirely for our sake?" Paul's reasoning, it is argued, arrogantly limits God's providential care to human beings.[47] The least original complaint is that Paul's thinking lacks any consistency. Augustine writes that when he was a Manichaean he had regarded Paul's writings as full of contradictions and out of step with the Law and the Prophets (*Confessions* 7.21.27). Whether one classifies Manichaeanism as a heterodox form of Christianity or as a separate religion, his view of Paul was certainly widespread among pagan critics. Macarius's anonymous pagan ridicules the "hear no evil, see no evil" policy on the eating of idol meat in 1 Cor. 8–10 and finds at least three different

---

47. Plutarch (in, e.g., *De sollertia animalium* and *De esu carnium*) and others make a case for the ethical treatment of animals, but no one convicts Paul of violating their dignity until the modern period.

positions taken in the letters on the matter of marriage and virginity. He also faults Paul for misrepresenting the gospel, though this appears to be for tactical reasons and not out of any genuine desire to valorize fidelity to Jesus, since the pagan writer elsewhere scorns the ignominious nature of Jesus's death and compares him unfavorably to Apollonius of Tyana (*Apocriticus* 3.1–3). "It·is high time to let Paul's confusions rest in peace," he declares (4.2), but this rest will not last for long.

Muslims

During the Middle Ages, criticism of the apostle issues from a new direction. In his Letter to the Galatians (1:17), Paul mentions a visit to "Arabia," likely referring to the Nabataean kingdom near Petra in present-day Jordan. If he ever made it to the Arabian Peninsula, no account of his travels has survived. Not until the rise and spread of Islam in the seventh and eighth centuries do we hear what the Arabs thought of Paul. Nowhere does he appear in the Qur'an, notwithstanding the claims of some Christian and Muslim apologists to have detected covert allusions in its pages praising or condemning him. Late in the eighth century, however, he emerges as a leading character in narratives about the origins of Christianity that are uniformly hostile in their evaluation of his role in history.[48]

One of the earliest surviving references is found in *The Book of the Wars of Apostasy and Conquest* of Sayf b. 'Umar al-Tamīmī (d. 796), written in the eighth century but only discovered in the early 1990s.[49] Sayf's primary interest is in the divisions that wrack the early Muslim community when the infamous Ibn Saba' incites a rebellion against the third caliph, 'Uthmān b. Affān, in the middle of the seventh century. Ibn Saba' is described as a recent Jewish convert to Islam who travels far and wide and writes letters to his followers that contain what Sunni Muslims consider to be theological errors. Among these are the notion that Muhammad would soon return to the earth and that the legitimate successor to the Prophet is 'Alī, Muhammad's cousin and son-in-law.[50]

48. Michael R. Licona (*Paul Meets Muhammad*) constructs a fictional dialogue between Paul and Muhammad that summarizes many of the most common Muslim objections to the central Christian beliefs about Jesus.

49. Anthony, "Composition of Sayf b. 'Umar's Account," provides an English translation; see also Barzegar, "Persistence of Heresy." Al-Damīrī relays a similar story in the fourteenth century, but the work of al-Kalbī (d. 763) that he cites has not survived; see van Koningsveld, "Islamic Image of Paul," 205.

50. See Barzegar, "Persistence of Heresy," 215.

To the parallels between Ibn Saba' and Paul that are apparent to anyone familiar with the biblical portrait, Sayf adds many more in a colorful narrative that does not appear in earlier sources. Paul is introduced as a king who, shortly after the ascension of Jesus, initiates a persecution of his followers but is unable to destroy the movement. Recognizing the wide appeal of the Christian proclamation, Paul decides to disguise himself as a commoner and approach the Christians as a convert "with the intent to lead them astray." This he does by telling a story of an encounter with Jesus on the road that is reminiscent of the account in Acts. The Christians receive him and build a house for him from which he issues proclamations calling for changes in their customs: they need no longer worry about clean and unclean foods ("Everything from the beetle to the elephant is licit [*halāl*]"); they are to change their direction of prayer; and they are not to seek revenge when wronged. Sayf says that they abandon warfare (*jihad*) in response to the third instruction.

A fourth and final instruction proves to be too much for some members of the community. Paul declares to an audience of four—Ya'qūb, Nastūr, Malkūn, and "the Believer"—that in Jesus "God most High appeared to us and then concealed himself." The first three figures represent the three main divisions of Eastern Christianity (Jacobite, Nestorian, Melkite) from an early Muslim perspective. Three of the men accept this revelation, interpreting it in slightly different ways, but the Believer is horrified. He curses Paul, seeks God's forgiveness, and tries to convince the others that Paul has brainwashed them, something that ought not to have been possible since they were companions of Jesus. But to no avail. Ya'qūb, Nastūr, and Malkūn return to Paul, who orders them to hunt down and kill the Believer and his companions. (At this point, the Believer notes that Paul has already changed his own teaching in calling for a war against those who rejected his innovations.) A remnant escapes to Syria, where they hide in caves and wander about for generations. A remnant of this remnant is able to preserve their monotheistic faith until the coming of Muhammad, when they convert to Islam.[51] The account concludes, "And the like of Paul in this community is Ibn Saba'."

This narrative makes Paul the root of evil on at least three different levels. First, and most deplorable in the eyes of Muslims from antiquity to the present, he invents the notion of Jesus's divinity. Making anything a "partner" alongside or equal to God (*shirk*) is the gravest of sins listed in the Qur'an and a violation of the most basic Islamic creed, the *Shahāda* ("There is no God

51. Muhammad al-Qaysī identifies this remnant with the Knights Templars, described as crypto-Muslims who, in a letter allegedly suppressed by Pope Clement V, have maintained devotion to the truth as proclaimed by Jesus and the imams instead of the false teachings of Paul the Jew. See van Koningsveld and Wiegers, "Polemical Works of Muhammad al-Qaysī," 168–75.

but God"). The Qur'an contains numerous warnings about *shirk* specifically in reference to Jesus (4:171; 5:73, 116; 112:1–4), and one of the most popular poems praising Muhammad in the Sunni Muslim world, the *Qasidah Burdah* ("Poem of the Mantle") of the Sufi al-Būsīrī (d. 1295), urges the reader to "renounce what the Christians claim concerning their prophet" (3.29–30). Second, Paul introduces deviations in Muslim practice in areas such as diet and prayer. His nefarious influence extends to military matters as well in that he persuades the Christians to eschew war as a means of righting wrongs, a somewhat inconvenient characterization for observers who regard "holy war" only as a later departure from authentic Muslim teaching. Even more startling, Sayf has Paul paraphrase Jesus's saying from the Sermon on the Mount about turning the other cheek (Matt. 5:39–40) when he articulates this pacifist heresy. Third, Paul's machinations become the source of the sectarian strife that plagued the Near East in late antiquity. Ibn Saba' is a latter-day Paul, responsible for the split between Sunni and Shiite, at least from a Sunni perspective.[52] So Paul not only leads astray and divides the followers of Jesus; he is also to blame for the later schisms within the Islamic *ummah*.

Versions of Sayf's narrative are repeated by a number of prominent Muslim commentators throughout the medieval period, including Abū Isḥaq al-Thaʿlabī (d. 1035), Abū Muhammad al-Baghawī (d. 1122), and Abū ʿAbd Allāh al-Qurṭubī (d. 1273).[53] A point of emphasis in many retellings is Paul's Jewishness. Ibn Ḥazm (d. 1064) tells of a group of rabbis who bribe Paul to feign belief in Jesus so as to mislead the Christians with ideas about his divine status. Such behavior is typical of Jews, according to Ibn Ḥazm, who proceeds to highlight the inconsistencies found throughout Paul's letters on matters such as circumcision.[54] Hypocritical and deceitful, Paul is the last person on whom the Christians should have based their religion. The anti-Jewish character of these stories is even more explicit in al-Qarāfi (d. 1285). He relates a story about Paul revealing contradictory doctrines about the nature of Christ to three kings with the intention of corrupting the religion of the Christians and of sowing discord among them. Paul did this "because he was a Jew and he used to fight and kill many Christians."[55] The following day Paul committed suicide in the hope that his "martyrdom" would confirm the truth of his teaching. Al-Qarāfi

---

52. Van Koningsveld, "Islamic Image of Paul," 201–2; cf. Barzegar, "Persistence of Heresy," 220, 223. The same comparison is made by Abū Bakr al-Khallāl (d. 923).

53. Barzegar, "Persistence of Heresy," 226.

54. Pulcini, *Exegesis as Polemical Discourse*, 125; cf. Anthony, "Composition of Sayf b. ʿUmar's Account," 193–94.

55. Van Koningsveld, "Islamic Image of Paul," 205–6; cf. Fritsch, *Islam und Christentum im Mittelalter*, 49–50. Pseudo-al-Wāqidī likewise depicts Paul as an example of Jewish malevolence in his *Futūḥ al-Shām* (Barzegar, "Persistence of Heresy," 226). That the anti-Judaism of

reports that Paul was successful, citing the trinitarian confusions of the Christians as evidence. They had followed the religion of Islam for thirty-one years, and they would have avoided falling into heresy were it not for Paul.[56]

Whereas Muslim anti-Paulinism frequently underscores Jewish subversion, writers like ʿAbd al-Jabbār (d. 1025) move in a different direction. Al-Jabbār belonged to the Muʿtazil school, which emphasized the value of reason in theological speculation. His *Confirmation of the Proofs of Prophecy* rehearses many of the standard Muslim arguments for the validity of Muhammad's message and includes a lengthy section on the origins of Christianity featuring Paul as the main character.[57] Here Paul remains "a wicked and evil Jew." His lust for power, however, manifests itself when he becomes a Christian. The Jews mock him when he reports having a vision of Jesus and a mystical communion with God in heaven for fourteen days. When they hand him over to Roman officials, he abjures his Jewish faith, claiming to be not only a Roman citizen but even a devotee of the cult of Caesar. He takes Paul as a Roman name and insinuates himself into the imperial household, gaining the favor of the women by altering Jewish divorce laws and of the men by relaxing the laws pertaining to circumcision and eating pork.[58] In this manner, writes al-Jabbār, "Paul tore himself away from the religion of Christ and entered the religions of the Romans. If you scrutinize the matter, you will find that the Christians became Romans and fell back to the religions of the Romans. You will not find that the Romans became Christians."[59] So successful is Paul in his plan to get revenge against the Jews, according to al-Jabbār, that the Roman siege of Jerusalem in 70 CE is ascribed to his influence. Yet his luck eventually runs out. Though he claims that he can heal the sick, he is unable to heal himself when he contracts elephantiasis in his leg.[60] Revealed as a fraud,

this text is more pronounced than its anti-Christian stance is surprising given that it was likely produced during the Crusades.

56. On this score, al-Isfarāʾīnī (d. 1079) is more reliable than the fourteenth-century commentators al-Damīrī, who states that eighty-one years separate Jesus and Paul, and al-Dimashqī, who believes they are separated by one hundred fifty years. See Ebied and Thomas, *Muslim-Christian Polemics*, 397, 403; and Anthony, "Composition of Sayf b. ʿUmar's Account," 198n120.

57. A translation of the Paul material is found in Reynolds and Samir, ʿAbd al-Jabbār, "Critique of Christian Origins," 98–106. See also S. M. Stern, "Abd al-Jabbār's Account."

58. On a number of points where al-Jabbār alleges that Paul is contravening Jewish law as upheld by Jesus, he actually paraphrases sayings of Jesus found in the Gospels and puts them in Paul's mouth. See Reynolds, *Muslim Theologian*, 103–4.

59. Reynolds and Samir, ʿAbd al-Jabbār, "Critique of Christian Origins," 103. Al-Jabbār is clearly fond of this witticism since he repeats it three times. Compare George Bernard Shaw's bon mot that "the conversion of a savage to Christianity is the conversion of Christianity to savagery" and thus the conversion of Paul "was no conversion at all" ("Prospects of Christianity," xcvii).

60. Reynolds and Samir suggest that "leg" here may be a euphemism for "genitalia" (ʿAbd al-Jabbār, "Critique of Christian Origins," lii n98).

Paul dies by crucifixion at the command of Nero. Having lost this battle, he nevertheless wins the larger war by getting Christians to forsake the religion of Christ. No better sign of Paul's victory can be seen than in the fact that, according to al-Jabbār, Christians stand when his letters are read during the Mass but sit for the reading of the Torah and the Gospels.[61]

Al-Jabbār introduces Constantine immediately following his account of Paul's death. Constantine codifies the paganization of Christianity initiated by Paul.[62] Both men exemplify a recurring charge made by medieval Muslim polemicists: they compromise the religion of Jesus, usually for self-serving reasons. According to the twelfth-century Persian religious historian ash-Shahrasātnī (d. 1153), Paul perverts the religion of Peter by injecting notions drawn from Greek philosophy.[63] Even abandoning the language spoken by Jesus—not Aramaic but Hebrew, according to al-Jabbār—is "a trick and a ruse" to enable Paul and Constantine to falsify the Gospels and the other scriptures.[64] "Hypocrite" is an epithet regularly hurled at Paul because he knows exactly what he is doing. This is the view of al-Tha'labī, a prolific commentator and contemporary of al-Jabbār. Although Paul recognizes the truth of Jesus's Islamic message, he does not embrace it. With malice afore-thought, Paul decides instead to infiltrate the community and bring it down from the inside. "Hellfire is our destiny," he says, since he and his fellow Jews have neglected Jesus's teaching, and so he devises "a trick so as to deceive them that they may enter hellfire."[65]

Throughout this period, Paul becomes a byword for any and every anti-Islamic impulse. He is by turns a scheming and treacherous Jew and a pagan who betrays Mosaic law and Israelite monotheism to curry favor with Rome. He perverts the customs of "true" Christians, which coincide with Muslim

---

61. Stern, "Abd al-Jabbār's Account," 134.

62. Ibn Kathir (d. 1373) places more of the blame on Constantine, under whose influence "the religion of the Messiah became transformed" by the addition of such doctrines as one finds in the Nicene Creed; see Barker and Gregg, *Jesus beyond Christianity*, 122. Whether Constantine converted to Christianity "as a ruse to corrupt it, for he was a philosopher, or out of plain ignorance," Ibn Kathir is not certain. Al-Dimashqī links Paul and Constantine in another way, claiming that Paul buried the true cross for Constantine's mother to discover it (Ebied and Thomas, *Muslim-Christian Polemics*, 32).

63. Quoted in Watt, *Muslim-Christian Encounters*, 69. In his *Book of Sects and Creeds*, ash-Shahrasātnī also accuses Paul, to whom he ascribes the Letter to the Hebrews, of corrupting the Scriptures by assigning divine attributes to Jesus.

64. Stern, "Abd al-Jabbār's Account," 135–36. Al-Tabarī (d. 923) puts it somewhat more gently in the sixth chapter of his *Book of Religion and Empire*, suggesting that Paul's eloquence and rhetorical sophistication made him more susceptible to pagan ideas, unlike other followers, such as Peter, Matthew, and Luke.

65. Reynolds, *Muslim Theologian*, 164.

practices, as well as their doctrines, above all by fabricating the idea of Jesus's divinity in various forms. Not only does he participate in the program of distorting the Scriptures, but his own letters even usurp the place rightfully belonging to the prophets and the unadulterated gospel. False prophets like Mani, who overzealously accommodated his teachings to the cultural milieu of second-century Persia, can be maligned by means of a fleeting association with Paul, whose declaration that he has become "all things to all men" (1 Cor. 9:22 RSV) is cited as a damning admission by Muslim critics.[66]

In their evaluation of Paul, Muslim authors turn the tables on their Christian opponents. John Damascene (d. 749) and other early Christian interlocutors viewed Islam as a Christian heresy. As early as the compilation of the Qur'an, Islam regards Christianity as a bastardized form of the religion of Jesus. What becomes Christianity begins as a turn away from the pristine faith of Jesus the proto-Muslim. What becomes Islam begins as a rejection of Pauline blasphemies.

The most ambitious and perhaps the most successful premodern example of this line of attack is found in a document that mentions Paul only twice. He appears in the prologue and in the final lines of the *Gospel of Barnabas*, a text consisting of 222 chapters that presents itself as a life of Jesus told by an eyewitness.[67] Although non-Muslim scholars universally regard it as a pseudepigraphical writing produced no earlier than the thirteenth century and possibly as late as the early seventeenth century due to the numerous anachronisms it contains, most Muslims believe it to be an authentic document, possibly even the original version of the gospel that was altered by the ancient church so as to conceal the true Islamic character of Jesus's prophetic message.[68] Despite the serious doubts about its authenticity, it has been a staple of Muslim presentations of early Christianity from the early modern period to the present.[69]

This narrative weaves together stories from canonical and noncanonical gospels that are harmonized with the Qur'an. Barnabas is portrayed as one of Jesus's original disciples. Jesus speaks many of the lines attributed to John the Baptist in the NT. In his many speeches, Jesus is exasperated that the people think he is God, and he constantly denies that he is the messiah.

---

66. Ibid., 169–70, on Muslim comparisons of Mani and Paul.

67. Ragg and Ragg, *Gospel of Barnabas*, remains the only full-length English translation.

68. On the date of composition, see Slomp, "'Gospel of Barnabas.'" The oldest manuscripts are in Spanish and Italian. The Spanish version contains a preface describing its "discovery" in the papal library, while Sixtus V was napping, by a friar who subsequently converted to Islam. Also in the Spanish preface is the (unsupported) claim that Ignatius and Irenaeus were critical of Paul; see J. Fletcher, "Spanish Gospel of Barnabas."

69. Leirvik, *Images of Jesus Christ in Islam*, 132–44.

That title belongs to Muhammad. Countering these pernicious errors is the purpose given in the prologue for the writing of the *Gospel of Barnabas*: "Many, being deceived of Satan, under pretence of piety, are preaching most impious doctrine, calling Jesus son of God, repudiating the circumcision ordained of God for ever, and permitting every unclean meat: among whom also Paul hath been deceived, whereof I speak not without grief" (preface). The final chapter reinforces the point: "Certain evil men, pretending to be disciples, preached that Jesus died and rose not again. Others preached that he really died, but rose again. Others preached, and yet preach, that Jesus is the Son of God, among whom is Paul deceived" (222).[70] Together these passages recapitulate the main complaints about Paul and the Christian church expressed by other medieval Muslim authors.

While the identification of Muhammad as the messiah is not orthodox Muslim teaching, the repeated accusation that Christians have tampered with the Scriptures (*taḥrīf*) is very much a mainstream view that has its origins possibly as early as the Qur'an (2:75; 4:46; 5:13).[71] In the *Gospel of Barnabas*, Jesus himself laments these alterations even before there is a written Scripture to alter: "Cursed be every one who shall insert into my sayings that I am the son of God" (53.6). Here Paul is not blamed for inventing the doctrine that Jesus is God or the son of God. Roman soldiers, under the influence of Satan, are said to have stirred up the people by saying that Jesus was God (69.6). Paul is simply among those deceived. Due to the dissemination of his writings, however, the baleful consequences of his credulity on this fundamental theological question are without parallel. At the same time as Luther and Zwingli in northern Europe are invoking Paul in their attempts to restore Christianity to its primitive state prior to its corruption by Roman Catholicism, further south Muslims are pushing the date of the supposed apostasy even earlier and implicating Paul in the process.

Whatever their differences, Christians, pagans, Jews, and Muslims could find common ground when they wanted to take Paul to task. They disparage his character as well as his theology. He can be a liar, a hypocrite, and an inconsistent thinker. He is frequently condemned as unfaithful to his supposed master, Jesus—at least when Jesus is not being portrayed as illiterate, unstable,

70. Ragg and Ragg, *Gospel of Barnabas*.
71. Thomas, "Bible in Early Muslim Anti-Christian Polemic." As early as the fourth century one finds Emperor Julian asserting that the Christian church has altered the teachings handed down by the apostles (*C. Galil.* 327B–C).

or involved in sorcery. Modern observers may be surprised to see how often moral laxity is added to the list of sins. Many comments are based on hearsay or garbled retellings of old legends, but as time passes it is somewhat more common to find critics who have actually read Paul's letters. And while there appears to be some literary interdependence between the various authors, the vast differences—is Paul a conniving Jew or an idolatrous Roman?—cause one to wonder whether they are talking about the same man. Muslim writers are more prone to fanciful accounts, perhaps owing to the greater distance that separates them from the events they seek to interpret. Jews tend to ignore Paul and focus on Jesus and the problems posed by the Gospel narratives. European pagans eventually disappear or become Christian, Muslim, or, in rarer cases, Jewish. Even though it is unlikely that most ordinary non-Christians gave him much thought at all, attitudes toward Paul present in microcosm the main lines of their briefs against the Christian religion as a whole.

3

THE ENLIGHTENMENT AND BEYOND

Jesus, Paul, and the Rise of Modern Biblical Scholarship

Martin Luther, one of Paul's greatest admirers, altered the religious and political landscape of Europe. The contributing factors for the changes he brought about are not always those one might suspect, and many of the effects are not at all what he would have anticipated, much less desired. His own writings testify to the pivotal role played by Paul in the spiritual crisis that led to the events of 1517 in Wittenberg and beyond. Romans and Galatians in particular prompted soul-searching of a kind that transformed his understanding of himself and his relationship to God. Without Paul, then, one could argue that Luther would never have called into question the doctrines and practices mentioned in his Ninety-Five Theses. But without Johannes Gutenberg and the advent of the printing press over half a century earlier, it is unlikely that Luther's eager students would have translated, reproduced, and distributed them so widely, causing matters to come to a head with church authorities. At the very least, the related Reformation notions of *sola scriptura* and the priesthood of all believers might have seemed moot without the increased access to the Bible made possible by movable type.

Paul influenced Luther, and Luther in turn influenced Paul's legacy in an unparalleled fashion. Together they also illustrate the law of unintended consequences. Justification by faith becomes the heart of the gospel for much of Protestant Christianity. On this score, Luther would be delighted. He loved

Galatians like he loved his wife—"I have betrothed myself to it," he says in one of his table talks, "it is my Katie von Bora"—because it so forcefully articulated this doctrine.[1] How to understand the relationship between faith and works was a major point of contention between Luther and his Catholic opponents.[2] It was also, if many scholars are correct, a question on which Paul and James took divergent positions. Luther sided with Paul against James, whom he saw as critical of Pauline teaching.

Luther negotiates this putative conflict in a way that echoes for the next several centuries. To extend the aural metaphor, how much distortion is involved in these reverberations is not immediately clear. Conflicts within the canon, be they real or only apparent, pose acute problems for interpreters who hold a high view of Scripture and subscribe to the doctrine of *sola scriptura*. In order to resolve this tension, Luther adverts to a form of *Sachkritik*. "Content criticism" and "theological criticism" are standard translations for this technical term.[3] While it is usually associated with Rudolf Bultmann, its application to Luther is not inappropriate given his willingness to recognize a de facto "canon within the canon" with adherence to Pauline teachings on sin and grace as the criterion for inclusion. *Sachkritik* operates under the assumption that authors do not always say exactly what they mean. The interpreter's prior understanding of what constitutes the basic subject matter of a text (the *Sache*) sets the parameters for what that text can mean. "What is said" is thus interpreted in light of "what it means."

Hermeneutical operations of this sort are not infrequently performed in an arbitrary manner. For Luther, *was Christum treibet*, "what shows thee the Christ," is the key that unlocks Scripture. Not all Scripture proclaims the good news in the same way or with the same degree of purity. "What does not teach Christ is not apostolic, not even if taught by Peter or Paul," he writes in the preface to James in his 1522 German translation of the NT. Conversely, "what does preach Christ is apostolic, even if Judas, Annas, Pilate, or Herod does it."[4] Luther had little doubt that Paul's writings possessed this apostolic character, and his decision to place Hebrews, James, Jude, and Revelation at the end of this edition of the NT was motivated by the judgment that their contents were incommensurate with Pauline teaching. (He breaks from the

1. Quoted in Mattox, "Martin Luther's Reception of Paul," 112.
2. Only recently (e.g., with the 1999 Joint Declaration on the Doctrine of Justification) have Protestant and Catholic theologians begun working together to understand and undo the mutual condemnations issued in the Reformation and Counter-Reformation; see Aune, *Rereading Paul Together*.
3. R. Morgan, "*Sachkritik* in Reception History."
4. See Dillenberger, *Martin Luther*, 36.

long-standing tradition that Hebrews was written by Paul.) The selection of *was Christum treibet* as a touchstone for interpreting the Bible within a Christian framework is not by any means without merit, but its relative simplicity invites elaboration. In the following centuries, theologians and biblical scholars elaborate that seemingly clear and simple message in the course of justifying principles and practices that would perhaps be anathema to Luther, all the more so if he were to learn that they cite him as a guiding light. Whereas Luther embodied the critical spirit that gave rise to modern biblical scholarship in acknowledging the diversity of voices within the canon and in questioning ecclesiastical tradition, he had only cracked open the door. Not content to ignore or reconcile any tensions that may be felt, others would come along during the Enlightenment to kick down the door and pit Jesus against Paul, appealing not to "what proclaims Christ" but, more often than not, to "what Christ proclaimed."

Sixteenth-Century Rumblings

The strategy of driving a wedge between Jesus and Paul had been employed prior to the early modern period. It was long a staple of anti-Christian polemic produced by Jews and Muslims. Isaac of Troki, a sixteenth-century Polish-Lithuanian rabbi, stands in continuity with this tradition. Readily available editions of the NT furnished him with ample material with which to carry out his program of refuting the claims of Christianity in his *Ḥizzuk 'Emunah* (*Faith Strengthened*). The second part of his work is a syllabus of errors committed by the NT authors. Chapters 67–93 deal mainly with Paul, who he says is misinformed about Israelite history, ignorant of the Hebrew language, and guilty of twisting the Scriptures, quoting them out of context and ignoring the intent of the original authors. (Isaac's treatment of Paul's writings occasionally exhibits the same tendencies.) In his critique of Pauline inconsistency, he highlights differences between Acts and the Pauline Epistles, a step later interpreters will take to undermine the reliability of Acts. He refers to Paul's circumcision of Timothy in Acts 16:3, positively contrasting it with the church's later abandonment of the practice, only to cite it as evidence of hypocrisy on the next page.[5] Not surprisingly, he also takes the side of James against Paul on faith and works, a topic that may have come up in his debates

---

5. Isaac of Troki, *Faith Strengthened*, 278–89. After quoting Paul (Gal. 5:3) on the necessity of maintaining the whole law for those who are circumcised, he remarks, "These words ought to be kept in constant remembrance by those Christians who urge us to abandon our holy faith and adopt their religious observances" (285).

with Lutherans.[6] Unlike many other polemicists who castigate Christians for failing to follow Jesus's example, however, Isaac never goes the route of calling Paul the founder of Christianity, generally reserving that title for Jesus. This "kitchen sink" approach in which Isaac pulls out every imaginable argument against Christianity may belie the claim made in the preface that he is primarily concerned to address the flagging zeal of his coreligionists. But this may be a false choice. Attacking Christianity and affirming Jewish identity are not mutually exclusive, as can be seen in a wide range of historical contexts.

Once they were translated into Latin in the seventeenth century, Isaac's writings were used by later critics of Christianity, as were those of the more radically skeptical Spinoza.[7] This development was a momentous one. Not since late antiquity had there been wholesale attacks on Christianity except by Jews and Muslims. Occasional murmurs can be heard prior to the seventeenth century. Erasmus was sometimes accused of denigrating Paul.[8] Andreas Bodenstein von Carlstadt, another collaborator and, later, critic of Luther, had suggested a tripartite division of the NT in his 1520 *De canonicus scripturis libellus*, with Paul's letters placed behind the Gospels but ahead of most of the Catholic Epistles and Revelation on the grounds that Paul's words do not have the same authority as those of Christ.[9] Reservations such as this are mild, however, compared to the frontal assaults that would occur during the Enlightenment.

The Deists of the Seventeenth and Eighteenth Centuries

England witnessed the beginnings of modern anti-Paulinism late in the seventeenth century. Its emergence was a part of the broader development of critical approaches to the study of the Bible taken by a number of Enlightenment figures associated with Deism.[10] John Locke's belief in divine revelation and miracles usually marks him as a precursor to, rather than a full-fledged proponent of, Deism. His view, set forth in *The Reasonableness of Christianity* (1695), that true revelation can be deduced from and never conflicts

---

6. Ibid., 18–19 (on Luther), 288–89 (on faith and works).

7. Surprisingly, Spinoza actually appeals to Paul in his attacks on traditional Judaism; see Langton, *Apostle Paul in the Jewish Imagination*, 234–42. It has been argued, however, that his remarks contained veiled criticisms of Paul that discerning readers were able to detect (Bagley, "Spinoza," 255–65).

8. Tinsley, *Pierre Bayle's Reformation*, 46–47.

9. Beard, *Martin Luther*, 401. Carlstadt disagreed with Luther's view that James contradicted Pauline teaching; see Sider, *Andreas Bodenstein von Karlstadt*, 94–97.

10. Reventlow, *Authority of the Bible*, 393–94, 289–334, 354–83; Baird, *History of New Testament Research*, 1:31–57.

with reason inspired later Deists to argue, quite reasonably, that revelation thus appears to be superfluous. Beyond simple belief in Jesus as the Messiah, little is required of the Christian except to lead a moral life, for which Jesus's example as recorded in the Gospels is the surest guide. "But 'tis not in the Epistles we are to learn what are the Fundamental Articles of Faith," according to Locke, since in Paul "they are promiscuously, and without distinction mixed with other Truths in Discourses that were (though for Edification indeed, yet) only occasional."[11] For Locke, most of the teachings contained in the letters are adiaphora, and to make them essential to the faith is to court precisely the sort of intolerance that causes civil unrest. As is the case with Carlstadt's comments, this hardly constitutes an attack on Paul, but Locke's responses indicate that some readers viewed his stance as tantamount to "contempt of the epistles" and turning them into "waste paper."[12] When he turns his full attention to the letters in *A Paraphrase and Notes on the Epistles of St. Paul to the Galatians, Corinthians, Romans, Ephesians*, published posthumously in 1705, he largely steers clear of controversy by focusing on historical rather than theological questions. His most critical comments have to do with Paul's writing style, which is characterized by "confusion, inextricable obscurity, and perpetual rambling," though he is inclined to write this impression off as a natural consequence of approaching the letters with insufficient familiarity with their context.[13] (Less forgiving is Voltaire, who observes disingenuously in his 1764 *Philosophical Dictionary* that Paul's writings "are so sublime, it is often difficult to understand them."[14])

Locke was often linked by his conservative critics with John Toland, the Irishman whose *Christianity Not Mysterious* (1696) set off the Deist controversy that would last for decades.[15] There he argues that a "natural religion" had been practiced by all humanity before its corruption with various ceremonies, sacrifices, and complicated theological speculations. Irrational doctrines like the Trinity violate the simple principles of this religion and introduce divisions between Christianity and the monotheistic religions with which it is in needless conflict, Islam and Judaism. His most thorough exposition of this thesis is found in *Nazarenus; or, Jewish, Gentile, and Mahometan*

---

11. Locke, *Reasonableness of Christianity*, 166. He believes that there is no danger in questioning doctrines "delivered in the Epistles, which are not contained in the Preaching of our Saviour and his Apostles, and are therefore by this Account not necessary to Salvation" (167).

12. Ibid., xlii–lvii.

13. Quoted in Wainwright, *John Locke*, 1:111. Cardinal Pietro Bembo, a friend of the Renaissance pope Leo X, allegedly refused to read Paul's Epistles to avoid contaminating his Ciceronian Latin; see Reinach, *Short History of Christianity*, 75.

14. Voltaire, *Philosophical Dictionary*, 5:200.

15. Sullivan, *John Toland*, 109–40; Reventlow, *Authority of the Bible*, 294–308.

Christianity (1718). On the Jewish side, he had learned of groups such as the Ebionites and the Nazarenes from his reading of patristic literature and was aware that they had rejected Paul's letters.[16] He deems these groups to be "the Primitive Christians most properly so call'd, and the only Christians for some time" and aims to describe them "in a truer light than other writers."[17] "The Original Plan of Christianity" was never that the Jews, "whether becoming Christians or not," should cease observing the law of Moses.[18] Any notion to the contrary is due to Paul's gentile converts who "did almost wholly subvert the TRUE CHRISTIANITY," which is obscured by "the rubbish of their endless divisions, and . . . the almost impenetrable mists of their sophistry." In arguing for the historical primacy of this form of Jewish Christianity, Toland simultaneously hopes to establish as most authentic a form of the faith that will be most conducive to religious and political harmony.[19] Just as the gentile forms of Christianity aligned with Paul had no more legitimacy than Jewish forms, so also the various Christian denominations have no basis for laying claim to a more pristine heritage than their rivals.[20] "Live and let live" is the moral of Toland's story.

Toland's treatment of Islam likewise has an anti-Pauline edge. He mentions the *Gospel of Barnabas* on the title page of *Nazarenus* and later quotes its first and last verses, which disparage Paul. While modern scholars regard it as a late-medieval forgery, for Toland it demonstrates that "this notion of Paul's having wholly metamorphos'd and perverted the true Christianity . . . and his being blam'd for so doing by the other Apostles" is not a Muslim fabrication but, rather, "was the constant language and profession of the most ancient sects."[21] He never explicitly approves this judgment, but in equating the Muslim message of the *Gospel of Barnabas* with that of the early Ebionites and

---

16. Toland, *Nazarenus*, 29, 80–81.

17. Ibid., iii. In *Amyntor* (64) Toland had already referred to the Ebionites and the Nazarenes as "the oldest Christians." The Welsh Deist Thomas Morgan is frequently but incorrectly quoted as a critic of Paul in the mold of Toland. When Morgan states that "St. Paul then, it seems, preach'd another and quite different Gospel from what was preach'd by Peter and the other Apostles," however, he is writing in the voice of Theophanes, a Jewish-Christian interlocutor and not in the voice of Philalethes ("Lover of Truth"), who represents Morgan's own convictions (*Moral Philosopher*, 1:80). Morgan looks on Paul as "the great Free-thinker of his Age, the bold and brave Defender of Reason against Authority" (71).

18. Toland, *Nazarenus*, vi.

19. Matt Jackson-McCabe ("Invention of Jewish Christianity," 69–70) contends that the very category of Jewish Christianity "was a byproduct of Toland's attempt to lay claim to the mythic source of Christian authority—Jesus and the apostles—for his own Enlightenment ethos of rationality, universal humanity, and tolerance."

20. F. Jones, "Genesis, Purpose, and Significance," esp. 94–96.

21. Toland, *Nazarenus*, 24.

characterizing the Ebionites, who saw Paul as "an intruder on the genuin[e] Christianity," as the original Christians, Toland certainly implies that he takes a similarly dim view of Paul's influence.[22] Whether this exemplar of Enlightenment skepticism sincerely believed the *Gospel of Barnabas* to be an ancient document is unclear.[23] The dominant impression is not that he wants to hail Islam as a superior religion—he shows little interest in Muslim teachings apart from Islam's strict monotheism, and Muslims would take exception to his categorization of Islam as a sect of Christianity—but to relativize the absolutist claims of Christianity and neutralize the authoritarian impulses that he associates with dogmatism. In this regard Toland made common cause with Socinianism, an antitrinitarian movement that originated in the mid-sixteenth century and sought to construct a counternarrative to the official historiographies put forward by both Catholic and Protestant orthodoxies of the day.[24] Research into Islamic texts was also a key ingredient in revisionist efforts like those of Henry Stubbe, who had incorporated medieval Muslim legends about Paul's alleged role in the corruption of Christianity in his *Account of the Rise and Progress of Mahometanism* (1671), just a few decades before Toland took the lead in promoting the *Gospel of Barnabas* among European thinkers.[25]

While he has little to say about the commonalities between Islam, Judaism, and Christianity, Thomas Chubb shares Toland's desire to recover and reassert the primacy of the religion of Jesus in *The True Gospel of Jesus Christ Asserted* (1738). The essence of this religion is to repent of one's sins and follow the moral example set by Jesus. Had Jesus never lived, however, the duty of the individual to lead a moral life would be unchanged. If Christianity is essentially a reiteration of timeless moral truths—a claim made explicit in Matthew Tindal's Deist manifesto *Christianity as Old as Creation; or, the Gospel a Republication of the Religion of Nature* (1730)—then it makes little chronological sense to regard Jesus as the founder of a new religion. At the same time, it would be a mistake to conclude that Chubb thus sees Jesus as simply continuing in the traditional Judaism into which he was born since Chubb essentially sees no place in the Christian

22. Ibid., 16, 29. His allusions to the anti-Pauline Pseudo-Clementine literature likewise reinforce this impression (23). One of Toland's earliest critics, Thomas Mangey, suspected that his use of the *Gospel of Barnabas* was intended "to prove our whole Christianity to be no other than a gross Blunder." See Lurbe, "John Toland's *Nazarenus*," 55.

23. Jackson-McCabe, "Invention of Jewish Christianity," 74–75.

24. Mulsow, "Socinianism," 578–85; see also Sullivan, *John Toland*, 135–36, on Toland's use of the *Gospel of Barnabas* to defend Unitarianism as the primordial, and therefore normative, form of Christianity.

25. Champion, "'I Remember a Mahometan Story.'"

Bible for the OT, with its many ceremonial requirements and its morally ambiguous God.[26]

Judaism deviated from the universal religion of nature before the advent of Jesus, according to Chubb, and after his death the Christian church did much the same thing by insisting on assent to such doctrines as original sin, the Trinity, the incarnation, and imputed righteousness, which were nowhere contained in Jesus's own teachings. The gospel, moreover, "is not an historical account of matters of fact."[27] Here Chubb anticipates the position most famously articulated by G. E. Lessing that the "accidental truths of history can never become the proof of necessary truths of reason."[28] Included among the historical facts that are not integral to the gospel is the death of Jesus, and it is merely the "private opinion" of certain of his followers that the cross atones for the sins of the world. And "any of their reasonings, or conclusions founded on, or drawn from such opinions" are not a part of the gospel.[29] Along with John, he singles out Paul as a prime example of a biblical author whose writings "were in many instances very abstruse, and much above the capacities of the common people," replete with "unintelligible propositions, which [are] liable to a thousand difficulties and perplexities."[30] Christ's preaching, by contrast, "was plain and intelligible, and level to the lowest understanding, as indeed it ought, and must needs be."[31] The perspicuity that, according to Luther and other Reformers, characterizes all of Scripture is here limited to the words of Jesus.

Peter Annet is considerably more direct in his treatment of Paul than either Toland or Chubb, who now and then concede that Paul has worthwhile things to say. So forceful are his criticisms, in fact, that he is compelled to publish them anonymously. Before turning his full attention to the apostle, he had already, in *The Resurrection of Jesus Considered* (1744), expressed grave doubts about Paul as a credible witness for the proclamation of the risen Lord. A few years later, he launches a full-scale attack in *The History and Character of St. Paul, Examined* (ca. 1748). This work resembles others in which he attacks Joseph, Moses, and David. In training his sights on Paul, however, Annet takes aim at the figure who was, "properly speaking, the author of a new religion."[32] At the outset he states that Christianity's legitimacy is contingent on the credibility

26. Reventlow, *Authority of the Bible*, 393–94.
27. Chubb, *True Gospel*, 43.
28. See Chadwick, *Lessing's Theological Writings*, 53.
29. Chubb, *True Gospel*, 46.
30. Ibid., 49–50. Chubb refers specifically to Paul's outline of salvation history in Rom. 9–11.
31. Ibid., 49.
32. Annet, *History and Character of St. Paul*, 46–47. On Annet more generally, see Herrick, *Radical Rhetoric*, 125–44.

of Paul's conversion and status as an apostle. Having already dissected the Gospels and found them wanting, he cannot imagine that Paul's writings can be any more reliable, and "therefore the Christian tradition is the least of all histories to be regarded for genuine and uncorrupted truth."[33]

Before making his case, Annet sets out the standard terms of the debate:

> [Paul] either was an imposter, who said what he knew to be false, with an intent to deceive, or he was an enthusiast, who by the force of an overheated imagination imposed on himself, or he was deceived by the fraud of others; and all that he said must be imputed to the power of that deceit; or what he declared to be the cause of his conversion, and to have happened in consequence of it, did all really happen; and therefore the Christian religion is a divine revelation.[34]

Imposter, enthusiast, or true apostle: these are the options available to the impartial observer, though Annet also allows that the information on which any decision must be based has been falsified by an unknown writer. From his study of patristic literature, he is aware that groups like the Cerinthians, Marcionites, and Encratites called into question both Acts and Paul's letters. More inclined to trust Acts than the letters, he uses both in arguing that Paul is an unreliable guide.

Annet engages in a ferocious ad hominem attack in building a case for Paul as an imposter. Because he was of the working class but too lazy for manual labor, Paul decided to turn informer by spying on the Christians on behalf of the high priest. But he ends up joining the Christians after contemplating the personal risks in persecuting them, "for they were not Quakers, as Malchus's ear was a proof."[35] His famous conversion was thus insincere, motivated by cowardice as well as by the favorable prospects of advancement in the new sect. Annet also repeats ancient rumors about Paul seeking the hand of the high priest's daughter in marriage and even aspiring to the office of high priest. Rebuffed on both counts, he sought to spite the Jews by going over to their enemies. Readers should not be fooled by Paul's reports on these affairs. "None complain more of being meanly used," says Annet, "than those that are most proud. . . . Great profession of piety and humility oft shew a want of it."[36] If vanity and insincerity were Paul's only flaws, perhaps his testimony would not be entirely tarnished. When one adds dishonesty to the list, no defense remains: "He that will dissemble and lie, and deceive, and

33. Annet, *History and Character of St. Paul*, 12.
34. Ibid., 16.
35. Ibid., 35.
36. Ibid., 41.

curse, and swear, and forswear, may be esteemed a very pious saint, but is a very immoral man."[37]

In attributing Paul's teaching and behavior to "enthusiasm," Annet is speaking a language imbued with social and political meanings peculiar to early modern England, albeit with parallels in France and Germany. "Enthusiasts" were individuals who believed themselves to enjoy privileged, direct communication with God and were possessed by excessive or misdirected religious emotions.[38] Especially in the years following the Glorious Revolution of 1688, enthusiasm included advocacy of political or sectarian causes in the public square. It was odious in the eyes of the Anglican establishment because it was widely regarded as the catalyst for the bloody English Civil War of 1642.[39] Continental Europe similarly wanted to avoid a repeat of the ravages caused by the Thirty Years' War. Writing in the same decade as Annet, David Hume provides a vivid sketch:

> Hope, pride, presumption, a warm imagination, together with ignorance, are, therefore, the true sources of ENTHUSIASM. . . . Being founded on strong spirits, and a presumptuous boldness of character, it naturally begets the most extreme resolutions; especially after it rises to that height as to inspire the deluded fanatic with the opinion of divine illuminations, and with a contempt for the common rules of reason, morality, and prudence.[40]

Whereas enthusiasm was usually associated with Protestant sects, superstition was the corresponding Catholic vice. No more sympathetic to one than to the other, Deists like Annet tended to agree with the assessment of Joseph Addison that "an Enthusiast in Religion is like an obstinate Clown, a Superstitious Man like an insipid Courtier. Enthusiasm has something in it of Madness, Superstition of Folly."[41] Neither is commensurate with tolerance or political stability.

Hume's enthusiast and Annet's Paul are clearly birds of a feather. Annet frequently links Paul to Methodist preachers John Wesley and George Whitefield,

37. Ibid., 97; cf. 66. Annet compares Paul's solemn affirmations of his truthfulness to those he heard about stories of witches and spirits when he was a child, adding, "We seldom hear a man say, he does not lie, unless he is very apt to lie . . . seriously and strenuously" (25).

38. J. Goldstein, "Enthusiasm or Imagination?"

39. Heyd, "Reaction to Enthusiasm."

40. Hume, "Of Superstition and Enthusiasm," 74, 77.

41. Joseph Addison, in the *Spectator*, October 20, 1711. He continues, "Most of the Sects that fall short of the Church of England have in them strong Tinctures of Enthusiasm, as the Roman Catholick Religion is one huge overgrown Body of childish and idle Superstitions." While Annet may focus on Paul's "Protestant" faults, he regards the Roman Catholic Church as a vile and hopelessly corrupt institution (*History and Character of St. Paul*, 7, 47).

the prototypical enthusiasts in eighteenth-century England. Fresh air or an emetic would normally be prescribed for those in the habit of cursing anyone who disagreed with them as Paul did. The violent mood swings seen in Paul's letters are likely due to the irregular circulation of his bodily humors.[42] Paul may not be an incorrigible liar, but the dreams and visions he constantly invokes are easily manipulated by others. The discrepancies in the three accounts of his conversion contained in Acts suggest that they are the product of delirium.[43] Psychophysical factors are likewise behind the many contradictions and non sequiturs scattered throughout his letters, as Paul "had too much heat to reason cooly, and too great a crowd of tumultuous ideas to range them in good discipline."[44]

Although his treatment is the most thorough Deist critique of Paul, Annet generally eschews one of the most popular approaches, that is, highlighting the disagreements between Paul and Jesus. He implies that Christians look to Paul for guidance only because the foundational belief in Jesus's resurrection is so unstable. But it is a mistake to make assent to any miracle, as Paul does with the resurrection in 1 Cor. 15, the sine qua non of authentic Christian faith. When "the church is brought to hang on this single thread," it is bound to snap.[45] There is a viable alternative, however, for those with ears to hear. Annet concludes with a call to natural religion, which by its very nature has no need for the dubious supernatural claims that define historic Christianity: "Whatever may be proved true concerning St. Paul, does not at all concern the truth of religion, whether he was a wise man or an enthusiast, an honest man or an imposter; but the religion of him that stands on St. Paul must fall with him."[46] The strident, sarcastic tone he adopted likely contributed to his conviction for blasphemy at the age of seventy, for which he was sentenced to stand in the pillory, but his ideas spread to the continent when his work was translated into French by the famous atheist Baron d'Holbach in 1770 and later translated back into English in 1823.[47]

The foremost German counterpart to the English Deists is Hermann Samuel Reimarus. In his early writings he rejects miracles as a violation of the laws of nature and the concept of divine revelation as contrary to the tenets of natural religion. Cognizant of Annet's fate, perhaps, he decided not to publish

42. Annet, *History and Character of St. Paul*, 25–27.
43. Ibid., 53–57, 65: "It was to be sure the abundance of visions and revelations that made him abundantly forgetful." See also 96: "The giddy headed man that changes from one sort of superstition to another, tho' he may be called a convert, is not the better man."
44. Ibid., 31.
45. Ibid., 19; cf. Herrick, *Radical Rhetoric*, 36–37.
46. Annet, *History and Character of St. Paul*, 106.
47. Herrick, *Radical Rhetoric*, 142–43.

his more provocative treatise, *Apology for the Rational Worshippers of God*.
Shortly after Reimarus's death in 1768, Lessing began to publish the *Apology*
in the form of "fragments of an anonymous author." The seventh fragment,
"On the Purpose of Jesus and His Disciples," refers to Paul.[48] According to
Reimarus, Jesus had no plans to found a new religion separate from Judaism.
This was the work of his disciples, for whom the crucifixion was definitive
proof that Jesus was mistaken about the nearness of the kingdom of God.

The disciples had expected to gain worldly wealth and status when they
forsook their trades to follow Jesus—indeed, Jesus had promised he would
give them these things when he came into his kingdom—and they were not
about to let his failed mission dash their hopes and dreams of financial and
political power. Membership in Jesus's entourage procured for them many
benefits. They had learned from their master that traveling preacher "was not
an unremunerative occupation" and were loath to experience the disgrace of
appearing again to their neighbors as ordinary fishermen or, worse, as beggars
after their "high and mighty expectations" had been frustrated.[49] Thinking
and acting quickly, they stole his body from the tomb and fabricated the Easter story out of whole cloth. The disciples then spun an elaborate theology
about the salvific effects of Jesus's death as allegedly foretold in OT prophecies. Unlike Annet, who depicts Paul as bumbling about in a charismatic fog,
Reimarus considers him to be the cleverest of the disciples. And although he
mocks Paul's logic and rhetoric, he has to acknowledge the superior forensic
skill he displays in his jousts with the Pharisees and Sadducees in Acts.[50] On
this score, at least, he is a worthy successor to Jesus. His Scripture-twisting,
question-begging sermons enabled the disciples to sustain the fraud they had
successfully perpetrated even as their predictions about the imminent return
of Jesus were proven wrong.

Lessing's judgment of Paul is less caustic, but his publication of Reimarus's
fragments was motivated by a shared desire to undermine revealed religion
and to create a climate in which a more rational alternative might flourish.
(Another of the fragments is titled "The Toleration of Deists.") For neither
Reimarus nor Lessing is Jesus an infallible teacher, but he is to be preferred
to Paul and others who preached in his name. In a 1780 essay Lessing states
the Scriptures contain the clear and simple religion of Christ as well as the
"uncertain and ambiguous" passages that are the source of endless division.

---

48. Translated as "Concerning the Intention of Jesus and His Teaching" by Ralph S. Fraser
in Talbert, *Reimarus: Fragments*, 59–269.
49. Ibid., 245; "it follows with all moral certainty that the possession of worldly wealth
and power was also the object of the apostles in the fabrication of their new doctrine" (243).
50. Ibid., 251–52, 256–57.

But the reader should be aware that "the religion of Christ and the Christian religion are two quite different things" and are incompatible insofar as the latter regards Jesus as more than human and as an object of worship.[51]

Across the Atlantic, pamphleteer Thomas Paine was no less indefatigable in opposing what he saw as the superstition and "moral mischief" accompanying the spread of Christianity.[52] He inspired the American colonists in their fight for independence from Great Britain and later moved to France in support of the revolution of 1789. When he ran afoul of Robespierre, he was imprisoned for ten months and passed the time writing part 1 of *The Age of Reason*, in part to provide a Deist alternative to the militant atheism of the Reign of Terror. Republican sentiment and theological conviction for Paine went hand in hand, and while the trajectory of his literary career may suggest that the former precedes the latter, they were firmly wedded well before he addressed the Bible in the 1790s.

The relationship between Paul and Jesus is an animating concern for Paine, as it had been for Annet and Reimarus. "Had it been the object or the intention of Jesus Christ to establish a new religion," Paine asserts, "he would undoubtedly have written the system himself, or procured it to be written during his lifetime." As he did not see fit to do so, it is only natural that the NT is full of contradictions, and consequently its authors must resort to all manner of equivocation and linguistic sleight of hand in order to reconcile them. Of these authors, Paul is the preeminent "manufacturer of quibbles" in a religion "interlarded with quibble, subterfuge, and pun" and "very contradictory to the character of the person whose name it bears." Christianity is "a religion of pomp and of revenue in pretended imitation of a person whose life was humility and poverty."[53]

Paine wrote part 2 after he escaped the guillotine and was freed from prison. He describes Paul as violent and prone to fanaticism, citing Annet's work as a source for the ancient smears against Paul with which he concurs.[54] With access to a copy of the Bible, he was able to document in detail the Pauline doctrines he opposed, such as original sin, the atonement, redemption by

51. Lessing, "Religion of Christ." Lessing's friend J. G. Herder similarly observes that the teaching of Jesus "was simple and comprehensible to all: God is your Father and you are all brothers one of another. . . . Whoever contributes to bringing back the religion of Jesus from a meretricious slavery . . . to that genuine Gospel of friendship and brotherliness, of convinced, spontaneous, free, glad participation in the work and intent of Jesus as they are clearly set forth in the Gospels" has performed a valuable service (quoted in Kümmel, *New Testament*, 83).

52. Walters, *Revolutionary Deists*, 113–44.

53. Paine, *Age of Reason*, 16, 18–19.

54. Paine, *Age of Reason: Part the Second*, 85–86. He refers to Boulanger, the pseudonym used by d'Holbach in his French translation of Annet.

means of the cross, and the resurrection of the body.[55] Elsewhere he essentially dismisses his letters as authoritative because it is impossible to trust that they were written by Paul. He does the same with nearly every other book in the canon. That the Scriptures were dependent on the political dictates of ecclesiastical hierarchies for their canonical status is, for Paine, reason enough to reject them. Whether it is Paul or, more likely, someone else writing in his name, the author is a predecessor to the priestly caste that manipulates the Scriptures to benefit despots up to the present day.[56] For good measure, however, he says that Paul's letters are not worthy of study even if he wrote them. Romans, which contains "the stupid metaphor of the Potter and the clay," has "nothing in it that is interesting except it be to contending and wrangling sectaries."[57] The happiness of the human race requires that all nations hark back to an age from which sectarian strife was absent. Reformation thinkers identified this era as the time of Jesus and his apostles, including Paul. This primitivist impulse takes Paine back much further—to Adam, the first Deist.[58] It is an understatement to say that Paine meant to relativize the claims of Christian orthodoxy. "Of all the systems of religion that ever were invented," he declares, "there is none more derogatory to the Almighty, more unedifying to man, more repugnant to reason . . . than this thing called Christianity."[59] Other Deists of the time likely shared this view. Few were willing to state it so unambiguously.

The critical spirit embodied by Renaissance humanists and Reformation theologians produced a truly impressive body of biblical scholarship in terms of both quantity and quality. British Deists over the following two centuries pioneered many of the approaches now regarded as quintessentially modern, even though they were philosophers, craftsmen, political propagandists, and the like rather than biblical scholars by training. John Locke and Peter

55. Ibid., 89–95. Elihu Palmer, an admirer of Paine and founder of the Deistical Society of New York in 1796, was similarly exercised by Paul for his espousal of the doctrine of original sin, arguing that it eroded moral responsibility (Walters, *Revolutionary Deists*, 191).

56. Davidson and Scheick, *Paine, Scripture, and Authority*, 27–36, 62–65. Paine's anti-Catholic rhetoric, found also in his earlier political writings, was widespread but not universal in colonial America.

57. Paine, "Of the Books of the New Testament," 344. He regards Tertius, the scribe who inserts his personal greeting in Rom. 16:22, as the true author. Throughout this essay, he takes the subscripts included in the King James Version that refer to Paul's scribes as proof that Paul did not write any of the letters ascribed to him.

58. Paine, *Age of Reason*, 55.

59. Paine, *Age of Reason: Part the Second*, 102.

Annet, Paul's chief antagonist during the Enlightenment, struck a particularly modern note by insisting that Paul be judged by the same standards that are applied to figures of other times and places, anticipating the heightened methodological self-awareness of nineteenth-century writers like Benjamin Jowett, who laid down the then-controversial principle that the Bible should be read "just like any other book."[60] The Renaissance and Reformation zeal for textual discovery and the recovery of older sources turned up evaluations of Paul that had lain dormant in Christian Europe for a millennium. Such writers' credulity when presented with ancient legends discrediting Paul, to be sure, often overcame their otherwise hypercritical faculties. (As Peter Gay observes, "Even the sane among the deists had a paranoid view of history and politics: they saw conspiracies everywhere.")[61] Whether the anti-Paulinism of the Enlightenment was the catalyst for or the consequence of the newer, more skeptical assumptions about and methods for studying the Bible and traditional religion more generally is not entirely clear. That they continued to develop in tandem, at any rate, is apparent.

One aspect of Deist exegesis and argument that has drawn praise is its sensitivity to context. These writers recognize that neither Paul nor Jesus existed in a vacuum. Reimarus is especially astute in his treatment of Jesus in his Jewish setting. Jesus may not be universally admired—Voltaire and others thought of him as a deluded "prophet"—but when he is compared to Paul, it is never to the apostle's advantage. Any departure from the religion of Jesus—as opposed to the religion about Jesus—is seen as a perversion. But while many writers salute Jesus the Jew as a foil to Paul with the right hand, with the left hand they are denigrating Judaism as a barbarous deviation from the universal religion of nature. Paine, for example, describes the OT as "a history of wickedness that has served to corrupt and brutalize mankind," better understood as "the word of a demon than the word of God." Other Deists regularly associate Judaism with blindness, superstition, fraud, and tyranny.[62] So if Jesus's religion is superior to Paul's and yet Judaism is depraved, then either their high esteem for Jesus is insincere or else the implication is that he is not truly Jewish. This turns Jesus into a cipher for their own Deist convictions.

Finally, through no fault of his own, during the Enlightenment Paul became entangled in the politics of what Michael C. Legaspi calls "the death of Scripture" and the concurrent rise of biblical studies as a scholarly discipline. The

60. Jowett, "On the Interpretation of Scripture," esp. 377.
61. Gay, *Deism*, 10.
62. Lucci, "Judaism and the Jews."

havoc wrought by confessional particularities in the centuries following the Reformation led many thinkers to embark on the construction of a political theology that would sustain an irenic social order. Such a project required a Bible stripped of its scriptural properties, a process accomplished in part by embedding the Bible in an alien, ancient culture. A prodigious body of historical scholarship on Christian origins was one by-product of this process, but just as important for its producers was that it acted "as a prophylactic against fundamentalism."[63] This was in no way history for history's sake. Different witnesses describe the purported death of Scripture in different ways: Was it premeditated murder or simple manslaughter? Critics in the nineteenth century would come increasingly to consider it justifiable homicide so long as it prevented Paul from committing further crimes against humanity.

63. Legaspi, *Death of Scripture*, ix, 5–6.

4

THE NINETEENTH CENTURY

Paul's Cultured Despisers

"How could the doctrinal system of Paul arise on the basis of the life and work of Jesus and the beliefs of the primitive community?" Looking back over the nineteenth century from early in the twentieth, Albert Schweitzer says that answering this question is one of the "great and still undischarged task[s]" of biblical scholarship.[1] It was not for lack of trying. The failure to find a satisfactory answer is perhaps less striking than the fact that the question so thoroughly consumed the guild in the first place. That it did so is an indication that the Deist interpretation of Paul had moved closer to the mainstream by century's end.

The predominance of the critical approaches to Paul did not come about overnight. Schweitzer focused on Germany, and especially on the pivotal role played by Ferdinand Christian Baur beginning in the 1830s (see below). But German scholars had already cast a wary eye Paul's way a few decades earlier. Johann Gottlieb Fichte, the idealist philosopher who would deeply influence Hegel, situates Paul in the second of five stages of history through which the human race progresses, from the rule of instinct to the rule of reason. In his lectures of 1804, he says that there are actually "two very different forms of Christianity," one contained in the Gospel of John and the other, "degenerate

---

1. Schweitzer, *Paul and His Interpreters*, v.

form of Christianity," in the writings of Paul.[2] John's Jesus "knows no other God than the true God," appealing to reason rather than to miracles. Once he has become a Christian, Paul cannot admit that he had been in the wrong in having been a Jew and so feels compelled to unite the two systems: "Paul and his party, as the authors of the opposite system of Christianity, remained half Jews; and left unaltered the fundamental error of Judaism as well as of Heathenism."[3] Elsewhere Fichte softens his criticism, but only a bit: "I do not say that in Paul, generally, True Christianity is not to be found: when he is not directly engaged with the great problem of his life—the intercalation of the two systems—he speaks so justly and excellently, and knows the True God of Jesus so truly, that we seem to listen to another man altogether."[4] In other words, as a teacher Paul is trustworthy, even inspiring—except when he is speaking on what he thinks matters most.

Jefferson, Bentham, and Carlile

Anglo-American writers likewise remained preoccupied with the question of Paul's relationship with Jesus. In fact, it inspired one of the best-known and most curious products of American religious history, the Jefferson Bible. Officially christened *The Life and Morals of Jesus of Nazareth*, the Jefferson Bible began as a literal cut-and-paste job carried out with a straight razor. Thomas Jefferson read through the Gospels and excised the miracles as well as those passages where Jesus claims to be divine. Paul's letters, replete with references to Jesus as God's Son, are not included. The result is a portrait of Jesus much more in tune with Jefferson's own Deist philosophy than the canonical rendering. Interestingly, Rammohun Roy, the Bengali reformer known as "the father of modern India," produced a very similar "Bible" in 1820 titled *The Precepts of Jesus*. Jefferson and Roy were animated by the same unitarian impulse originating in Great Britain and spreading around the globe in a way made possible by empire.[5]

Jefferson describes his project in an 1803 letter to Benjamin Rush, a fellow signer of the Declaration of Independence. "To the corruptions of Christianity

2. Fichte, *Characteristics of the Present Age*, 98–99, 201, though Fichte states that this was "a necessary product of the whole spirit of the Age" (201). It was inevitable for this form of Christianity to appear, by Paul's hand or someone else's.

3. Fichte, *Way towards the Blessed Life*, 96.

4. Fichte, *Characteristics of the Present Age*, 100. Fichte believes that the doctrine of justification represents Paul's misunderstanding of Jesus by making his status as the Jewish messiah, demonstrated in his death, central to his significance; cf. Jüngel, *Justification*, 33–36.

5. Zastoupil, "'Notorious and Convicted Mutilators.'"

I am indeed opposed," he writes, "but not to the genuine precepts of Jesus himself." In this respect, Jefferson was influenced by English Deists such as Joseph Priestley and Henry St. John (Viscount Bolingbroke).[6] With his letter, Jefferson enclosed a "Syllabus of an Estimate of the Merit of the Doctrines of Jesus, Compared with Those of Others." This syllabus lays out his basic views about Jesus and the principles that guided the editorial decisions he made in putting his Bible together. He notes that Jesus, like Socrates, wrote nothing, but Socrates at least had a Xenophon to record his teachings. (Plato "only used the name of Socrates to cover the whimsies of his own brain.") In the case of Jesus, this task "fell on unlettered and ignorant men," and his doctrines "have been still more disfigured by the corruptions of schismatizing followers, who have found an interest in sophisticating and perverting the simple doctrines he taught, by engrafting on them the mysticisms of a Grecian sophist, frittering them into subtleties, and obscuring them with jargon."[7] Who might he have in mind?

An 1820 letter to Jefferson's personal secretary, William Short, gives the answer.[8] While there is much to admire in Jesus's teachings, it is mixed together with "so much ignorance, so much absurdity, so much untruth, charlatanism and imposture, as to pronounce it impossible that such contradictions should have proceeded from the same Being." Jefferson attributes this state of affairs "to the stupidity of some, and roguery of others of His disciples," and singles out Paul as "the great Coryphaeus" of "this band of dupes and imposters." Whether Paul was more dupe or imposter, he does not say. But in calling him "the first corrupter of the doctrines of Jesus," Jefferson intimates that Paul knew what he was doing. "Coryphaeus" was the title given to the leader of the chorus in ancient Greek drama. Were it not for "the palpable interpolations and falsifications of [Jesus's] doctrines" of those for whom Paul served as spokesman—which, in addition to the substitutionary theory of the atonement and the emphasis on faith over works, included the cruel and capricious nature of God associated by Jefferson with Calvin and the doctrine of predestination—there would have been no need to set things in order.[9] Were Jefferson to hear of Saul K. Padover dubbing him "the St. Paul of American democracy," he would not have taken it as a compliment.[10]

6. Koch, *Philosophy of Thomas Jefferson*, 9–14, 23–29. After a lengthy discourse on Paul's muddled reasoning, Bolingbroke comments that "where it is intelligible it is often absurd, or profane, or trifling" (*Works of Lord Bolingbroke*, 3:430). On the same themes in Jefferson's correspondence with John Adams, see J. Smith, *Drudgery Divine*, 7–9.

7. Quoted from Jefferson's "Syllabus," 3:508.

8. Quotations from Jefferson's letter are taken from Adams, *Jefferson's Extracts from the Gospels*, 391–94.

9. Sanford, *Religious Life of Thomas Jefferson*, 61, 144–46.

10. See Padover, *Thomas Jefferson on Democracy*, 1.

Jefferson did not want word of his Bible to get out while he was in office, and the fact that it was not published until well after his death suggests that most Americans would not have been receptive to his views. His contemporary and occasional correspondent, Jeremy Bentham, faced a similar situation in England. If ever a book could be judged by its cover, it would be his *Not Paul, but Jesus*, published under the pseudonym Gamaliel Smith in 1823. The title gives his answer to the dilemma faced by "every professor of the religion of Jesus," namely, "to which of the two religions, that of Jesus or that of Paul, he will adhere."[11] In the Gospels and the Pauline Epistles, it is clear that "two quite different, if not opposite, religions are inculcated; and that, in the religion of Jesus may be found all the good . . . [and] in the religion of Paul, all the mischief."[12]

Originally projected to appear in three volumes, only the first was published before Bentham died in 1832. In this first volume, he rehearses many of the standard arguments attacking Paul's integrity and consistency found in the work of previous writers like Peter Annet and Isaac of Troki, adding his own special points of emphasis. Paul's "conversion" was outward only; it was faked in order to bolster his credentials as a spokesman for Jesus and to secure the fame, wealth, and power he craved.[13] An inveterate liar, Paul fabricates such stories as the appearance of the risen Lord to five hundred disciples (1 Cor. 15:6) and invents the idea of the antichrist in 1–2 Thessalonians so as to keep his prophecies of the second coming from being proved false. The title of the final section of the final chapter asks the rhetorical question, "Paul, Was He Not Antichrist?" and supplies an answer in the affirmative: for those who look for an antichrist ("with or without horns and tail"), "they need not go far to look for one." As Bentham did not believe in demons, it is obvious that by this title he means "neither more nor less than that which is opposed to Christ," but this hardly diminishes the opprobrium he means to heap on Paul.[14]

Volume 2 of *Not Paul, but Jesus*, dealing with the history of the early church, was never published, and only very recently has volume 3 been transcribed and published (in 2013) under the auspices of University College London, where the philosopher's preserved corpse is still on display.[15] A glance at the contents of volume 3 reveals the reason for the delay. Under the rubric of

11. Bentham, *Not Paul*, xvi. See also McKown, *Behold the Antichrist*, 117–282.
12. Bentham, *Not Paul*, vii.
13. Ibid., 73, 395.
14. Ibid., 371–73.
15. A version of this material written in 1816 is available in Bentham, *Of Sexual Irregularities, and Other Writings on Sexual Morality*. Philip Schofield ("Jeremy Bentham") discusses the third volume in the context of Bentham's wider corpus.

"asceticism," it deals exclusively with differences between Jesus and Paul on "the pleasures of the bed." Bentham had already registered his opinion in volume 1 that Jesus did not advocate asceticism. He saw no harm in eating and drinking "unless with the pleasure it produced greater pain."[16] In this sense, Jesus was the first to espouse the philosophy that Bentham and John Stuart Mill articulate as utilitarianism, according to which moral actions are those that result in the greatest good or happiness for the greatest number of people, with "good" understood in terms of pleasure. By means of "hedonic calculus," it is possible to determine the aggregate amount of pleasure or pain produced by any act. Paul is bad at this basic math. Asceticism violates the principle of utility by increasing pain and decreasing pleasure in this life while unnecessarily complicating the equation with illusory punishments and rewards in an afterlife.

Insofar as "gratification accorded to the sexual appetite"—referred to by Bentham as "the sixth sense"—provides the greatest of pleasures, its condemnation prevents individuals from achieving happiness.[17] More than any other person, Paul bears responsibility for promoting the soul-crushing asceticism enforced by church and state to the detriment of its citizens. It originates in the law of Moses, but whereas Jesus criticizes the law, Paul seeks to retain it in this aspect, likely influenced by Stoics, who regard pleasure and pain as poor guides in the pursuit of virtue.[18] When he ushers in "the demon of asceticism," "those who on this ground relapsed into the doctrine of Moses and his hypocrite spawn the Pharisees gained the ascendant" while "those who adhered to the doctrine and practice of Jesus were driven out of the field."[19] For Paul, the only licit sexual activity takes place "in the ordinary mode," within marriage for the purpose of procreation. Such a restriction, according to Bentham, is arbitrary and decidedly nonutilitarian. He first attempts to explain away most of the supposed biblical prohibitions against "unnatural" sexual relations. He then argues that, since Jesus nowhere explicitly condemns homosexuality, one may conclude that he approves of it. Nothing can be found in the Gospels indicating disapproval of sexual activity "in whatever shape and from whatever source derived."[20] Bentham is somewhat selective in his references to the cultural background of early Christianity in making this

16. Bentham, *Not Paul*, 394.

17. Bentham, *Not Paul*, 3:54–55.

18. Schofield, "Jeremy Bentham," 64–65. He sees Jesus as essentially Epicurean; see Bentham, *Not Paul*, 3:196n42.

19. Bentham, *Not Paul*, 3:110.

20. Ibid., 111; cf. 122: "By Jesus and his religion, no gratification in any shape from this source had been placed in the catalogue of sins."

argument from silence, mentioning the permissive attitude found in ancient Greece but dismissing the proscriptions found in the OT as misinterpretations or as the ravings of a mind obsessed with uncleanness. More controversial, he further speculates that Jesus likely engaged in relations with the women who attended him in his ministry and also partook of "the eccentric pleasures" with "the Beloved Disciple" in the Fourth Gospel and with the naked youth—a male prostitute, he suspects—in Mark 14:51–52.[21]

Along with homosexuality, Bentham endorses a number of other "irregularities" that "the principle of utility could not without inconsistency condemn," such as prostitution, polygamy, contraception, divorce, abortion, and infanticide (or, as he euphemistically calls it, "the power of breeding-up or not during early infancy").[22] Pleasures unnecessarily forgone and pains endured are not the only evils laid at Paul's feet. For commending "ordinary" sexual relations to the exclusion of all other kinds, Bentham blames Paul for the overpopulation that Thomas Malthus describes as a looming disaster in his 1798 *Essay on the Principle of Population*.[23] Against the traditional view that homosexuality poses a threat to human survival because of its sterility, Bentham argues that it not only increases happiness but also provides a more practicable remedy to the dangers of overpopulation than the abstinence prescribed by Malthus.

Bentham's reluctance to go public with these ruminations may have had something to do with the experience of Richard Carlile, his friend and fellow agitator who spent several years in jail on blasphemy charges related to his publication of Thomas Paine's *The Age of Reason*.[24] Carlile continued to publish his radical newspaper *The Republican* while incarcerated at Dorchester. He refers to Paul as "that loveless cripple" who founded Christianity in an 1825 essay "What Is Love?" that appeared in print the following year as *Every Woman's Book*, often cited as the earliest English sex manual to tout the health benefits of sexual pleasure and to include instructions on contraception.[25]

An open letter to the presiding judge at his blasphemy trial illustrates the degree to which Carlile attributed the defects of Christianity to the personal hang-ups of Paul, "the originator of that horrid Christianism . . . which has

21. Ibid., 177. He recognizes that the question is one of "extreme delicacy" but feels compelled to address it on the grounds of "the comfort of mankind and the sound principles of penal justice."

22. Ibid., 57–67.

23. Ibid., 30–36. See also Levy, "Malthusianism or Christianity."

24. Carlile praises Paine for having the courage to criticize Paul openly; see Wiener, *Radicalism and Freethought*, 33–54. Carlile had also published a number of Bentham's works.

25. Carlile, "What Is Love?," 551; see also Bush, *What Is Love?*

both degraded, stupefied, and desolated Europe to this day."[26] Drawing on the physical description in the *Acts of Paul and Thecla*, he mercilessly ridicules him as short, lame, and ugly. "Almost every town furnishes an eccentric and a crippled shoe-maker that much resembles this portrait of Paul . . . the little crooked dog [who] has done more mischief, by the crookedness of his mind, than any other man who has lived."[27] Lazy but clever—like most short men—this "comical little character" is "a perfect adept in the art of deceit."[28]

The latter half of the letter lampoons Paul in the form of a satirical dialogue in which Carlile imagines the recipients of 1 Corinthians responding to the instructions contained in that letter.[29] Speaking for the other women, Priscilla says that she would rather listen to Paul's sermons than receive one of his "holy kisses" and that she would hate a man with crooked thighs, "even though he were a saint." (Shuddering, she adds, "Lord! It must be like a crab creeping about one!") The Corinthians are not persuaded by Paul's arguments about relations between the sexes, as "there is nothing natural about this Saint Paul, and it is clear that he knows nothing about nature." Charges of ignorance and inconsistency are punctuated with a swipe at his virility: "Had Saint Paul been man enough to marry, he would have learnt better how to make laws for women." As if this were not scandalous enough, Carlile also refers to the lewd acts condemned by that "vile hypocrite" in Rom. 1:26–32 and promises to publish a literal translation "with suitable notes and graphic illustrations."[30]

Ferdinand Christian Baur and the Tübingen School

More influential, if less titillating, than the attempts of Bentham and Carlile to situate Jesus and Paul in their historical context was that of F. C. Baur. Although certain aspects of his presentation of early Christianity were anticipated by the English Deists John Toland and Thomas Morgan, Baur's impact and that of his Tübingen School on the field of NT scholarship is without equal.[31] The idealist philosophy of history of Fichte and, especially, Hegel provided the background for understanding this presentation and Paul's place in it. For Hegel, history can be viewed as an unfolding dialectical process in which an idea (the "thesis") emerges but proves unsatisfactory

26. Carlile, "To the Christian Judge Bailey," 678.
27. Ibid., 678, 681.
28. Ibid., 677, 681.
29. Ibid., 687–89.
30. Ibid., 683.
31. Lincicum, "F. C. Baur's Place," 139–41. For a broader assessment of his legacy, see H. Harris, *Tübingen School*.

and thus generates a competing idea ("antithesis") until a new idea is produced as a result ("synthesis"). This "compromise" in turn becomes a new
thesis, and the process continues. It would not be accurate to see Baur as
simply trying to prove the truth of Hegel's system, but there is no doubt
that the schema proved heuristically useful as he considered the history of
the early church.

Baur took the first step in reconstructing this history in an 1831 essay on
the divisions in the Corinthian church, where Paul's law-free gospel, popular
among gentiles, came into contact with Peter's law-observant Jewish Christianity, representatives of which cast aspersions on Paul for not having been
a disciple of Jesus.[32] These two opposing tendencies remained in conflict,
according to Baur, until their "reconciliation" in the second century in the
form of "early Catholicism," which drew its institutional forms from the early
Christian community that was still immersed in Judaism.[33] The book of Acts
harmonizes the Petrine and Pauline factions, and in so doing, presents a version
of history that is not at all true to first-century realities. As one might expect
from a nineteenth-century Lutheran, Baur's views of "early Catholicism" and
of the Judaism from which it was derived were not complimentary. For Paul,
by contrast, he has high praise. Paul is "the first to lay down expressly and
distinctly the principle of Christian universalism as a thing essentially opposed
to Jewish particularism," and if ever "hierarchical Catholicism should again
overgrow evangelical Christianity," Paul stands ready to reassert "the original
Christian consciousness in its most vital element."[34]

Where does this leave Jesus in relation to Paul? Side by side, as it turns
out. "Is it possible to speak in any real sense of the essence and contents
of Christianity," Baur asks, "without making the person of its founder the
main object of our considerations? . . . Is not its whole meaning and significance derived from the person of its founder?"[35] Jesus, notwithstanding "the
cramping and narrowing influence of the Jewish national Messianic idea,"
is the original embodiment of the principle of universalism subsequently
taught by Paul, who "introduced Christianity to its true destination as a
religion for the world."[36] According to Baur, the primitive Jewish-Christian
community in Palestine, albeit in closer chronological proximity to Jesus,

32. Baur, "Christuspartei."

33. On the category of "early Catholicism" as used by Baur and his followers, see Neufeld,
"'Frühkatholizismus'"; Harris, *Tübingen School*, 198–207; and Thielman, *Theology of the
New Testament*, 484–93.

34. Baur, *Church History*, 1:47, 113. "The narrow limits of Jewish particularism" (180) is
a recurring theme in Baur's work.

35. Ibid., 23–24.

36. Ibid., 49.

had a looser grasp than did Paul of Jesus's purported intentions to transcend Judaism.

Baur reoriented NT scholarship to such a degree that modern students largely take his thesis-antithesis-synthesis for granted. Several aspects have been rejected by conservative and liberal scholars alike, such as his theory that Revelation is one of the earliest documents in the NT and that it was written in part to combat Pauline teaching. In broad strokes, however, the Tübingen model fairly describes a consensus that still obtains among critical scholars, most of all in its account of Christianity beginning in theological diversity and only later arriving at greater doctrinal conformity under the aegis of the Roman church. Even those unpersuaded by the exegetical arguments on which this model is based find it difficult to break free from it. It was no part of Baur's agenda to denigrate Paul in this outline of Christian history. But he establishes a framework wherein it becomes possible to arrive at a radically different assessment of Paul, one that emphasizes his distance and deviation from the historical Jesus rather than an underlying organic unity in the Hegelian realm of "Spirit" of which Jesus's companions had only a faint grasp.

The Tübingen model requires that each NT document be situated chronologically in this developmental history of early Christianity. Baur saw Christianity evolving along a trajectory that led him to accept only four of the Pauline Letters as authentic—Romans, 1–2 Corinthians, and Galatians. Because the other letters do not exhibit the same type or degree of conflict, they do not fit into this trajectory. Rather than adjusting the model, Baur concluded that they must have been written at a much later date. On the question of dating and authorship, he went beyond even the most skeptical position embraced today. One might describe Baur's stance as anti-Pauline in a qualified sense in that he denied Pauline authorship for some letters that Paul actually wrote on the grounds that they contain "non-Pauline" elements.

Baur was not the first writer to cast doubt on the authorship of the letters. Friedrich Schleiermacher had paved the way in 1807, arguing that the literary style of 1 Timothy was not that of Paul and was thus proof of pseudonymity.[37] Few writers would go to the same extreme as Bruno Bauer or the Dutch Radicals, who would argue that none of the letters are authentic, but it was in this period that the question became a defining feature of Pauline scholarship.[38]

37. Schleiermacher, *Über den sogenannten ersten Brief des Paulus an den Timotheus.* J. E. C. Schmidt had expressed doubts about the authenticity of 1 Timothy three years earlier but did not attract the same attention as Schleiermacher did with his open letter. See Patsch, "Fear of Deutero-Paulinism." Whereas Schleiermacher only questioned the authorship of 1 Timothy, Baur would reject all three Pastoral Epistles (*Die sogenannten Pastoralbriefe*).

38. Schweitzer, *Paul and His Interpreters*, 118–28.

By putting the issue of authorship front and center, Baur and Schleiermacher affirmed a precedent whereby critics of Paul need not accept or reject in toto the thirteen-letter Pauline corpus. Schleiermacher had previously sought to defend Christianity against its enemies, who in his view misunderstood the true nature of religion, the "cultured despisers" mentioned in the subtitle of his 1799 treatise *On Religion*. In retrospect, it looks as if he is handing them a scalpel with which they might inflict death by a thousand cuts on the writings of its most prominent spokesman. While it does not appear that this was his intention—he repeatedly states that he wants to prevent religion from becoming a "dead letter"—his ambivalence toward Scripture is evident. He tells his readers that they are correct to look down on "the paltry imitators who derive their religion wholly from someone else or cling to a dead document by which they swear and from which they draw proof. Every holy writing is merely a mausoleum of religion."[39]

The Tübingen School did not have the last word on the relationship between Paul and Jesus. Baur's disciples as well as his critics produced a prodigious body of scholarship in the ensuing decades, respectively refining or finding fault with his portrait of early Christianity.[40] Their ambitious research programs, executed in the course of attempting to settle the question, helped to establish NT studies as a serious academic discipline. The achievements of the Quest for the Historical Jesus were the most noteworthy fruit of this labor. Together with the "solution" to the synoptic problem arrived at by H. J. Holtzmann, the Quest arose in conjunction with the Jesus-Paul debate if only for the reason that, in order to assess Paul's continuity with Jesus, one must first gain a clearer view of Jesus's life and message. In his masterful 1906 survey of the Quest, Albert Schweitzer documented its successes and also some of the overconfident reconstructions of Jesus's biography. Comparative study of myth and religion gave rise to creative "deconstructions" of Jesus's biography as well, with a growing number of "Christ myth" proponents arguing that Jesus never existed.[41] This theory remained on the fringe, but its advocates joined the chorus of writers claiming that Paul founded Christianity—on the grounds that a nonexistent Jesus could not possibly have done so himself.

---

39. Schleiermacher, *On Religion*, 50.

40. On the early response to Baur in Germany, see Furnish, "Jesus-Paul Debate"; and in the United States, see E. A. Clark, *Founding the Fathers*, 106–12, 169–202.

41. The most prominent advocate of the "Christ myth" position was Bruno Bauer; see Schweitzer, *Quest of the Historical Jesus*, 137–60. Richard Carlile also subscribes to the mythicist theory, which explains why his criticism of Paul is not articulated as a betrayal of Jesus's teachings ("To the Christian Judge Bailey," 673).

Development and Decline

Nineteenth-century discussion of Jesus and Paul took place against the back-drop of a larger preoccupation with historical processes of development and change, of which Hegelian dialectic and, later, Darwinian evolution stand as two prominent examples.[42] This emphasis on change and development, however, did not displace a much older tendency to accentuate decline as the defining characteristic of history, at least as it applies to the church. Hege-sippus in the second century says that the church had continued as "a pure and uncorrupted virgin" until the reign of Trajan, when "the sacred choir of the apostles became extinct and the generation of those who had been privi-leged to hear their inspired wisdom had passed away" (Eusebius, *Hist. eccl.* 3.32). Many of the Protestant reformers believed that the church underwent a "Great Apostasy" the further it strayed from the simple teachings of Jesus and extrapolated doctrines and institutions not found explicitly in the NT, a view that pervades Matthias Flaccius's *Magdeburg Centuries*, the most com-prehensive ecclesiastical history written during the sixteenth century. Several denominations formed in the post-Reformation period with an explicit goal of reviving the original form of Christianity practiced in the apostolic age. In the wake of the Second Great Awakening, Restorationist movements such as the Campbellites preached "no creed but Christ" and endeavored to call "Bible things by Bible names" in pursuit of this ideal, sometimes resisting the label "denomination" inasmuch as it implied that they were not in possession of the faith practiced before divisions set in and most of Christendom deviated from the teachings of Jesus. For these movements, there was little question of Paul being out of step with Jesus. While few claimed access to new revelations that made it possible to span the vast chronological gap separating the present from the ancient Christian past, as did the Latter-Day Saints under Joseph Smith, these diverse movements shared a conviction that a vital connection to the church's roots in the apostolic era had been severed by the time of the Council of Nicaea.[43]

Development and decline are two sides of the same coin. The common denominator they share is change, and everyone acknowledged that the shape of Christian faith and practice had changed—at some point, in some ways, to some degree. Protestants in this setting tended to regard this change as mainly for the worse, at least until the long medieval slide into ignorance and

---

42. Meeks and Fitzgerald, *Writings of St. Paul*, 397.

43. R. T. Hughes and C. L. Allen, *Illusions of Innocence*; R. T. Hughes, *American Quest*; Manning, "'That Is Best, Which Was First'"; Hammond, *John Wesley in America*; and Wilcox and Young, *Standing Apart*.

superstition was arrested in the Reformation. Jesus is an outlier in this view of history, representing a temporary reprieve from the widespread malaise expressed by Roman writers like Livy. Once he was gone, the bleak status quo reasserted itself. Early Catholicism's concern for "externals" such as law and priesthood was seen as a resumption of degenerate Jewish religion under a new guise.

Catholics, needless to say, saw things differently. While the notion that Catholic theologians recognized no difference between the church of the nineteenth century and the one purportedly founded by Jesus is a caricature, it is true that their telling of Christian history emphasized the static over the dynamic. The Protestant insistence on basing doctrine and practice on "Scripture alone" was part of a larger strategy, along with emphasis on the Pauline doctrine of justification by "faith alone," for staking a claim to closer continuity with Jesus than one found in Catholic tradition. Observance of special holy days or spiritual disciplines, monastic orders, sacramentalism, veneration of Mary and the saints—for Protestants these constituted illegitimate departures from the teachings of Jesus. For Catholics, they represented the authentic development of elements already present in seed form though in no way visible during the church's infancy. John Henry Newman contended that "from the history of all sects and parties in religion, and from the analogy and example of Scripture, we may fairly conclude that Christian doctrine admits of formal, legitimate, and true developments . . . contemplated by its Divine Author."[44] Drawing on the analogy of the emergence in adulthood of inherent traits not apparent during childhood, he argued that change of some sort was to be expected in the history of so complex a religious system founded on divine revelation. (That Newman's thinking on development was not simply a reactionary, rearguard attempt at salvaging religious belief in the face of scientific discoveries that threatened to undermine it was apparent from the fact that Darwin did not publish *On the Origin of Species* for another decade.) But one person's development is often another person's devolution. Protestant commentators on occasion conceded that first-century audiences may not have been as capable of appreciating the manifold richness of Jesus's teachings as later audiences but were discomfited by assertive gestures such as the formal definition of the dogma of papal infallibility at the First Vatican Council in 1870 that asserted a prerogative to adjudicate cases where there was disagreement.[45]

Development and decline often occur gradually, organically, and impersonally, but sometimes it is anything but accidental or incidental, fostered instead

44. Newman, *Development of Christian Doctrine*, 113.
45. E. Clark, *Founding the Fathers*, 172–73.

by an active agent. That agent, in the eyes of a growing number of observers, was Paul. Baur actually saw development—understood in a Hegelian or "spiritual" sense if not in terms of visible ecclesiastical institutions—as a phenomenon that resulted in world-historical progress. In pushing back the point of departure into the apostolic era and implicating Paul in the process, he made both Catholics and Protestants nervous. In the paradigm inaugurated by Baur, the NT itself—the putative basis for distinguishing legitimate development from illegitimate deviation—thus became a product of the very conflicts it had previously been thought to predate. Paul's critics embraced the concept of theological or moral development in the abstract—at least in that they saw Paul as a backward thinker whose inordinate influence hindered progress as construed by Enlightenment thinkers—yet simultaneously deployed the primitivist rhetoric of decline to undermine his position and impugn his character.

However influential Baur's theories were, especially among scholars, it was not as if everyone else attended to the finer points of his arguments or waited for the disagreements to be settled before forming their opinions. Ralph Waldo Emerson was well acquainted with German biblical scholarship and its approach to the relationship between Jesus, Paul, and the early church. In letters to his brother William, a theology student in Göttingen, he expressed particular interest in the work of scholars who provided the strongest arguments against the divine authority of the NT.[46] He drew on this scholarship in the 1832 sermon that led to his departure from the ministry at Second Church Boston, the only one of his sermons to be published during his lifetime.[47] Emerson had requested permission to discontinue celebration of the Lord's Supper and laid out his reasoning in this sermon. Jesus did not intend to establish a perpetual observance, he said, citing the fact that of the four Gospels only Luke suggests otherwise by including the instruction "Do this in remembrance of me" (22:19). Paul indicates in 1 Cor. 11:23–26 that it had become a regular ordinance, but "his mind had not escaped the prevalent error of the primitive church," that is, the belief that the second coming of Christ would shortly occur, a crucial fact that "diminishes our confidence in the correctness of the Apostle's view." Emerson also urged his Unitarian audience to abandon the Pauline understanding of the communion rite for the way in which it made Jesus more than human.

Emerson's reliance on an argument that presupposed eyewitness testimony in Matthew and John is curious given his familiarity with German skepticism

46. Hurth, *Between Faith and Unbelief*, 22–27. See also Roberson, *Emerson in His Sermons*, 193–98.

47. Quotations here are taken from *Emerson's Complete Works*, 11:9–29.

about the authorship of the Gospels and their late date of composition relative to the letters. Equally striking is the ease with which he jettisoned primitivist rhetoric and rationales in making the case that "the opinion of St. Paul, all things considered, ought [not] alter our opinion derived from the evangelists."

> We ought to be cautious in taking even the best ascertained opinions and practices of the primitive church, for our own. If it could be satisfactorily shown that they esteemed it authorized and to be transmitted forever, that does not settle the question for us. We know how inveterately they were attached to their Jewish prejudices, and how often even the influence of Christ failed to enlarge their views. On every other subject succeeding times have learned to form a judgment more in accordance with the spirit of Christianity than was the practice of the early ages.[48]

Here and elsewhere one has the impression that, had Baur's theories crossed the Atlantic more quickly, Emerson would have found in them an affirmation of his own. But the most surprising aspect of the sermon is his admission that even if he believed that Jesus had enjoined his disciples to institute a permanent observance, he would not adopt it if it were to prove "disagreeable to [his] own feelings." Such transparency when it comes to explaining one's reasons for preferring Jesus to Paul is exceedingly rare.

Baur's influence in Catholic countries was somewhat limited until Ernst Renan published his multivolume *Histoire des origines du christianisme*. His reading in German theology led him to abandon his plans to enter the priesthood in 1845 and embark on an academic career. The first volume in his history, *La vie de Jésus* (1863), was enormously successful. More historical novel with footnotes than conventional biography, it went through over twenty printings and was translated into more than a dozen languages.[49] The second volume focused on the activities of the apostles, including a brief introduction of Paul, whose conversion he attributed to the effects of a stroke.[50]

The third volume is devoted entirely to Paul. Renan's reconstruction of Paul's ministry is heavily indebted to the conflict scenario sketched by Baur. It is a stirring, if embroidered, portrait that highlights familiar themes in its final pages. Renan does not refer to Paul as the founder of Christianity but "founder of Christian theology, . . . the true president of those great Greek Councils, which make Jesus the keystone of a system of metaphysics."[51] Al-

---

48. Ibid., 21.
49. Schweitzer, *Quest of the Historical Jesus*, 180–92.
50. Renan, *Apostles*, 171–73.
51. Renan, *Saint Paul*, 326–27.

though Paul's influence waned in the Middle Ages, Renan observes, it waxed anew with the Reformation. Contemplating where Paul stands in relation to Jesus and Peter, Renan remarks that Paul was no saint. He was haughty, argumentative, and opinionated. His writings lack charm and grace, and his "paradoxical contempt for reason" impeded scientific progress. He is a man of action, not an artist or an intellectual. Luther reminds Renan of Paul more than any other figure, as both men share "the same frantic attachment to a thesis embraced as the absolute truth."[52] By this time, Renan has strayed far from his orthodox Catholic roots but, despite the influence of Baur, has little affinity for the alternative. "After having been for three centuries, thanks to orthodox Protestantism, the Christian teacher *par excellence*," he says, with optimism and relief, "Paul sees in our day his reign drawing to a close."[53]

Jesus, on the other hand, "lives more than ever." In the final paragraph Renan reiterates his opinion "that the part taken by Paul in the creation of Christianity, should be ranked far below that of Jesus":

> It is no longer the Epistle to the Romans, which is the resumé of Christianity—it is the Sermon on the Mount. True Christianity, which will last forever, comes from the gospels—not from the epistles of Paul. The writings of Paul have been a danger and a hidden rock—the causes of the principal defects of Christian theology. Paul is the father of the subtle Augustine, of the unfruitful Thomas Aquinas, of the gloomy Calvinist, of the peevish Jansenist, of the fierce theology which damns and predestinates to damnation. Jesus is the father of all those who seek repose for their souls in dreams of the ideal. What makes Christianity live, is the little that we know of the word and person of Jesus. The ideal man, the divine poet, the great artist, alone defy time and revolutions.[54]

That he ranks Paul behind Jesus is no surprise. That he also places him beneath medieval mystics such as Francis of Assisi and Thomas à Kempis is also a sign of an aesthetic sensibility that conditions his adverse evaluation of Paul.

Coming at the end of a work largely devoid of direct criticism, this harsh assessment catches the reader off guard. It comes into sharper focus, however, when one understands it as a complement to the characterization of Jesus in his first volume, where Jesus himself is said to undergo a process of dialectical development. Born a Jew, he overcomes "almost all the defects of his

52. Ibid., 329–30.
53. Ibid., 330. In *The Apostles* (176), Renan had already attributed the survival of Christianity as more than a Jewish sect to "this ungovernable Paul," the prototype of the Christian "disengaged from all authority who will believe only from personal conviction." "Protestantism thus existed five years after the death of Jesus," he adds, "and St. Paul was its illustrious founder."
54. Renan, *Saint Paul*, 330.

race" such as "harshness in controversy," and only the innate pugnacity of the Semitic mind can bring him to compromise his refined style, "in spite of himself."[55] By the end of his brief ministry, "he appears no more as a Jewish reformer, but as a destroyer of Judaism"; indeed, "Jesus was no longer a Jew" and preached "the religion of man, not the religion of the Jew."[56] Christianity will fulfill its potential in returning to Jesus, but not by returning to Judaism.

For the lapsed Catholic Renan, this idealized Christianity would have little in common with a dogmatic faith derived from the Letters of Paul the combative Pharisee. Jewish contemporaries like Abraham Geiger faulted Renan for perpetuating the worst aspect of German scholarship, namely, its anti-Jewish orientation, without retaining its historical rigor.[57] Geiger, one of the first Jewish scholars to enter the fray in the 1860s, believed that Renan got the Jesus-Paul relationship exactly backward. Jesus was thoroughly and proudly Jewish. Upon his death and elevation to the status of the divine Logos, however, Christianity "almost cease[s] to represent a tendency within Judaism," and then Paul's decision to spread the word of Israel's God beyond its borders—"a mighty step in the advance of mankind"—brings with it a brand of messianic belief that "place[s] itself beyond the pale of Judaism" when observance of the law is deemed nugatory.[58] For Geiger, it is no coincidence that Christianity's departure from Judaism and its entry into the pagan world came at a time of cultural degradation. Devoid of "any peculiar native spiritual power," Rome could only imitate the Greeks on a superficial level. Paul facilitated this process by borrowing the strategy of Euhemerus, the fourth-century BCE Greek writer who argued that the gods were nothing more than embellished versions of venerable heroes from more ancient times.[59]

Leo Tolstoy also read Renan but manifests nothing like the anti-Semitism one sees in Renan's writings or in much of the German scholarship with which he is also acquainted.[60] In *My Religion* (1882), Tolstoy places the cleavage between Jesus and Paul in a broader pattern of religious evolution

---

55. Renan, *Life of Jesus*, 229.

56. Ibid., 168, 309.

57. Almog, "Racial Motif"; Heschel, *Abraham Geiger*, 154–57; Heschel, *Aryan Jesus*, 33–38.

58. Geiger, *Judaism and Its History*, 143–44. Adolf von Harnack represents a dominant strand of liberal Protestant thinking at the end of the nineteenth century, essentially agreeing with Geiger that it was Paul "who delivered the Christian religion from Judaism" (*What Is Christianity?*, 176). But unlike Geiger, Harnack praises Paul for removing "the Jewish limitations attaching to Jesus's message" (180). On Harnack's response to Geiger, see Wiese, *Challenging Colonial Discourse*, 159–69.

59. Geiger, *Judaism and Its History*, 147–48, 149–51.

60. Medzhibovskaya, *Tolstoy*, 187–88. His personal library included a copy of Renan's works on Jesus and Paul (ibid., 197n78).

than at a particular stage in a Hegelian dialectic pitting Jews against gentiles. Adherents of all religions wander from the precepts of the founder and find someone to justify their deviations, though this tendency is nowhere as pronounced as it is in Christianity. Whereas Jesus proclaims the most elevated of all doctrines,

> the arbitrary separation of the metaphysical and ethical aspects of Christianity entirely disfigures the doctrine, and deprives it of every sort of meaning. The separation began with the preaching of Paul, who knew but imperfectly the ethical doctrine set forth in the Gospel of Matthew, and who preached a metaphysico-cabalistic theory entirely foreign to the doctrine of Jesus; and this theory was perfected under Constantine, when the existing pagan social organization was proclaimed Christian simply by covering it with the mantle of Christianity.[61]

Tolstoy's earlier conversion to a radical faith had been precipitated by a moving encounter with the Sermon on the Mount, to which he alludes here. Its true meaning had been concealed from him by the learned commentaries he had studied. Theologians, according to Tolstoy, do little more than distract the believer from the unequivocal ethical demands of the gospel with futile speculations and empty ceremony. "Pseudo-Christianity" lacks vitality because it makes no demand on the believer.[62]

Tolstoy is frequently called a Christian anarchist due to his stance that, if only Christians were to interpret the Sermon on the Mount literally and put it into practice, there would be no need for the state. Jesus tells his disciples not to judge, swear oaths, or resist evil. The state engages in these activities and compels citizens to cooperate—often on the threat of violence in the event they do not comply. By aligning itself with the power of the state, the church allowed itself to become corrupted. This unholy alliance was ratified in the time of Constantine. Muslim critics had earlier drawn a line from Paul to Constantine in tracing a theological decline that led to the trinitarian dogmas of Nicaea and Chalcedon. In this view, Paul and Constantine were villains for introducing pagan religious concepts and thereby corrupting true Christianity. Tolstoy draws a line that accentuates the political rather than the theological dimension. Paul's part in this sorry tale becomes clearer a few

---

61. Tolstoy, *My Religion*, 219. He makes a similar criticism in "Church and State," written in the same period: "This deviation begins at the time of the apostles, especially with that lover of teaching, Paul: and the wider Christianity extends, the more it deviates and appropriates the methods of that very external worship and dogmatism the denial of which was so positively expressed by Christ" (*Church and State*, 17).

62. Tolstoy, *My Religion*, 220.

pages later in *My Religion*, where Tolstoy paraphrases Paul's admonitions to obey the governing authorities in Rom. 13:1–7.[63] Whatever themes Tolstoy shares with other critics before and after him, the rise of the nation-state in nineteenth-century Europe and his antagonistic stance toward the Russian Orthodox Church and the czarist regime it supported are among the ingredients that give to Tolstoy's anti-Paulinism its special flavor.

Fin de Siècle Anti-Paulinism

The increasingly bitter criticism of Paul coincided not only with heightened interest in processes of development and change but also with the tide of suspicion directed toward received tradition that began to swell earlier during the Enlightenment. Nowhere is this bitterness more palpable than in the writings of Friedrich Nietzsche. His personal correspondence also illustrates just how small the "Republic of Letters" remained at the end of the nineteenth century. In a letter sent to Richard Wagner in April 1873, Nietzsche says that he is sending a copy of Renan's book on Paul and will forward a copy of a book by Franz Overbeck he had promised, along with another by Paul de Lagarde.[64] Like Tolstoy, Nietzsche had read Renan, but he was no admirer. His *Antichrist* can be read in part as a critique and parody of Renan and his valorization of a romantic Jesus.[65] Overbeck was Nietzsche's friend and housemate who had him placed in an asylum when he lost his sanity near the end of his life. Overbeck was a radical skeptic who asserted that Christianity had abandoned its world-denying character as soon as it began accommodating itself to the surrounding culture. He believed that "all the beautiful sides of Christianity are connected with Jesus, all the ugly with Paul."[66]

Paul de Lagarde has been credited with first inspiring in Nietzsche a profound distrust of the apostle Paul. He regarded the German church as spiritually bankrupt and sought to revive a national religion consonant with the character of the German *Volk* in its flourishing, prior to the cultural decay that set in with industrialization.[67] Lagarde's career as a brilliant philologist is now overshadowed by his role in propagating odious racial theories. Paul, "who even after his conversion remains a Pharisee from top to toe," is the Jewish

---

63. Tolstoy, *My Religion*, 227. Tolstoy's diaries reveal considerable antipathy toward Paul for his teachings about the role of human governments (see Maude, *Life of Tolstoy*, 2:39–40).
64. Middleton, *Selected Letters of Friedrich Nietzsche*, 117–18.
65. Shapiro, "Nietzsche contra Renan"; Santaniello, *Nietzsche, God, and the Jews*, 123–31.
66. Quoted in Baird, *History of New Testament Research*, 2:144.
67. F. Stern, *Politics of Cultural Despair*, 35–52, 90–94.

foil to the Aryan Jesus.[68] The glorification of Jesus's death—perpetuated in the Catholic Eucharist—is a Jewish perversion that negates the vigor of his life and teachings by introducing an alien theory of atonement. Were it not for Paul's influence, moreover, the church would not be burdened with the OT and would be able to jettison these and other vestigial elements.[69] While Lagarde is not representative of all nineteenth-century German scholarship on the question, the portrait of Paul as the Jewish nemesis of the Aryan Jesus was filled out in greater detail by German scholars in the ensuing decades.[70]

Nietzsche stands apart from most nineteenth-century critics in that he cared so little about the question of Paul's particular ethnic or religious identity. To be sure, it was on account of "this apostle who was so greatly troubled in mind and so worthy of pity" that "the ship of Christianity threw overboard no inconsiderable part of its Jewish ballast" and sailed into gentile waters. But throughout aphorism 68 of *Morgenröte* (*The Dawn of Day*, first published in 1881), it would matter little if the ship had sailed in the opposite direction.[71] Had it not been for Paul, "one of the most ambitious and importunate of souls that ever existed, . . . there would have been no Christian kingdom." No one bothered to read his writings with truly open eyes for over fifteen centuries, or else "it would have been all up with Christianity long ago." Before his conversion, an event that Nietzsche appears to attribute to epilepsy, Paul was violent, malicious, melancholy, and hungry for power. His "ungovernable ambition" did not diminish but, rather, instilled in him the conviction that he possessed the key to understanding the ultimate meaning of the law and that "history would henceforth revolve around him." Not only have all sins been expiated by the death of Christ; sin itself has been abolished. In arriving at this realization, Paul became "the inventor of Christianity."

As an indictment of Paul, Nietzsche's description in *The Dawn of Day* is relatively bland when compared to his comments in *The Antichrist*, written several years later and first published in 1895.[72] Subtitled *Attempt at a Critique of Christianity*, it was one of his last works. Its title has been interpreted as intended to be a mocking parallel to "anti-Semite." To label

---

68. Lagarde, "Über das Verhältnis," 29. When Jesus calls himself "Son of Man," according to Lagarde, one should understand him to be saying "I am not a Jew" (F. Stern, *Politics of Cultural Despair*, 41–42).

69. Lagarde, "Über das Verhältnis," 30–31.

70. Hans Rollmann notes that many of Lagarde's contemporaries regarded his ideas as fanciful ("*Paulus Alienus*," 33–38).

71. Quotations are from J. M. Kennedy's translation of Nietzsche, *Dawn of Day*, 66–71.

72. Quotations from *The Antichrist* are from the translation of Walter Kaufmann in *The Portable Nietzsche*. Sections 39–43 have Paul as their primary focus. On Nietzsche's interpretation of Paul, see Kaufmann, *Nietzsche*, 343–48; and Havemann, "*Apostel der Rache*," 184–260.

Nietzsche a philo-Semite would be inaccurate, but his anti-Semitism may
have been exaggerated as well, due in part to his sister's hand in shaping his
legacy.[73] Here Nietzsche has nothing positive to say about Christianity. It is
not that Christianity has been tainted—Christianity itself is the contami-
nant: "The Christian church has left nothing untouched by its corruption;
it has turned every value into an un-value, every truth into a lie, every integrity into a vileness of the soul. . . . I call Christianity the one great curse,
. . . the one immortal blemish of mankind."[74] Unlike Lagarde, he does not
deny that Christianity flows out of Judaism. Any difference between Jesus
and Paul is not due to the fact that one is more or less Jewish than the
other—they are "perhaps the two most Jewish Jews [*jüdischesten Juden*]
who ever lived."[75] Christianity is not so much a reaction against Judaism
as it is an amplification of the worst elements of Judaism without any of
its redeeming features.

Paul plays a central role in this regression in that he "reduce[s] being a
Christian . . . to a matter of considering something true." Nietzsche ridicules
this Pauline emphasis on faith at the expense of practice and declares that
"there was only one Christian, and he died on the cross."[76] There have been
no true Christians since then. Even Jesus's first followers misunderstood him
and his death from the outset. They did not perceive that his life demonstrated
his freedom from *ressentiment* and were unwilling to forgive those responsible
for his death. Paul, "with that rabbinical impudence which distinguishes him
in all things," substituted faith in Christ for the obligation to live a life like
Christ's.[77] Jesus's supposed disciples were consumed with a desire for revenge
and retribution despite his abolition of the very concept of guilt. "On the
heels of the 'glad tidings,'" says Nietzsche, "came the *very worst*: those of
Paul. In Paul was embodied the opposite type to that of the 'bringer of glad
tidings': the genius in hatred, in the vision of hatred, in the inexorable logic
of hatred."[78] Like many other writers, Nietzsche distinguishes between the
Jesus of history and the Christ of faith, preferring the former to the latter
as well as to Paul. Any praise of Jesus, however, is tempered by the fact that

73. Kaufmann, *Nietzsche*, 298–303.
74. Nietzsche, *Antichrist*, §62.
75. See Kaufmann, *Nietzsche*, 43.
76. Nietzsche, *Antichrist*, §39.
77. Ibid., §41. Paul promotes "the lie of the 'resurrected' Jesus" because he has no use for
his life. Only the gullible will believe that Paul is being honest when he dresses up his "halluci-
nation" of the risen Jesus as an authentic vision: "What he himself did not believe, the idiots
among whom he threw his doctrine believed" (§42).
78. Ibid., §42. Paul is a "hate-inspired counterfeiter" who "invented his own history of
earliest Christianity."

Nietzsche seems to have conceived of Jesus in the image of the title character of Dostoevsky's *The Idiot*.[79]

The emphasis on postmortem judgment from which one—but not one's enemies—is spared was part of Paul's ploy to gain sway over the herd. In introducing the doctrine of the resurrection and, along with it, of personal immortality, Nietzsche further argues that Paul devalued all the accomplishments that can be attained in this life and encouraged mediocrity. His criticism of Paul on this point should be understood in relation to the *Übermensch*, a concept Nietzsche first explores in *Also sprach Zarathustra*. This "higher type of man" is that toward which humanity ideally moves, and Paul's bourgeois "slave morality" stands in the way of the "revaluation of all values" that only the *Übermensch* can effect. In siding with all that is weak and base, Christianity wages war against "all that is noble."[80] That everyone has an eternal soul of infinite value in God's eyes "is an intensification of every kind of selfishness into the infinite," and it is to this "miserable flattery of personal vanity" that Christianity owes its triumph. Paul praises the dregs of society and thereby validates the noxious egalitarian impulse, the "lie of the equality of souls" that constitutes "the greatest, the most malignant, attempt to assassinate *noble* humanity."[81] On this score, Nietzsche sees little difference between Jesus and Paul: "I do not like at all about that Jesus of Nazareth or his apostle Paul that they put so many ideas into the heads of little people, as if their modest virtues were of any consequence . . . ; they have led astray, to the point of self-destruction, the brave, magnanimous, daring, excessive inclinations of the strong soul."[82] Epicurus had resisted this tendency, a latent form of Christianity, and would have succeeded in preserving the *imperium Romanum*, the most magnificent achievement in human history. "Then Paul appeared, . . . the Jew, the eternal Wandering Jew par excellence" whose genius lay in recognizing how the symbol of a crucified god could unite all the outcasts if he could project onto the savior their own cowardly and effeminate yet vengeful emotions.[83]

---

79. Kaufmann, *Nietzsche*, 340–41.

80. Nietzsche, *Antichrist*, §5. Nietzsche twice quotes 1 Cor. 1:20 ("Has not God made foolish the wisdom of this world?") to suggest that Paul is personally to blame for the resulting decadence (§§45, 51; see also §24 for "the Christianity of Paul" as a weak, decadent movement).

81. Ibid., §43.

82. Nietzsche, *Will to Power*, 122.

83. Nietzsche, *Antichrist*, §58. In *The Wanderer and His Shadow* (1880), Nietzsche similarly suggests that the Calvinistic notion that the damnation of souls to hell serves to glorify God originated with Paul as a projection of his own vanity (§85).

In terms of content and style, nothing quite compares to Nietzsche's animadversions. The closest analogue may be Søren Kierkegaard, whose withering attacks on "Christendom" now and then include asides that express ambivalence about Paul, who "has already relaxed in relation to the gospels." "As early as 'the apostle' the scaling down process begins," he says, "and it seems as if the natural man gets off a little easier in becoming a Christian."[84] Yet admiring, even reverential references far outweigh the occasional criticism, and he is much less apt to blame the corruption on Paul than on the *Kulturprotestantismus* of Danish Lutherans or even Luther's own misreading of Paul.[85] Furthermore, his articulation of these themes in his journals of the 1840s owes virtually nothing to the German scholarship that undergirds much criticism of Paul in this period.[86]

Other critics may fit more snugly than Kierkegaard into one category of anti-Paulinism or another, but taken as a whole, the nineteenth century marks a turning point. In no previous era did so many feel so emboldened to air their grievances against the apostle. A desire to distinguish "the religion of Jesus" from "the religion about Jesus" animated many of the pioneers in the emerging discipline of historical criticism, and those who faulted Paul for fabricating the latter increasingly seized on the conclusions of scholars in various ancillary fields in making their case. Does Paul's purported betrayal of Jesus represent a compromise or, conversely, a recrudescence of core Jewish convictions? Opinion remained divided on this and other questions at century's end. The industry and inventiveness on display in the search for answers were remarkable, so much so that twentieth-century critics as often as not did little more than recycle the arguments of their predecessors.

84. Hong and Hong, *Søren Kierkegaard's Journals and Papers*, 3:105–6, 303. Other comments critical of Paul are commonly attributed to Kierkegaard on many internet websites, but they are greatly embellished or not found in his published works.

85. Brandt, "Paul," 190–91; cf. Hong and Hong, *Søren Kierkegaard's Journals and Papers*, 3:855.

86. Although he is acquainted with F. C. Baur's work, he finds it to be of little value in understanding Paul's thought; see Müller, "Kierkegaard," esp. 307–8.

5

YESTERDAY AND TODAY

Jesus versus Paul in the Public Square

Unde malum? To solve this theological conundrum—"Whence evil?"—writers over the past century have turned increasingly to Paul, not because they think he knows the answer but because they think he is himself the answer. More than anyone else, he is seen as the source of the mischief that Christianity has unleashed on the world. The further one travels into modernity and beyond, the more challenging it is to provide a comprehensive summary of the case against Paul. Much of the heavy lifting takes place in the nineteenth century. In the meantime, Paul's critics have followed most of the same lines of attack, either repeating earlier arguments or applying them to new circumstances. But the twentieth and twenty-first centuries have witnessed new trends as well. This chapter, organized topically rather than chronologically, surveys contemporary anti-Paulinism in both its older and newer incarnations.

Inside the Academy

Adolf Deissmann, a pioneer in the study of Christian letters in their ancient social context, was fully aware that modern readers often see in Paul a figure of considerable ambiguity. He is widely viewed as "darksome as well as great." Deissmann was not convinced that the problem lies with Paul:

The darkness, however, is largely due to the bad lamps in our studies, and the modern condemnations of the apostle as an obscurantist who corrupted the simple gospel of the Nazarene with harsh and difficult dogmas, are the dregs of doctrinaire study of St. Paul, mostly in the tired brains of gifted amateurs.[1]

No one looking out over the landscape of anti-Paulinism can deny that it is heavily populated with amateurs, both gifted and ungifted. The observations of such nonspecialists, however, frequently parallel or overlap with those of scholars carrying out their research in relative anonymity.

The study of Paul at the turn of the twentieth century was related to the study of Jesus in a manner not witnessed prior to the publication of Albert Schweitzer's seminal work *The Quest of the Historical Jesus* in 1906. Schweitzer makes a compelling case that scholars and amateurs alike tend to project their own values and concerns onto Jesus, and that most attempts at writing his biography reveal much more about the author than the subject. The paucity of reliable data available for reconstructing his life and ministry aids this unconscious tendency, creating a vacuum that historians are eager to fill. The reception of Schweitzer's work was such that many scholars, wary of making the same embarrassing mistakes as their predecessors, abandoned the Quest. Skepticism about the received accounts of Jesus's life could be so strong that his very existence as a historical personage was called into question. A common corollary was that, since a nonexistent Jesus could not possibly have founded Christianity, someone like Paul must have done it.[2] In rare instances, this extreme skepticism extended to Paul. Peter Jensen argues that, like many other biblical figures, "Paul" was fabricated using details borrowed from the *Epic of Gilgamesh*.[3] Doubts about Paul's existence are never voiced by critics who hold him responsible for alleged evils perpetrated by the church in Jesus's name, however, since people who never lived make poor scapegoats.

With firsthand knowledge of Jesus out of reach, many scholars found firmer ground in the preaching of the early church. Paul's writings provide the earliest and most substantial source for reconstructing this proclamation. On theological grounds, Rudolf Bultmann is content with the fact that Jesus's proclamation constitutes only "a presupposition for the theology of the New

1. Deissmann, *St. Paul*, 4.
2. E.g., Brandes, *Jesus: A Myth*, 56. Albert Schweitzer (*Paul and His Interpreters*, 235) also mentions Arthur Drews drawing this conclusion.
3. P. Jensen, *Moses, Jesus, Paulus*. More recently, Thomas L. Brodie contends that Paul as well as Jesus was "a work of imagination" whose letters are works of historicized fiction that flesh out a persona created by the early church to serve as "a paradigm of the gospel of Christian freedom" (*Beyond the Quest*, 146–47). Swedish filmmaker Lena Einhorn "solves" (or compounds) the problem by arguing that Jesus and Paul are actually the same person; see Einhorn, *Jesus Mystery*.

Testament rather than a part of that theology itself."[4] He regards Paul, along with John, as the preeminent theologian of early Christianity whose writings suffice for the cultivation of authentic Christian faith. Many interpreters regard Paul's statement in 2 Cor. 5:16 (RSV) that "even though we once regarded Christ from a human point of view, we regard him thus no longer" as not only a statement of ignorance about the particulars of Jesus's life and teaching or of an altered understanding of his significance, but also of outright indifference. Paul knows little about Jesus and cares less. Other interpreters were less comfortable than Bultmann with the discontinuity they perceived. Schweitzer believed that Paul's Hellenistic background diverted him from the apocalyptic-eschatological orientation of Jesus, casting a long shadow over the subsequent development of Christianity. "The fateful thing," he says, "is that the Greek, the Catholic and the Protestant theologies all contain the Gospel of Paul in a form which does not continue the Gospel of Jesus, but displaces it."[5]

Insofar as disputes about the continuity between Jesus and Paul persist, it is clear that the conventional wisdom that Schweitzer brought the Quest to a resounding halt is not entirely accurate. After all, only by making certain assumptions about the thrust of Jesus's thought can one speculate about its coherence with Paul's. William Wrede's book on the "messianic secret" in the Gospels is the last of the works Schweitzer reviews in his survey of the Quest, but just a year later he would publish an equally important book on Paul that attracted a larger readership than most scholarly works. Looking back from the period between the two world wars, it is to Wrede's ideas that Bultmann was responding.[6] For turning Christianity into a religion of redemption centered on Jesus's death rather than on his ethical teachings, Wrede says that Paul deserves the title "second founder of Christianity." To describe the character of the central conception of this Christianity, he says, "we cannot avoid the word 'myth.'" "We do not employ it with the desire to hurt anyone's feelings," he continues, explaining that it is not a term of contempt.[7] He was correct to sense that readers might take offense and view his description as negative.[8] If his final assessment serves as a guide, their suspicions were not

---

4. Bultmann, *Theology of the New Testament*, 1:3; see also "Significance of the Historical Jesus."

5. Schweitzer, *Mysticism of Paul*, 391–92.

6. Bultmann, "Jesus and Paul," 183–84.

7. Wrede, *Paul*, 179.

8. See Victor Paul Furnish's discussion of the early reactions in Europe and the United States: "Jesus-Paul Debate," 29–30. On the relationship between Wrede and unambiguously anti-Pauline authors like Ernst Renan and Paul de Lagarde, see Rollmann, "*Paulus Alienus*." Wrede's prediction (*Paul*, 179) that "even liberal theology" would shrink from his conclusions would prove true, but only in the short run.

without basis: "This second founder of Christianity has even, compared with the first, exercised beyond all doubt the stronger—not the better—influence."[9]

Whatever disagreements persist about the proper resolution of the Jesus-Paul debate, then as now, there is widespread agreement that it is no trivial matter. Wrede's summary—"Jesus or Paul: this alternative characterizes, at least in part, the religious and theological warfare of the present day"[10]—is still apposite in many ways. If Paul can rightly be called the founder, according to J. Gresham Machen, a staunch conservative who left Princeton to found Westminster Theological Seminary in 1929, then Christianity faces an unparalleled crisis:

> For—let us not deceive ourselves—if Paul is independent of Jesus, he can no longer be a teacher of the Church. Christianity is founded upon Christ and only Christ. Paulinism has never been accepted upon any other supposition than that it reproduces the mind of Christ. If that supposition is incorrect—if Paulinism is derived not from Jesus Christ, but from other sources—then it must be uprooted from the life of the Church. But that is more than reform—it is revolution. Compared with that upheaval, the reformation of the sixteenth century is as nothing.[11]

Those less enthralled by the apostle's legacy, who bemoan the gulf they see between Paul and Jesus on such issues as sexuality, Jewish law, and the status of women, nevertheless concur that the question is of central importance. As James Tabor puts it, "Christianity, as we . . . know it, *is* Paul and Paul *is* Christianity."[12]

Paul among the People

Machen was not just a biblical scholar and theologian but also a first-rate polemicist who took part in the culture wars of the 1910s and 1920s. That he frames the issue in the same terms as his opponents demonstrates the extent to which the Jesus-Paul debate had entered the mainstream of public discourse. One such opponent was H. L. Mencken, the sharp-tongued scourge of fundamentalists best remembered for his reporting on the Scopes Monkey Trial of 1925. While Mencken was not drawn to Machen's conservative faith, he wrote an obituary expressing respect for his refusal to alter Christian doctrine for the purposes of making it more palatable to modern sensibilities.

9. Wrede, *Paul*, 180.
10. Ibid., 181.
11. Machen, "Jesus and Paul," 548.
12. Tabor, *Paul and Jesus*, 24, emphasis original.

Paul appears in Mencken's *Notes on Democracy*.[13] Mencken is no senti-mentalist when it comes to the common man, abhorring democracy's way of valorizing mediocrity and sanctifying the opinions of "the eternal mob." His views on culture generally and Paul in particular echo those of Nietzsche, whose *Antichrist* he had translated as part of a program of introducing the German's philosophy to American audiences. The common man is "lazy, improvident and unclean," and his guiding principles are "the inventions of mountebanks." Christianity has not made any positive difference, though this is not the fault of Jesus. "Is it argued by any rational man," he asks, "that the debased Christianity cherished by the mob . . . has any colourable likeness to the body of ideas preached by Christ?" Not at all, according to Mencken: "The plain fact is that this bogus Christianity . . . is the invention of Paul and his attendant rabble-rousers—a body of men exactly comparable to the corps of evangelical pastors of today, which is to say, a body devoid of sense and lamentably indifferent to common honesty." Here he has in mind figures like William Jennings Bryan, "the Great Commoner." For Mencken, linking Paul to Bryan is the worst insult conceivable. (He also wrote an obituary for Bryan, in which he describes him as "ignorant, bigoted, self-seeking, blatant and dishonest.")[14]

To their discredit, the rabble had rejected Jesus because his ideas were too logical and his ethics too demanding:

> What it yearned for was the old comfortable balderdash under a new and gaudy name, and that is precisely what Paul offered it. He borrowed from all the wandering dervishes and soul-snatchers of Asia Minor, and flavoured the stew with remnants of Greek demonology. The result was a code of doc-trines so discordant and so nonsensical that no two men since, examining it at length, have ever agreed upon its precise meaning. But Paul knew his mob; . . . He knew that nonsense was its natural provender—that the unintelligible soothed it like sweet music. He was the *Stammvater* of all the Christian mob-masters of today.[15]

Paul's place in Christendom was usurped by Peter in the Middle Ages, but he always remained "the prophet of the sewers." His star rose again with the Reformation, when he resumed his role as "arch-theologian of the mob," whose "turgid and witless metaphysics makes Christianity bearable to men

13. Mencken, *Notes on Democracy*, 64–68.
14. Mencken's obituary of Bryan appeared in the July 27, 1925, edition of the *Baltimore Evening Sun*.
15. Mencken, *Notes on Democracy*, 66–67.

who would otherwise be repelled by Christ's simple and magnificent reduction of the duties of man to the duties of a gentleman."[16]

Was Paul little more than a rabble-rouser? Mencken was not alone in this view. His contemporary, Cambridge philosopher Alfred North Whitehead, had a similar bone to pick. As a proponent of process theology, he rejected the dualistic element he found in Paul's writings. But Whitehead was more troubled by Paul's role in promulgating Christian theology, "one of the greatest disasters of the human race" in that it involved the captivation of Northern European culture by "Hebraic thought," with its "view of life that came in through the slave and proletarian populations."[17] (The sentiment echoes those of Nietzsche, though, when asked, Whitehead said that he had not read *The Antichrist*.) He attributes to Paul "their view of how life may be well lived even though you are an underdog." Paul "did more than anybody else to distort and subvert Christ's teaching," and as a consequence it is "impossible to imagine anything more un-Christlike than Christian theology."[18] Love, not fear, is the way to finding God, and that is why the modern world needs "the help of John and not of Paul."[19]

For Adolf Hitler, too, Paul was a man of the people in a decidedly negative sense. His wartime table talk was replete with references to Christianity as a form of Bolshevism. Christianity, the religion "fabricated" by Paul, "is nothing but the Communism of today." Given the circumstances—Germany had invaded the Soviet Union earlier in 1941—his obsession with Bolshevism is understandable even if its connection to Paul is somewhat opaque. Paul "distorted with diabolical cunning the Christian idea," thereby establishing "a rallying point for slaves of all kinds against the élite, the masters and those in dominant authority."[20] Just as Paul discovered that "he could succeed in ruining the Roman State by causing the principle to triumph of the equality of all men before a single God," the Bolsheviks are bent on sowing anarchy and destruction. Paul's "egalitarian theories had what was needed to win over a mass composed of innumerable uprooted peoples, . . . the abject rabble of the catacombs." Hitler saw in the Christian conquest of the noble Roman spirit and destruction of its cultural treasures a parallel to the "frightful leveling-down" taking place in Russia in the name of Marx, to whom he frequently compares Paul.[21]

---

16. Ibid., 68.

17. Whitehead, *Dialogues*, 60.

18. Ibid., 307. When he asserts that "the first interpreter of the New Testament was the worst, Paul" (134), he does so apparently unaware that Paul's letters are likely the earliest surviving Christian writing. By that token, he was in no position to interpret "the New Testament."

19. Whitehead, *Religion in the Making*, 64.

20. Trevor-Roper, *Hitler's Secret Conversations*, 586.

21. Ibid., 63–65.

Other writers in the first half of the century took a diametrically opposed view of Paul. Compared to Jesus, Paul was an elitist, not a man of the people. H. G. Wells and George Bernard Shaw, both members of the Fabian Society, believed that the early church under Paul's influence abandoned the socialist teachings of Jesus soon after his death.[22] The definitive statement of this position came in Bouck White's 1911 *The Call of the Carpenter*, a novelistic biography of Jesus lavishly praised by Eugene V. Debs, five-time presidential candidate on the Socialist Party ticket.[23] Two years after it appeared, White's portrait of Jesus as a socialist agitator seeking to awaken the proletariat to revolution led to his dismissal from the ministry at Holy Trinity Episcopal Church in Brooklyn. Whereas "Jesus declared war on the capitalism of his day" in the hope of establishing a brotherhood of equals,

> Paul was a stockholder in Rome's world corporation. And that stock by slow degrees had blinded him to the injustice of a social system in whose dividends he himself shared. This explains in large part why he accepted the political status quo and preached its acceptance by others . . . , and he was personally too much the gainer from Rome's empire of privilege to share the insurrectionary spirit of the Son of Mary.[24]

"Both by birth and training," writes White, "he was unfitted to enter into the working-class consciousness of Galileans" who "had not his advantage of a university education."[25] In reinterpreting the Christian faith so as to make it acceptable to the Romans, Paul believed that he was doing it a favor. His error on this point was due to a congenital blind spot insofar as his personal makeup was "imperial rather than democratic."[26] White suspects that while "Paul would probably have cast a first stone against the woman taken in adultery, . . . he is strangely silent concerning the social sinners of the day." His

22. See Vedder, *Socialism*, 212–13, 435–79. Harold Bloom's final judgment of Paul, whose genius he does not deny, is a negative one on the same grounds: "You can read and reread all the authentic epistles of Paul, and never know that Jesus, like Amos and the other prophets, and like William Blake in a later time, spoke for the poor, the ill, the outcast" (*Genius*, 142).

23. On the reception of White's book, see Burns, *Radical Historical Jesus*, 91–95, 191–92.

24. White, *Call of the Carpenter*, 235.

25. Ibid., 227, 231. In a 1930 essay, Erich Fromm applies insights from Marxist social psychology and discerns a similar evolution. Christianity begins among "poor, oppressed, uneducated people feeling common suffering, common hatred, and common hope," but "gradually another social element, the educated and the well-to-do, began to infiltrate the communities" through the work of Paul, "one of the first Christian leaders that did not stem from the lower classes" (*Dogma of Christ*, 51–52).

26. White, *Call of the Carpenter*, 227. Later, however, when speaking of Paul's "apostasy from the Jewish race with its intense traditions of democracy," White seems to assume that this mind-set is acquired rather than inherited (233).

"Roman reverence for property" inclined Paul to believe that "huge inequalities of fortune were ordained of God" and that their root cause—capitalist exploitation—was of little interest.[27]

Did Paul's theology corrupt his social ethics, or did it instead act as a buttress for his socioeconomic interests? Either way, White suggests, the result is the same. Peter and "the other Galilean workingmen" attempted to carry on the revolution started by Jesus, but it was put down when Paul "annexed himself to the movement and reinterpreted the life of Jesus from that of a workingman into the career of a mystical personage aloof from the economic facts of life."[28] In the end, "Christianity did not change Paul so much as Paul changed Christianity."[29]

During the Gilded Age this critique germinated in the "Jesusism" of freethinkers such as D. M. Bennett, who identified Jesus as a communist.[30] It came to fruition in the Progressive Era with White and kindred spirits like Lyman Fairbanks George, the author of "A Rythmical Protest in Fourteen Cantos" titled *The Naked Truth of Jesusism*. Best described as a book-length composition of free verse largely bereft of poetic expression and sensibility, it is reminiscent of Lucretius and his Epicurean epic *De rerum natura*: earnest, angry, and relentlessly ideological, complete with an invocation of the muse ("Jesus, I sing, and the pure simple faith of First Ages").[31] On the first page, George declares his intention "to restore Jesus's sayings to their original purity." This urgent task involved clearing away any number of distortions and misconceptions for which Paul, among others, was responsible. Paul succeeded in appropriating Jesus with "Edenlike serpentine suavity":

> Snatch from their hands the true Gospel, as Jesus proclaimed it,
> And with a cultured and scholarly unction repolish it—
> Soften its harshness against acquiescence to Caesar,
> Mold it for uses imperial, then to annex it.
> Thus would he Christianize Caesar and Romanize Jesus![32]

In bringing about this malformation, Paul must "curb the sedition of working-men converts," a task that came all too naturally since he was "too biased to enter the working class consciousness."[33] Not even Judas was guilty

---

27. Ibid., 238.
28. White, *Letters from Prison*, 156.
29. White, *Call of the Carpenter*, 229.
30. Bennett, *Champions of the Church*, 49.
31. George, *Naked Truth of Jesusism*, 7.
32. Ibid., 81.
33. Ibid., 82, 93.

of the same wrongs as Paul, George says. Lest it be said that George is totally lacking in originality, he employs a unique image in comparing Paul to Jesus. "Paul was a penguin," but Jesus was "a storm-eagle" swooping down to feed his fledglings and inspire them with the Marxist slogan "Workers, UNITE!"[34] References throughout to monopolies, union organizing, and workers' compensation regulations mark the poem as a product of its time.

Paul's pro-Roman proclivities have invited criticism, as his admonition to "be subject to the governing authorities" (Rom. 13:1) is seen as, at best, a disconcerting quietism that encourages indifference to the lot of the colonized or, at worst, as "a pact with the devil" meant to buy time for his project of spreading the good news to the ends of the earth before God would fulfill his apocalyptic promises.[35] His most direct statement on the nature of political power readily lends itself to the defense of tyrants and totalitarian regimes, and it has been routinely invoked in support of the divine right of kings. He is "the ideological guardian of the processes and structures of imperial power," routinely deployed "as one of the ideological weapons in the arsenal of Death."[36] Late in the twentieth century there emerged an anti-imperial reading of Paul that construed Rom. 13 and other texts as intended to subvert imperial claims in general and the so-called *Pax Romana* in particular.[37] Neil Elliott identifies "a very specific historical moment" for his conversion to this perspective, namely, George H. W. Bush's launching of the first Gulf War in 1991, while many others have followed his lead in the wake of the invasion of Iraq in 2003 under George W. Bush.[38] Once it is recognized that Paul is engaged in an ongoing program of resistance, covertly constructing an alternative to the power structures reflected in the ubiquitous propaganda disseminated by Rome, he becomes a useful resource in combating imperialist ideologies, especially when they are associated with American foreign policy.

Not so fast, say many scholars who are otherwise sympathetic to Elliott's political concerns. According to Jeremy Punt, "One has to be careful not to try

---

34. Ibid., 83–84. Alongside George's unique image of Paul as a penguin, one might add A. N. Wilson's allusion to Kenneth Grahame's *The Wind in the Willows* in describing him as a "spiritual Mr. Toad" who "gets out his big drum and beats and bangs it for all he is worth (*Paul*, 217).

35. Nelson-Pallmeyer, *Jesus against Christianity*, 273. According to Nelson-Pallmeyer, "Paul's fundamental betrayal of Jesus" consists of his embrace of apocalyptic images and expectations of God (268–69). He also criticizes Paul for seeing Jesus as the fulfillment of prophecies from Isaiah concerning the vindication of Israel before the nations since this Jewish sense of being specially chosen by God—part of the "violent legacy of monotheism"—"gives way often and easily to imperial pretensions and desires for revenge" (270).

36. Blumenfeld, *Political Paul*, 283; N. Elliott, *Liberating Paul*, x, 3–24. See also Ditchfield, "Divine Right Theory."

37. See Lull, "Paul and Empire"; and C. D. Stanley, *Colonized Apostle*.

38. N. Elliott, *Liberating Paul*, xiv.

so hard to rehabilitate Paul that one becomes oblivious to Paul's own tendency to assert a subtle form of hegemony," as his anti-imperial challenge "contain[s] the very sentiments that would allow these letters to establish and sustain hierarchy and imperialism, domination and entrenched power, and the ideological manipulation of others in the history of the Christian church and Western world."[39] "Paul's politics of meaning," says Elisabeth Schüssler Fiorenza, "often seems not very different from the hegemonic discourses of domination and empire."[40] These critics commonly remark that, far from serving as an ally in the struggle against various "subordinationist schemes," Paul in fact "reinscribes" the very arrangements seen as endemic to oppressive societies.[41]

Slavery comes up in many of these critiques, be it in the Nietzschean form of aspersions cast on Paul's "slave mentality" or, alternatively, on his disregard for the welfare of the downtrodden. Criticism of Paul in connection with literal slavery as a living (or recently deceased) institution mounted in the nineteenth century, especially in the United States. It would have been cold comfort for slaves in the antebellum South to hear that Paul was not their enemy since ancient Roman slavery was not race based. Documentation is scarce, but suspicion of Paul on this basis was undoubtedly common among blacks before the turn of the century. Harriet Beecher Stowe has one of her slave characters in chapter 11 of *Uncle Tom's Cabin* snort in disgust when a white man quotes Paul's exhortation to "remain in the state in which he was called."[42] Howard Thurman, a black theologian who mentored Martin Luther King Jr., recalls a similar reaction when reading the Bible to his illiterate exslave grandmother. She never allowed him to read from Paul's letters—except for 1 Cor. 13—because "Old man McGhee" would always have a white minister preach to his slaves on the obligation to obey their masters.[43] Although a few of the texts cited in proslavery arguments are of disputed authorship (Eph. 6:5; Col. 3:22; 1 Tim. 6:1–2), others cannot be dismissed as lightly. That Paul has the opportunity to condemn slavery and instruct Philemon to free Onesimus in unambiguous terms but fails to do so is a sin of omission that many find hard to forgive.

39. Punt, "Postcolonial Approaches," 204.
40. Schüssler Fiorenza, "Paul and the Politics of Interpretation," 50.
41. E.g., Zerbe, "Politics of Paul," 73.
42. First Corinthians 7:20 RSV. For a similar slave reaction to sermons on Paul's Letter to Philemon and the belief that "there existed somewhere a real Bible from God" that did not contain Paul's comments supporting slavery, see Raboteau, *Slave Religion*, 294–95; see also M. V. Johnson, J. A. Noel, and D. K. Williams, *Onesimus Our Brother*.
43. Thurman, *Jesus and the Disinherited*, 30–31. On the interpretation of the household codes containing these injunctions to slaves, see Martin, "*Haustafeln* (Household Codes)." More generally on African American attitudes toward Paul, see Callahan, "'Brother Saul.'"

To the extent that slavery predates the rise of Christianity and exists in parts of the world uninfluenced by Paul's writings, he cannot be held uniquely accountable for the institution. Is it anachronistic to blame Paul for the evil inflicted on blacks under the American system of slavery? Many of his critics suspect that, since he was unable or unwilling to call for its abolition then, he would probably be on the wrong side of the question were he alive today. Delores S. Williams, who coined the term "womanist theology" to describe a perspective ignored by black liberationists and feminist theologians alike, looks at Paul and doubts that any message of freedom "can be taken seriously by today's masses of poor, homeless African Americans, female and male, who consider themselves to be experiencing a form of slavery—economic enslavement by the capitalistic American economy."[44]

Other writers look beyond slavery in lamenting Paul's legacy for blacks. James Baldwin traces back to Paul a destructive attitude in Western culture that denigrates the physical dimensions of human existence. In a 1968 speech delivered to the World Council of Churches charging the church with complicity in racism, he declared, "There is a sense in which it can be said that my black flesh is the flesh that Saint Paul wanted to have mortified."[45] Albert B. Cleage Jr., founder of the Shrine of the Black Madonna and of the Pan African Orthodox Christian Church, saw Paul as betraying Jesus politically as well as theologically. Jesus, the Black Messiah, sought to "root out the individualism and the identification with their oppressor" that had corrupted Israel.[46] Paul was Jewish, but in taking his message to the gentiles, he "attempted to break the covenant which the Black Nation Israel had with God."[47] "'Apostle to the Gentiles' meant Apostle to the white people," writes Cleage, and while Greece and Rome had at least been touched by the civilizing hand of Africa, the hinterland was much more primitive.

> Paul's distortion of Jesus could even be taken to Europe where there were nothing but heathens, pagans and barbarians who lived in caves and ate raw meat. They accepted violence as a way of life. These were the white barbaric European Gentiles who now dominate the world. The Apostle Paul kept trying to change the religion of Jesus to meet their needs and so he lost the concept of the Black Nation which gave the teachings of Jesus meaning.[48]

44. Williams, *Sisters in the Wilderness*, 146–47.
45. Baldwin, "White Racism or World Community?," 371–76 (quote on 374).
46. Cleage, *Black Messiah*, 3–4.
47. Ibid., 44.
48. Ibid., 89–90.

By preaching the resurrection and a "spiritualized" Jesus, Paul distracted the oppressed from the realities of their oppression in the here and now. Black Christians suffering injustice in a white man's land "do not need the individualistic and otherworldly doctrines of Paul and the white man." According to Cleage, "This is a corruption of the religion of Jesus by the Apostle Paul for the white Gentiles."[49]

The Pauline Psyche

Why has the Christian church so often been on the side of the strong and powerful against the weak and oppressed? "A part of the responsibility seems to me to rest upon a peculiar twist in the psychology of Paul," writes Howard Thurman, who believes that it "hung very heavily upon the soul of the apostle" that he was not one of the original twelve disciples. Paul was "of a minority but with majority privileges" like Roman citizenship, thus combining in his person an inferiority complex with a guilty conscience.[50] With the birth of psychology as a formal discipline, a new approach to Paul gained popularity: criticism as diagnosis. That few observers who study Paul in this manner have any clinical training has not been a deterrent. Nor has the fact that the basis for any diagnostic assessment consists of secondhand literary sources, handled with little regard for the difficulties involved in sifting through the differences in personality type and mode of expression across boundaries of time and culture.[51] Gerd Theissen is sympathetic to psychological interpretations yet acknowledges that such methods do not yield uniform results, noting that Paul's thought can be addressed variously as the expression of a neurotic defense mechanism, as liberation from neurotic compulsions, or as the fulfillment or the overcoming of fantasies of omnipotence.[52] Explanatory categories of this sort hardly suggest a portrait of Paul as the epitome of robust mental health.

Theissen's tone is neutral and descriptive, however, in comparison with that of other armchair analysts. "If Paul had lived today," according to Max

---

49. Ibid., 4, 93. In Paul one finds "a religion addressed primarily to persons who are seeking an individual escape from death and punishment for sin" (92). See also Hendricks, *Politics of Jesus*, 85: "Paul transformed Jesus's concern for collective social, economic, and political deliverance for his entire people into an obsession with the personal piety of individuals. Paul seems to have no room in his faith for thoughts of earthly freedom; it is heaven that holds his complete attention."

50. Thurman, *Jesus and the Disinherited*, 31–32.

51. See, most recently, J. C. Hughes, "If Only the Ancients Had Had the DSM."

52. Theissen, *Psychological Aspects*, 27.

Dimont, "he might have ended up on a psychiatrist's couch" because through-out his life "he was overwhelmed with an all-pervasive sense of guilt which pursued him with relentless fury."[53] For William James, Paul is an example of the discordant personality plagued by religious melancholy, self-loathing, and despair.[54] Carl Jung compares him to those converts who "are the worst fanatics" on account of the internal doubts they are compelled to suppress. Paul's "psychogenic blindness" is a function of "an unconscious unwillingness to see."[55] Terrance Callan classifies Paul in Freudian terms as an example of the phallic personality type, to which he attributes Paul's need for recognition and applause.[56] Gerd Lüdemann likewise invokes Freud, suggesting that Paul "was afflicted with an overpowering superego, a phenomenon which, in that unsophisticated age, he quite readily projected on the heavens and mistook for the voice of God."[57] William Hirsch believes that Paul shares with Jesus an unfortunate condition: "Paul, too, was a paranoiac . . . whose thoughts and actions all rested on delusions and hallucinations." His writings, "which laid the foundation stone of the Christian religion, are in every way characteristic of the insanity at the bottom of them."[58]

Pauline Sexuality

Many writers who regard Paul as mentally unstable believe that unresolved personal difficulties with sexuality lie at the root of the problem and that his personal fixations in turn have caused unnecessary anguish for countless individuals living in societies that have been influenced by his writings. "Of all mankind's ideas," according to the popular historian Barbara Tuchman, "the equating of sex with sin has left the greatest train of trouble" in that, through Paul's formulation of the doctrine of original sin, it has "conferred

53. Dimont, *Jews, God, and History*, 141. The schism between Christians and Jews "was both the decision and the accomplishment of one man, another Jew, the real builder of the Christian Church" (140).

54. James, *Varieties of Religious Experience*, 170–71. Cf. Klausner, *From Jesus to Paul*, 425: "We find in him also the characteristics of a thorough melancholiac."

55. Jung, "Psychological Foundations," 8:307–8.

56. Callan, *Psychological Perspectives*, 130.

57. Lüdemann, *Paul*, 244. Surprisingly, Freud himself speaks highly of Paul and has little to say about his psychosexual development; see Westerink, "Great Man from Tarsus."

58. Hirsch, *Religion and Civilization*, 179, 207. Paul's vision of Christ on the road to Damascus was a function of the delusions of grandeur emanating from his "diseased brain" (184–87). See also Herbert J. Muller: "However profound, his thought was essentially an un-critical rationalization of his intense, peculiar experience, . . . the extremities of both his hopes and his fears, and it naturally yielded some dubious dogma when it was read literally by later Christians" (*Uses of the Past*, 158).

permanent guilt on mankind."[59] These critics are often unaware or uncon-
vinced that the judgment expressed in 1 Cor. 7:1—"It is well for a man not to
touch a woman"—belongs to a faction of the Corinthian church that denies
the goodness of sexual pleasure and not to Paul. His preference for celibacy,
recommending marriage only for those who will otherwise "be aflame with
passion" (7:9), is seen as deprecating even conjugal relations. "A great change
from the divine view" was Mark Twain's wry commentary on Paul's advice to
avoid sexual intercourse.[60] Oskar Pfister, an early protégé of Jung and Freud,
asserts that whereas Jesus's views on marriage "were infinitely more delicate and
profound," those who follow Paul's instructions "are in danger of descending
the steep path towards a fear neurosis, unless they happen to achieve adequate
compensation in the form of powerful sublimations."[61] Ernest Hemingway
has a character voice a similar complaint in *A Farewell to Arms*. Rinaldi, the
promiscuous Italian army surgeon, baits a priest over dinner by referring to
Paul as "the one who makes all the trouble." "He was a rounder and a chaser,"
says Rinaldi, "and then when he was no longer hot he said it was no good.
When he was finished he made the rules for us who are still hot."[62]

Rinaldi would no doubt endorse the judgment of Frank Harris, the Irish-
born editor of the *Saturday Review* whose autobiography was parodied by
Hemingway in 1927 in his only contribution to *The New Yorker*. In the preface
to *My Life and Loves*, which was banned in the United States and England
for its nude photographs and graphic descriptions of sexual relations, Harris
declares that one of his chief aims in writing "the first chapter in the Bible of
Humanity" is to counter the baleful influence of "Paulism," a hypocritical
creed that has "dirtied desire, degraded women, debased procreation, vul-
garized and vilified the best instinct in us."[63] The churches have imposed this
creed to their own detriment:

> The silly sex-morality of Paul has brought discredit upon the whole Gospel.
> Paul was impotent, boasted indeed that he had no sexual desires, wished that
> all men were even as he was in this respect, just as the fox in the fable who had
> lost his tail, wished that all other foxes should be mutilated in the same way
> in order to attain his perfection. I often say that the Christian churches were
> offered two things: the spirit of Jesus and the idiotic morality of Paul, and they

59. Tuchman, *Distant Mirror*, 211.
60. Twain's remark in this "Letter from the Earth" is meant to highlight ethical inconsistencies on the part of God as much as to skewer Paul (*Bible according to Mark Twain*, 256).
61. Pfister, *Christianity and Fear*, 267. For Pfister's sketch of Paul as a neurotic Jew in search
of liberation from feelings of guilt, see "Entwicklung des Apostels Paulus."
62. Hemingway, *Farewell to Arms*, 184.
63. F. Harris, *My Life and Loves*, xiii–xiv, xviii.

all rejected the highest inspiration and took to their hearts the incredibly base and stupid prohibition. Following Paul we have turned the Goddess of Love into a fiend and degraded the crowning impulse of our Being into a capital sin.

The reader should not be distracted by the prurient content of Harris's memoir. His only desire, he says, is to benefit humanity by removing hindrances to the fulfillment of its deepest and most sincere longings. Prudery and judgmentalism cause only harm to the average man since his dearest wish is "to be healthy and strong while gratifying all his sexual appetites."[64]

Lawrence Durrell similarly elevates sex to the level of a sacrament and, not coincidentally, magnifies Paul's culpability in thwarting its expression in *Clea*, the last installment of his *Alexandrian Quartet*. Extracts from the journal of one character, Pursewarden, compose a chapter of the novel that reflects Durrell's own view that "culture means sex, the root-knowledge, and where the faculty is derailed or crippled, its derivatives like religion come up dwarfed or contorted."[65] He elaborates the theme that sex is "the university of the soul" with specific reference to D. H. Lawrence's novella *The Man Who Died* (originally published as *The Escaped Cock*). Lawrence reimagines Jesus, the titular character, awaking in his sepulcher after the crucifixion, embarking on a quest to find a woman who can connect him to the physical world, and eventually arriving in Egypt, where he impregnates a priestess of Isis. "How wonderful the death-struggle of Lawrence," writes Durrell's Pursewarden, "to realize his sexual nature fully, to break free from the manacles of the Old Testament." Durrell shares with Lawrence the view that healthy cultures embrace the sensual: "His struggle is ours—to rescue Jesus from Moses. For a brief moment it looked possible, but St. Paul restored the balance and the iron handcuffs of the Judaic prison closed about the growing soul forever." The resurrection ought to have meant "the true birth of free man," but thanks to the one "who invented the perversion of Original Sin, that filthy obscenity of the West," emancipation has yet to arrive.[66]

Aleister Crowley, notorious British occultist, also fulminates against the puritanical sense of guilt and sin that he considers "a modern invention due principally to the tyranny of a Pauline priestcraft." Alluding to Paul's "thorn in the flesh," Crowley says,

We do not know enough about Paul to be perfectly sure from what bodily infirmity he suffered. But there is a great deal of evidence in his treatment

64. Ibid., xvii.
65. Durrell, *Clea*, 141.
66. Ibid., 142.

of the sex question to make us suspect that he was some kind of sexual degenerate. Any man who is abnormal sexually, if he should combine with this defect a powerful intellect and some degree of personality, is a far more dangerous wild beast than any dragon of fable. Paul was evidently a monster of this type.[67]

From a man dubbed "the Wickedest Man in the World," whose guiding moral dictum was "Do What Thou Wilt," this amounts either to unfair criticism—the pot calling the kettle black—or the highest praise.

Criticism of Paul for his negative attitude toward specifically homosexual behavior was the loathing that dared not speak its name prior to the twentieth century because of taboos that have only recently begun to relax. When novelist James Baldwin thought back on his youth, he recalled having been "bull-whipped" through the Scriptures, including the writings of "the helplessly paranoiac Saint Paul."[68] His own experience is hinted at in his later comment that "no matter what Saint Paul may thunder, love is where you find it."[69] Whatever ostracism he may have felt as an African American homosexual and son of a Baptist minister did not translate into sympathy for Paul, who "with a most unusual and stunning exactness, described himself as a 'wretched man.'"[70]

Why was Paul so wretched? The hypothesis that his personality and views on sex stem from repressed homosexual impulses has been put forward by various writers over the last several decades.[71] Controversial filmmaker Pier Paolo Pasolini wrote a screenplay that depicts Paul as a closeted homosexual in 1960s New York who contracts a mysterious illness when he first senses the nature of his desires.[72] Episcopal bishop John Shelby Spong has claimed in several books that Paul's "ill-informed, culturally biased prejudices" are explained by "his own hidden secret," namely, the private disgust he feels over his own same-sex attractions:

I am convinced that Paul of Tarsus was a gay man, deeply repressed, self-loathing, rigid in denial, bound by the law that he hoped could keep this thing, that he judged to be so unacceptable, totally under control, a control so profound

67. Crowley, *Gospel according to St. Bernard Shaw*, 154.
68. Baldwin, *Devil Finds Work*, 11.
69. Ibid., 70.
70. Baldwin, *Fire Next Time*, 32.
71. E.g., H. Fischer, *Gespaltener christlicher Glaube*, 52–56.
72. Maggi, *Resurrection of the Body*, 21–106. While the sexual aspect of this work is provocative, Pasolini is more interested in exploring other issues related to his Marxist political philosophy.

that even Paul did not have to face this fact about himself. But repression kills. It kills the repressed one and sometimes the defensive anger . . . also kills those who challenge, threaten or live out the thing that this repressed person so deeply fears.[73]

Spong has popularized the theory that these unbidden desires are the mysterious "thorn in the flesh" about which Paul complains in 2 Cor. 12:7. He is the main authority cited by R. W. Holmen for his historical novel, *A Wretched Man*, in which Paul is portrayed as a tormented homosexual. (Holmen speculates that 1 Cor. 9:27—"I pommel my body and subdue it" [RSV]—may be a reference to masochistic self-flagellation.)[74] Holmen's title is taken from Rom. 7:23–24, Paul's cri de coeur over his inability to avoid the sins he despises. Most scholars now interpret this passage as speech in character, serving a rhetorical rather than an autobiographical purpose, but this has not interfered with this approach to Pauline psychology.

Spong and others do not mean to slander Paul in suggesting that he was gay. Their agenda is to shift the traditional Christian teaching on homosexuality from condemnation to acceptance. (Spong himself was roundly criticized as elitist if not outright racist for suggesting, in the lead-up to the 1998 Lambeth Conference, that Anglican bishops from Africa opposed the liberalization of church teaching because they had only recently "moved out of animism into a very superstitious kind of Christianity.")[75] The object of their criticism is the traditional teaching, based on Pauline texts that are to be discounted because they supposedly issue from a warped psyche. In this reading, Paul can be as much a figure of pity as of reproach.

Compassion and forbearance are totally missing, however, from Gore Vidal's treatment in *Live from Golgotha*. The convoluted plot shifts back and forth from the late first century to the late twentieth century and involves a computer virus that threatens to erase the gospel from human memory. Alongside Timothy, who narrates the story, the main character is Paul or, as Timothy likes to call him, "Saint." To say that Vidal's characterization is unflattering would be an understatement. Paul is a compulsive liar, a shameless name-dropper, a cheapskate, a packrat, and a lousy tent maker with poor personal hygiene who was wrong about the timetable for the second coming of Christ. He struggles with dyslexia, attention deficit disorder, and epilepsy, which is played for comic effect. His narcissistic personality is fed by his missionary work because "the one thing that Saint could not live without

---

73. Spong, *Sins of Scripture*, 140; cf. Spong, *Rescuing the Bible*, 116–25.
74. Holmen, *Wretched Man*, 399–400.
75. Hassett, *Anglican Communion in Crisis*, 72–74.

was a live audience."[76] The compliments he is paid are hardly redeeming. Vidal portrays him as a virtuoso juggler and credits him with inventing tap dancing. Not only is he a marketing genius who "could sell a refrigerator to an Eskimo," but he also possesses the creative accounting skills needed to conceal the prodigious amount of money he raises.

The notion that Paul, not Jesus, "invented" Christianity is mentioned a few times but is largely taken for granted. More pervasive and more shocking is Vidal's presentation of Paul as unabashedly homosexual. He constantly harasses Timothy, sleeping with him and with virtually everyone else he can as he travels the Mediterranean. Vidal's Paul is no angst-ridden character struggling with forbidden passions. Virtually every character continuously engages in ribald banter, and Paul more than holds his own. He embodies the gay-male stereotype: sassy, campy, effeminate, an aficionado of theater and modern dance, with a flair for interior decorating. This characterization of Paul is not intended as a negative judgment that works by associating him with sinful behavior—Vidal's own sexual proclivities are well-known—but rather as a way of highlighting his hypocrisy, especially when it comes to sex. It is impossible to view this portrait and not sense the author's disdain for Paul personally and the faith he bequeathed to posterity.[77]

Paul on Stage and Screen

Playwrights have not been any friendlier to Paul than have novelists or psychologists, poking fun at imagined peccadilloes and linking him with conservative Christianity so as to tar the man and his message—at least as it has been put into practice—with the same brush. George Bernard Shaw vents his spleen in a lengthy preface to *Androcles and the Lion*. Like so many others, he finds original sin nonsensical and psychologically unhealthy. Paul's emotional swings are "a pathological symptom of that particular sort of conscience and nervous constitution which brings its victims under the tyranny of two delirious terrors: the terror of sin and the terror of death."[78] His conversion is a spectacular manifestation of these terrors, out of which he fabricates a new religion in the name of Jesus. More accurately, his conversion "is no

76. Vidal, *Live from Golgotha*, 27.
77. Vidal's negative view of Paul is anticipated in his 1964 historical novel about the Roman emperor Julian, "the Apostate." Paul "outdid all quacks and cheats that ever existed anywhere" (*Julian*, 299–300).
78. G. B. Shaw, "Prospects of Christianity," xcvi. H. G. Wells (*Outline of History*, 952–55) emphasizes the contradictions between Darwinism and Paul's teachings about a literal fall into original sin.

conversion at all." Rather, "it was Paul who converted the religion that had raised one man above sin and death into a religion that delivered millions of men so completely into their dominion that their own common nature became a horror to them."[79]

According to Shaw, Paul succeeds in "stealing the image of Christ crucified for the figure-head of his Salvationist vessel," even though there can be found "not one word of Pauline Christianity in the characteristic utterances of Jesus."[80] Going against the grain of much modern criticism, Shaw's beef with Paul has little to do with any supposed tendency toward asceticism and self-denial. To the contrary, he argues that the doctrine of the atonement associated with Paul's cross-centered gospel undermines the austere moral code enjoined by Jesus: "The notion that he was shedding his own blood in order that every petty cheat and adulterator and libertine might wallow in it and come out whiter than snow, cannot be imputed to him on his own authority."[81] (On the specific matter of sex, Shaw begs to differ with those like Frank Harris, his biographer and editor, who deride Paul as a puritanical killjoy. Striking a rare conciliatory note, Shaw rejects "foolish surmises" about Paul's personal life as examples of transference "by people so enslaved by sex that a celibate appears to them a sort of monster.")[82] The consequences of thus eroding moral responsibility, including a "violently anti-Christian system of criminal law," lead Shaw to declare, "There has really never been a more monstrous imposition perpetrated than the imposition of the limitations of Paul's soul upon the soul of Jesus." Paulinism nonetheless continues to have broad appeal to "untrained minds," he says, especially among the "negro piccaninnies" in Africa.[83]

Until recently, Paul's appearances in the public square had rarely included the theater. He appears as the main character in the work of Jim Grimsley, an award-winning novelist and playwright hailed as a leading voice on the American gay literary scene. In Grimsley's *The Lizard of Tarsus*, first staged in 1990, Jesus has returned to earth late in the twentieth century only to be incarcerated by Paul. Set in an interrogation room, the play dramatizes "one of the central confrontations that continue to invigorate and torment the

---

79. G. B. Shaw, "Prospects of Christianity," xcvii.

80. Ibid., c. Elsewhere Shaw decries "Crosstianity" and "the central superstition of the salvation of the world by the gibbet" ("Preface to Major Barbara," 183).

81. G. B. Shaw, "Prospects of Christianity," c–ci. His aim was "to make self-satisfied sinners feel the burden of their sins and stop committing them instead of assuring them that they could not help it, as it was all Adam's fault" (ibid., ci).

82. Ibid., xcix–c. Shaw was himself married but never consummated the union, living a celibate life until the death of his wife forty years later; see S. Peters, *Bernard Shaw*, 217.

83. G. B. Shaw, "Prospects of Christianity," cii–ciii.

weakened but still-presiding faith of our civilization," as novelist Reynolds Price describes it in his brief introduction to the published script.[84] Paul comes across alternately as self-important, self-absorbed, insincere, misogynistic, Machiavellian, prone to conspicuous consumption (he reads the *Wall Street Journal* and, literally, burns money), disinclined to worship Jesus, and generally uninterested in what Jesus has to say. Above all, Paul wants Jesus to confirm the story of his conversion so that he can quell mounting challenges to his authority as Jesus's spokesman and cornerstone of his church. Jesus initially disclaims any recollection of a meeting on the Damascus road, and his interactions with Paul range from passive aggressive to sarcastic to psychologically manipulative. He says that God is dead, refers to the Bible as "dead weight," and compares Paul to Judas Iscariot.

The climax occurs with the revelation that on the road to Damascus, Paul had a sexual encounter with a woman whose tongue he rips out when he hallucinates that she is a reptile. This denouement is foreshadowed earlier when Jesus tells a lengthy parable featuring a character who engages in incest with his brother, kills his wife and later his illegitimate son, locks his concubine in a basement for several years, and receives a pet lizard that is described as the Son of God who "has come to die for the sins of the world." Other transgressive elements in the dialogue include hints that Jesus and John shared an intimate relationship and that Paul's "thorn" was impotence or self-castration.

Grimsley's absurdist play was first performed not long after the 1988 release of Martin Scorsese's *Last Temptation of Christ*. It could almost be described as a transmutation of the scene near the film's conclusion where Scorsese has Paul telling a bewildered Jesus that the church no longer needs him. "You should understand by now. It's mine anyway. The message. If you don't give me the Word, I'll get it somewhere," says Grimsley's Paul, adding that he'll have to make "a few doctrinal corrections here and there" to any statement Jesus may make.[85] Deeper than Scorsese's influence is that of Dostoevsky and the story of "The Grand Inquisitor" embedded in his epic novel *The Brothers Karamazov*. Ivan tells Alyosha a parable about Christ reappearing in sixteenth-century Spain and working wonders before being arrested on the orders of a powerful cardinal. This inquisitor explains to Jesus that he has misjudged humanity's ability to handle free will and that his return interferes with the church's mission of saving humans from themselves. In presuming to know better than Jesus what is in the world's best interests, the inquisitor and the church he represents function as a tool in the devil's hands. It is no

84. Grimsley, *Lizard of Tarsus*, 69.
85. Ibid., 85, 87.

coincidence, one suspects, that Grimsley describes Paul as an "inquisitor" in the dramatis personae. Like Dostoevsky, Grimsley voices a trenchant critique of Christendom, however much they may differ in terms of substance and sophistication.

British playwright Howard Brenton has Paul meet Jesus in a different venue. His *Paul*, first staged at London's National Theatre in 2005, has the apostle playing the unwitting accomplice of James in a plan to capitalize on the legacy of his brother Jesus. Most of the play takes place in flashback mode as Peter and Paul await their execution by Nero. The encounter with the "risen" Jesus, who has in fact survived the crucifixion, is arranged by James during one of Paul's frequent epileptic seizures. The audience learns that the gentile mission was "never meant to be" but is delegated to Paul to get him out of the way, that Jesus marries Mary Magdalene to spite his wealthy parents, and that he begins to believe the "very beautiful lies" Paul tells about him. In Brenton's telling, Paul's career is built on a lie, only not one of his own devising.

Filmmaker Robert Orlando is less hostile than Grimsley but also less inclined to see Paul as an innocent or unwilling dupe in an unsavory plot as one finds in Brenton. One part animated narration of Paul's ministry and one part documentary, his 2013 release *Apostle Paul* bears the provocative subtitle *A Polite Bribe*.[86] It highlights the conflict between Paul with his law-free gospel and James with his commitment to his brother's insistence on Torah observance. James is willing to tolerate the mission to the gentiles on the condition that Paul take up a collection for the poor in Jerusalem. The gift was to be presented to the temple leadership in a "primitive money-laundering scheme." A riot erupts when Paul, accompanied by his gentile coworker Titus, tries to deliver it. Orlando intimates not only that James leaves Paul in the lurch when things get ugly but that it was James's secret hope that Paul would be eliminated. Paul dies, but the movement that would become the Christian church would survive, "the product of one man and his vision alone."

One might see *A Polite Bribe* as a piece of anti-James polemic as much as an example of anti-Paulinism given James's cynical dealing in leaving Paul to twist in the wind. The negative statements about Paul that appear on the website promoting the film and Orlando's reliance on the work of James Tabor and Gerd Lüdemann, however, do not suggest a sympathetic appraisal.[87] Nor

---

86. The subtitle is likely borrowed from a phrase of Lüdemann, *Paul*, 42.

87. Lüdemann, *Paul*, 246: Paul's "personal compulsion to be the original and the final authority, and his missionary zeal to retain the converts he had made and to add ever more by solving problems with ad hoc doctrinal solutions, led him to create a religion far different from that of Jesus." Cf. Tabor, *Paul and Jesus*, 157, 160: A mistaken belief that history would soon come to an end leads Paul to promulgate an "interim ethics"—one should live "as if" God's kingdom

does his inclusion of Jeffrey Bütz as a talking head alongside such widely respected scholars as John Dominic Crossan, Amy-Jill Levine, and N. T. Wright. Elsewhere Bütz has written on the way in which the church's preference for Paul over James signals a betrayal of Jesus on key teachings, as well as on the preservation of Jesus's Jewish message from the time of James down to the Founding Fathers of the United States via secret societies such as the Cathars and the Freemasons.[88] Together with the appearance of Bütz, the promotional blurbs for the DVD evince a conspiratorial bent that may discomfit some of the scholars providing sound bites in the film. "If Oliver Stone ever became a Bible scholar, he might turn out a movie a bit like *A Polite Bribe*," says one. Invoking the name of, arguably, the most famous conspiracy theorist in the United States somewhat undercuts the meticulous research that went into the making of the film.

Pauline Plots

Conspiracy thinking is not a new phenomenon. Nor are intricate theories about Paul's alleged role in Christian history. Their proliferation and circulation have certainly been aided by the onset of the information age. Just as it has for nearly every other subject, the internet provides access to scholarly resources once available only to those with access to university libraries. At the same time, it functions as a clearinghouse for all sorts of wild speculation and rumormongering. Rarely are they as far-fetched or unabashed as Holger Kersten and Elmar Gruber's *The Jesus Conspiracy*, which links Paul to a Vatican scheme to manipulate radiocarbon dating of the Shroud of Turin—not, as one might expect, to prove its authenticity but rather to invalidate it, because it allegedly shows Jesus surviving the cross and not having been raised from the dead, thus negating the central claim of Pauline Christianity.[89] As with

---

has already been realized—that has "resulted in incalculable human suffering and misery" because of his influence on Western thinking about sexuality, economic and social inequities, and religious and ethnic divisions. Herbert J. Muller laments the same effect but identifies a different cause, namely, Paul's doctrine of original sin. Throughout history, "the conviction that man's birthright is sin has encouraged an unrealistic acceptance of remediable social evils, or even callousness about human suffering" (*Uses of the Past*, 160).

88. Bütz, *Brother of Jesus*; Bütz, *Secret Legacy of Jesus*.

89. Settling this question about an alleged relic thus has far broader implications: "Although there are several most delightful passages in the texts of Paul, Christianity has his narrow-minded fanaticism to thank for numerous detrimental developments, which are diametrically opposed to the spirit of Jesus: the intolerance towards those of different views, the marked hostility to the body and the consequently low view of woman, and especially the fatally flawed attitude towards nature" (Kersten and Gruber, *Jesus Conspiracy*, 339).

the Christ-myth theory, which went underground for much of the twentieth century, Pauline exposés only occasionally offer anything of substance that has not been heard before. However much they may differ in tone, the line separating internet chatter or other popular treatments of Paul from academic treatments is sometimes blurred, perhaps because popular writers now have greater access to scholarship, even if they are not always able or willing to digest the content or appreciate the nuance that scholars typically bring to the topic.

Barrie Wilson illustrates this peculiar convergence. It is not unfair to categorize his *How Jesus Became a Christian* as a conspiracy theory since he consistently employs the shorthand "Jesus Cover-Up Thesis" when referring to his overarching argument. "I have come to some startling conclusions" after years of study, he informs the reader. These conclusions will not startle readers with any familiarity with the Jesus-Paul debate in its nineteenth-century iteration. The original Jesus Movement started by Jesus and led by his brother James is displaced by a new religion, the Christ Movement, forged by Paul in the diaspora. "Part of the excitement of this book consists of exploding the commonplace notion that Paul was somehow a faithful disciple of Jesus," says Wilson.[90] Paul shifts attention away from the "teachings of Jesus" to a completely different set of "teachings about the Christ." Followers of the Christ Movement are "very much aware" of "the big switch" they are making—"one of the most effective cover-ups of all time"—and the result is "Paulinity," a "brand-new religion entirely," named after the "Jewish dropout" who oversees an amazingly effective public relations campaign and later becomes the star of the revisionist historical fiction known as the Acts of the Apostles.[91] Because Paul and his fellow "Christifiers" are conscious of their systematic suppression of Jesus's voice, one sees a "guilt dynamic" that has them "lashing out at the witnesses," that is, the Jews who honored Jesus before his legacy was hijacked by Hellenists who want to destroy Judaism.[92] Wilson draws on a narrow range of the voluminous secondary literature and exaggerates the originality of his argument. His claim about the high degree of intentionality on Paul's part is the most novel aspect of his thesis, though even this is implicit in the work of some other scholars. Most surprising is that Wilson, while striving to present his thesis in as scholarly a manner as

90. B. Wilson, *How Jesus Became a Christian*, 1–2.
91. Ibid., 3, 5, 114, 129–30, 145. See also 109, 114: "Nothing in the early Jesus Movement prepares us for Paul. . . . The Christ and Jesus Movements are in fact, *different* religions, not rival interpretations of the same religion" (emphasis original).
92. Ibid., 170–71, 252. Wilson compares Paul to Antiochus IV, the Seleucid ruler who tried to eradicate Judaism in the Maccabean period.

possible, compares his work to Dan Brown's *The Da Vinci Code*—not at all
to distance himself from conspiracy theories as such but to claim that his
theory is more radical and has implications that are far more consequential
than Brown's.[93]

Hyam Maccoby and Robert Eisenman present theories that are at once
more thoroughly researched than those of Wilson and, in many respects, more
explicitly conspiracist in orientation. Both rely heavily on Ebionite attacks on
Paul from the patristic period. According to Maccoby, the NT gets it exactly
backward in claiming that Paul was a Pharisee and that the Pharisees in turn
were the mortal enemies of Jesus. Reared a god-fearing pagan, Paul was in
fact a convert to Judaism, despite what he says in his letters. When he was
frustrated in his attempts to rise in the Pharisee ranks, he joined the police
arm of the Sadducees. Proselytes sometimes become the most conscientious
of Jews, Maccoby observes, but they might also backslide into paganism or
concoct "weird religious fantasies . . . in which the Jews tended to figure as
the villains."[94] Feelings of failure or rejection lie behind such fantasies, and
"Paul was the greatest fantasist of all." His worldview incorporated narratives from the Hebrew Scriptures but was mainly based on gnostic redeemer
myths, "reinforced by powerful sado-masochist elements derived from mystery
religion."[95] To help legitimate his position, he fabricated a Pharisee past for
himself out of whole cloth. While many writers believe that Paul knew, and
perhaps cared, very little about the historical Jesus, Maccoby contends that
he knew all too well that Jesus engaged in political resistance against Rome
but suppressed this aspect of Jesus's ministry by repackaging him in a quiet-
ist theology. In so doing, Paul invented Christianity and, as the first writer to
assign to the Jews the role of "sacred executioner" fated to bring about the
Savior's death, became the father of Christian anti-Semitism.[96]

Eisenman likewise sees Paul as erasing Jesus's authentic teachings and
usurping the rightful place of his Jewish disciples in guiding the movement
he had started and defining its doctrine. His reconstruction of early Christianity is far more elaborate than Maccoby's and depends on idiosyncratic
readings of the Dead Sea Scrolls. Eisenman claims that James is the mysterious
Teacher of Righteousness thought to be the leader of the Qumran sect and
that the Spouter of Lies who appears as the Teacher's nemesis is a code name

93. Ibid., 107–8, 248, 252. David Aaronovitch (*Voodoo Histories*, 195–228) discusses the work
of Brown as well as that of Michael Baigent, Richard Leigh, and Henry Lincoln (*Holy Blood,
Holy Grail*, 1982) and other writers against the background of contemporary conspiracism.
94. Maccoby, *Mythmaker*, 204.
95. Ibid., 198.
96. Ibid., 203, 205.

for Paul, a non-Jew who betrays the "new covenant." He further speculates that Paul may have had a hand in the execution of John the Baptist by Herod and provided military intelligence to Nero during the Jewish revolt of 66–70.[97]

Social psychologists often account for the prevalence of conspiracy theories by describing the cognitive state of those who subscribe to them. To attribute the conspiracist tendencies of these approaches to Paul to the psychological state of their proponents would be uncharitable, even if they often exhibit extreme discontent with the status quo, appeal to secret knowledge, congratulate themselves on their appreciation of this gnosis, and manifest a Manichaean worldview that casts the history of the church as a struggle between darkness (= Paul) and light (= Jesus). Explaining Paul's "victory" over the religion of the Jesus movement as the result of his ideas finding favor in Rome likewise has elements in common with but cannot be reduced to a nativist anti-Catholicism that sees a powerful, secretive, hierarchical organization wielding undue influence over world affairs.[98] What leads many of Paul's critics to implicate him in nefarious plots? It may be their embrace of a robust hermeneutics of suspicion. Yet it is an inconstant embrace, by turns insufficiently suspicious of dubious historical claims and unwilling to concede that mainstream institutions may not always cloak their true origins or conceal ulterior motives by means of "official" narratives.

Paul and Misogyny

Among the accusations sometimes made against Paul is that he has conspired to doctor the historical record and erase the name of the primary witness to the resurrection. Each of the Gospels portrays Mary Magdalene as the first person to discover the empty tomb and bring the good news to the other disciples, yet Paul omits her name from the list of witnesses in 1 Cor. 15:5–8.[99] This may be the first of Paul's sins against women but, according to his critics, it is by no means his last. Books about Paul and the effect his teachings have had on women could easily stock a small library. In the West, it is perhaps the most common complaint against Paul one hears in the twentieth century. As the primary source of a "nonsensical anti-feminism" and an "antiwoman dogma inherent in the Christian liturgy," Paul "can be legitimately cast in

97. Eisenman, *James*, 529, 654–55.

98. See Barkun, *Culture of Conspiracy*, 131–36, on the relationship between American anti-Catholicism and conspiracy theories in the nineteenth century. In Paul's case, his purported "contamination" of Christianity with Roman religious ideas parallels the accusation that the Roman Catholic Church seeks to preserve or revive pre-Christian paganism.

99. Schaberg and Johnson-DeBaufre, *Mary Magdalene Understood*, 113–16.

the role of the first official Christian misogynist."[100] According to feminist theologian Mary Daly, Paul was an "arch-hater of life in general and women in particular."[101] While "there is a breath of charity in the Gospels," writes Simone de Beauvoir, through Paul "the fiercely antifeminist Jewish tradition is affirmed."[102]

As was the case with slaves, one may surmise that anti-Pauline feelings were present earlier if not at all prominent due to the general absence of female voices from the public square. This began to change with Elizabeth Cady Stanton's publication of *The Women's Bible*. The volume containing commentary on the NT appeared in 1898. Earlier female interpreters tended to explain away the harshness of Paul's comments by situating them in their original cultural context or to criticize their application by a male-dominated ecclesiastical hierarchy. Stanton is not afraid to take direct aim at Paul. She scoffs that his instructions on the veiling of women prophets in 1 Cor. 11 are based on "an absurd old myth" and states that the prohibition of women from teaching in 1 Tim. 2 is not an inspired teaching but "evidently the unilluminated utterance of Paul, the man, biased by prejudice."[103] It is unnecessary and unjust for modern believers to be limited by his cultural horizon: "Could Paul have looked down to the nineteenth century with clairvoyant vision and beheld the good works of a Lucretia Mott, a Florence Nightingale, a Dorothea Dix and Clara Barton, . . . he might have hesitated to utter so tyrannical an edict: 'But I permit not a woman to teach.'"[104] Moreover, the doctrine that sin originates with women, "planted in the early Christian Church by Paul, has been a poisonous stream in Church and in state," and it formed no part of the teaching of Jesus.[105] Even some of her fellow activists for women's rights were uncomfortable with her radical theological stances, however, and the National Woman Suffrage Association formally dissociated itself from *The Women's Bible* upon its publication.[106]

Two texts have supplied more fodder for Paul's critics than any other. In 1 Cor. 14:33b–36, he says that "women should be silent in the churches"

100. Seltman, *Women in Antiquity*, 185; Gilmore, *Misogyny*, 86–87.
101. Daly, *Pure Lust*, 8.
102. Beauvoir, *Second Sex*, 97.
103. Stanton, *Women's Bible*, 159, 163.
104. Ibid., 162.
105. Ibid., 163–64.
106. In his historical novel *Legacy*, James Michener has a character echo Stanton when she concludes a suffragist call to arms by linking political and religious objectives in debates over the Nineteenth Amendment: "Please cleanse your faiths of antique practices which deny women full partnership, because the women of America will no longer kowtow to the fulminations of St. Paul" (*Legacy*, 114).

and that "they are not permitted to speak, but should be subordinate." His remarks come in the context of a lengthy discussion of speaking in tongues, but the conclusion that "it is shameful for a woman to speak in church" has been applied more generally to suppress women's voices. In 1 Tim. 2:11–15, the author issues a similar mandate: "Let a woman learn in silence with full submission. I permit no woman to teach or to have authority over a man." A theological rationale accompanies the command. Women should remain silent because Eve led Adam astray and the rest of humanity into sin. They may nevertheless be saved "through childbearing." Critical engagement with these texts became especially intense as the movement for women's ordination in the church gained steam in many Christian denominations over the course of the twentieth century.

Inconsistency and ambiguity are commonly cited as factors militating against simple answers to questions about Paul's chauvinism. Treatment of objectionable passages displays the range of responses Paul elicits when it comes to his legacy for women, generally falling into one of three categories: (1) These and other texts show Paul to be implacably hostile to women, in patriarchal retreat from the egalitarian position staked out by Jesus.[107] (2) These texts are not written by Paul. The broad consensus that 1 Timothy is pseudonymous aligns with this approach. Many also regard 1 Cor. 14:33b–36 as an interpolation added to Paul's letter by members of a deuteropauline "school" seeking to domesticate his teachings. In this approach, Paul is not to blame so much as later church authorities unwilling to enact his emancipatory program.[108] (3) These texts have been misinterpreted. Rightly understood, passages from the undisputed letters—the Pastoral Epistles are still deemed highly problematic—in fact speak powerfully on behalf of the equal status and value of women. This third approach has become increasingly popular, especially but not exclusively among feminist interpreters one might otherwise expect to be among Paul's fiercest critics, as scholars recognize that an understanding of Paul in his ancient context does not readily yield a decision as to whether Paul is "for" or "against" women.[109]

107. E.g., Ruether, *Sexism and God-Talk*, 33–34; Schüssler Fiorenza, *Rhetoric and Ethic*, 149–73. Other feminist scholars have labeled the portrait of Jesus's ministry as a "discipleship of equals" as "a myth posited to buttress modern Christian social engineering." See K. Corley, *Women and the Historical Jesus*, 1.

108. Scroggs, "Paul and the Eschatological Woman."

109. Krause, "Paul and Women." Brian J. Dodd similarly notes that asking "*Was* Paul a sexist?" is not the same as asking "*Is* Paul a sexist?" in that the former attempts to compare Paul's views to those of his contemporaries while the latter involves speculation as to how Paul's views might "translate" into a modern setting (*Problem with Paul*, 21–22). Davina C. Lopez believes that Paul's ministry can be "re-imagined" from a feminist or queer perspective:

Paul's view of women is sometimes attributed to a Platonic dualism of flesh and spirit that he inherited from his Hellenistic background. Through its association of women with the material realm of flesh and sin, it is argued, this dualistic anthropology had dire consequences.[110] Whether it is a wariness about sexual relations that determines Paul's view of women (with whom men normally come into contact during intercourse) or a low view of women that determines his views on sex is not a matter on which critics agree. Whatever their sources, in his attitudes toward women Paul is still widely seen as arrogant, authoritarian, petulant, and uncompromising. His views are often cited as instances of "othering," in which one group establishes its identity by marginalizing another group through stereotyping and other invidious rhetorical strategies.[111]

A noteworthy expression of this view can be seen in a May 2013 sermon delivered by Katharine Jefferts Schori, the presiding bishop of the Episcopal Church in the United States.[112] The sermon in question, which attracted international attention, took as its text Acts 16:16–18, where Paul casts out a "spirit of divination" from a slave girl who has generated a steady income for her masters. Paul, "very much annoyed" that he has been stalked for several days by a demon-possessed girl screaming "These men are slaves of the Most High God, who proclaim to you a way of salvation," finally casts out the spirit, to the consternation of her owners, who are thereby deprived of a handsome financial windfall. Jefferts Schori believes Paul is motivated by something more than simple irritation. "Human beings have a long history of discounting and devaluing difference, finding it offensive or even evil," she says, noting that "some remarkable examples of that kind of blindness" are present in the day's reading. But she does not have the human traffickers who are using the girl for ill-gotten gain in mind. Rather, Paul is the one with distorted vision:

> She's telling the same truth Paul and others claim for themselves. But Paul is annoyed, perhaps for being put in his place, and he responds by depriving her of her gift of spiritual awareness. Paul can't abide something he won't see as beautiful or holy, so he tries to destroy it. It gets him thrown in prison. That's pretty much where he's put himself by his own refusal to recognize that she, too, shares in God's nature, just as much as he does—maybe more so!

"While I would not argue that Paul is perfect or even a feminist or gay man himself, I submit that characterizations of Paul as excessively dominating and irretrievably harmful suffer from a lack of complexity. Ancient Paul is not simply for or against contemporary women and LGBT people" (*Apostle to the Conquered*, 15).

110. Ehrensperger, *That We May Be Mutually Encouraged*, 41.

111. Schüssler Fiorenza, *Rhetoric and Ethic*, 180–87.

112. See Oppenheimer, "Sermon Leads to More Dissent."

Many commentators were surprised not that Jefferts Schori would criticize Paul but that she would take the side of slave owners exploiting a young girl, especially when she mentions the evil of slavery earlier in the sermon. For Paul, no good deed goes unpunished. He frees a girl from oppression by human and demonic forces and gets arrested. To add insult to injury, he is reproved for self-righteousness. It is difficult to tell whether the bishop's convoluted exegesis is a function of her desire to make a statement about the value of diversity regardless of the lectionary reading for the day or whether her hostility toward Paul is so great that, wherever she looks, she sees a cudgel with his name on it.

Anti-Paulinism achieves a bewildering diversity in the modern period. What new forms might it take in the future? Forecasting cultural trends can be difficult, but one might note that some writers have turned their gaze from Paul's sins against fellow humans to those perpetrated against nonhumans. Environmentalists begin in the 1970s to identify Christianity's anthropocentrism and human-animal dualism as a source of ecological degradation. Paul's part in this story has been a minor one, with critics focusing mainly on what they perceive as Paul's dismissive attitude toward animal welfare in 1 Cor. 9:9–10 (RSV): "Is it for oxen that God is concerned? Does he not speak entirely for our sake?" Peter Singer remarks in his animal rights manifesto *Animal Liberation* that Paul lacks even those few "flickers of concern for their sufferings" contained in the OT.[113]

Nearly all of Paul's critics have heretofore had some connection with Christianity, vestigial or otherwise, be it the early proponents of a Torah-observant form of the nascent messianic faith, the European Deist advocates of a universal religion of nature purified of such superstitious notions as resurrection and blood atonement, or Christians who believe that the apostle (or those speaking in his name) has compromised the progressive teachings of Jesus that form the basis of "authentic" Christian faith. Two important exceptions are Judaism and Islam. Whereas Hindus, Buddhists, and Daoists have had much to say about Jesus, they have largely ignored Paul. The question of Jesus's status is, in different ways, unavoidable for Jews and Muslims. Rejection of certain Pauline understandings of Jesus is a crucial aspect of Jewish and Muslim self-definition, however much these groups differ in terms of

---

113. Singer, *Animal Liberation*, 209. On this score, according to Singer, Jesus is no better, "show[ing] indifference to the fate of nonhumans" by unnecessarily inducing two thousand pigs to cast themselves into the sea during an exorcism in Mark 5:11–13 (ibid.).

the substance and emphasis of their respective critiques. In the future, their roles in the phenomenon of anti-Paulinism are likely to reward continued attention. To complement the surveys of premodern criticism among Jews and Muslims in part 1, chapter 6 in part 2 below will describe the contours of contemporary Jewish and Muslim engagement with Paul.

PART 2

Anti-Pauline Contexts, Subtexts, and Pretexts

6

IN THE TENTS OF SHEM

Paul among Jews and Muslims

As is so often true in human relationships, those with the strongest feelings about Paul are those who presumably know him best, namely, fellow Christians. Other monotheists—Jews and Muslims—likewise have strong reactions, though both have their doubts as to whether Paul belongs to their number when he honors Jesus as "Lord." The historical, geographic, and ideological proximity of the "peoples of the book" holds great promise for mutual understanding. But it can also exacerbate the disagreements, as greater familiarity all too often breeds greater contempt. Reflecting on his own feelings about Paul, Jewish "death of God" theologian Richard L. Rubenstein states that "one of the problems perennially bedeviling the Judeo-Christian encounter has been the fact that there has been too much rather than too little brotherhood," as "fraternal feelings are likely to become fratricidal" when, despite their shared heritage, the differences remain so deep.[1] Efforts at reconciliation through a rereading of Paul have begun to materialize among Jews, if not among Muslims.[2] Sibling strife, however, continues to beset relations among the heirs of Abraham in the modern period.

---

1. Rubenstein, *My Brother Paul*, 5, 115. The contributors to an ecumenical volume on Jesus and Paul acknowledge that efforts aimed at mutual understanding could backfire but believe the rewards to be worth the risk (Swidler et al., *Bursting the Bonds?*).

2. Meissner, *Heimholung des Ketzers*. John G. Gager ("Rehabilitation of Paul") argues that this rehabilitation process begins much earlier.

Paul: Jewish and/or Christian?

Jewish trepidation toward Paul, though its prevalence is sometimes overstated, has a very long history. Until the nineteenth century Paul played little or no part in Jewish engagement with Christianity, especially in comparison with the attention paid to Jesus. Jewish writers often reclaim Jesus as one of their own while highlighting those differences that point to Paul as the founder of a new religion. The first line of the nine-thousand-word entry on Paul in the 1906 *Jewish Encyclopedia* states forthrightly that he was the "actual founder of the Christian Church as opposed to Judaism." Many of the article's subheadings give a sense of the largely negative assessment Paul receives: "Not a Hebrew Scholar"; "His Epilepsy" (which accounts for the "irrational or pathological element" in his letters); "Anti-Jewish Attitude"; "Antinomianism and Jew-Hatred."[3] Kaufmann Kohler, the author of this article, was president of Hebrew Union College in Cincinnati and had been instrumental in formulating the Pittsburgh Platform (1885), a foundational document of American Reform Judaism. In Jesus Kohler saw "one of the highest types of humanity," a Jew who embodied "all those social qualities which build up the home and society, industry and worldly progress"—in other words, more like a Reform Jew than like Paul, an "irritable, ghost-seeing fanatic" whose writings are "a quaint mixture of Hellenistic philosophy, of semi-pagan mysticism . . . and oriental superstition."[4] The stark contrast was part of an attempt by Kohler to distance Judaism from Christianity by deflecting Orthodox criticism of Reform Judaism onto Paul while laying claim to the more authentically Jewish Jesus.[5] In this way he was able to preempt criticism of the sort later visited upon Sholem Asch—including accusations of apostasy from Judaism—over what many in the Jewish press saw as an excessively sympathetic reading of Paul in his 1943 novel *The Apostle*.[6]

Many of these views had already surfaced in such writers as Heinrich Graetz, whose thirteen-volume *Geschichte der Juden* (1853–76) was one of the most widely read histories among Jews in the nineteenth century.[7] "Christianity might have died a noiseless death if Saul of Tarsus had not appeared,"

---

3. Kohler, "Saul of Tarsus." In *The Origins of the Synagogue and Church*, Kohler repeats the claim that Paul is "the real founder" (247, 260).

4. Kohler, *Jesus of Nazareth*, 3; Kohler, *Christianity vs. Judaism*, 3 (quoted in Ariel, "Christianity through Reform Eyes," 184). Paul "made a caricature of the Law . . . [and] impregnated the Christian World with hostility to Judaism and the Jew" (Kohler, *Jewish Theology*, 438–39).

5. Langton, *Apostle Paul in the Jewish Imagination*, 66–67.

6. Norich, *Discovering Exile*, 74–95.

7. Graetz's discussion of Paul appears in volume 2 of the English translation: *History of the Jews*, 2:219–31. On Graetz's influence on Jewish perceptions of Jesus and Paul, see Heschel, *Abraham Geiger*, 136–37.

writes Graetz. Paul was "one-sided and bitter in his treatment of those who differed from him in the slightest degree," possessed only a limited knowledge of Jewish literature, and dispelled any doubts about his mission through a "nervous temperament and imaginative nature." His outreach to pagans is related to his belief in Jesus as the Messiah, in that the commandments of the Torah were thought to be nonbinding with the commencement of the messianic era. Paul's law-free gospel—which, according to Graetz, appealed especially to slaves and women but "appeared as a ridiculous absurdity" to "cultivated Greeks"—"directly aimed at destroying the bonds which connected the teachings of Christ with those of Judaism."[8]

Variations on these themes—that Paul was a self-hating Jew who rejected Torah and caricatured Judaism as a legalistic religion quite unlike anything taught by Jesus or practiced by other Jews in antiquity—appeared throughout the early twentieth century. Orthodox and Reform writers alike invoked Paul to situate themselves within the spectrum of opinion on such contested questions as what constitutes Jewish identity.[9] According to H. G. Enelow, a Reform rabbi, Jesus died a Jew, with no idea that he would be hailed as the founder of a new faith. His first followers, "simple folk, who had followed Jesus with their hearts, rather than their heads," would soon be joined by Paul, "the intellectual founder of the Christian religion." "Had he not founded the Christian church," says Enelow, "he might have become one of the greatest rabbis." Instead, he became the catalyst for a process in which "Jesus was removed more and more from the sphere and the sympathy of the Jews."[10] Orthodox rabbi Gerald Friedlander is less charitable in his interpretation of the divergence between the faith of Paul and the faith of Jesus. He asserts that Pauline teaching is at odds with the Sermon on the Mount, where Jesus tells his followers to beware of wolves in sheep's clothing. "Might it not be a warning against Paul and his followers?" he asks.[11] The renowned Hasidic philosopher Martin Buber likewise sees a contrast, though he stops short of identifying covert allusions to Paul in the Sermon on the Mount. Buber's *I and Thou* (1923) describes a mode of dialogical interpersonal and human-divine relations that he deems superior to the monological, impersonal I-It relationship and regards Paul rather than Jesus as "the real originator of the

8. Graetz, *History of the Jews*, 2:223–24, 228–29.

9. See Ronning, "Some Jewish Views of Paul"; Wiefel, "Paulus in jüdischer Sicht"; Hagner, "Paul in Modern Jewish Thought"; and Bird and Sprinkle, "Jewish Interpretation of Paul." On the concerns arising from political and social emancipation in the nineteenth century as the subtext for many Jewish readings of Paul, see Langton, *Apostle Paul in the Jewish Imagination*, 3–12, 30–31.

10. Enelow, *Jewish View of Jesus*, 156–58, 163.

11. Friedlander, *Jewish Sources*, 250.

Christian conception of faith."[12] Whereas Jesus exemplifies Jewish *ĕmûnâ* (faith as trust) that originates in the history of the Jewish nation, Paul's "faith" is properly understood as Greek *pistis* (faith as assent to a proposition) that originates with and emphasizes the individual.[13]

Leo Baeck takes a slightly different tack, faulting Paul not for a hyperrationalistic or impersonal approach to faith but for being overly "romantic." Baeck had risen to prominence in 1905 with the publication of *The Essence of Judaism*, a response to Adolf von Harnack's *The Essence of Christianity*. He became chairman of a group representing the German Jewish community after Hitler's rise to power in 1933. His criticism of Paul appears in "Romantic Religion," which was published in 1938 but almost immediately destroyed by the Gestapo, five years before he was sent to Theresienstadt.[14]

In this essay, Baeck divides the different types of piety into two categories, the classical and the romantic. Judaism and Christianity respectively represent these two types. When a German Jew writing in 1938 says that the finest illustration of the romantic disposition is to be found in nineteenth-century Germany, one may infer that the comparison is not meant to flatter. For the romantic, "everything dissolves into feeling; everything becomes mere mood; everything becomes subjective." Agitation, excitement, the passivity of the visionary, a certain "feminine" aspect—these characterize the romantic, who "lacks any strong ethical impulse." "Trait for trait," he says of Paul, "we recognize in his psychic type the features that distinguish the romantic."[15] Under Paul's influence, Judaism and paganism come together to form something new:

> What is called the victory of Christianity was in reality this victory of romanticism. . . . And it became victorious in a world which had become weary and sentimental; it became the religion for all those whose faint, anxious minds had darted hither and thither to seek strength. It represented the completion of a long development. For what had been most essential in the ancient mysteries is preserved in this Pauline religion.[16]

12. Buber, *Two Types of Faith*, 44.
13. Ibid., 170–74. Buber had already formulated a negative view of Paul in an essay first published in 1918, describing "the sweet poison of faith" commingled with Jesus's teachings that he transmitted to the nations, "a faith that was to disdain works, exempt the faithful from realization, and establish dualism in the world." Writing near the end of World War I, he says, "It is the Pauline era whose death agonies we today are watching with transfixed eyes" ("Holy Way," 127–28).
14. An earlier version had appeared in 1922. On Paul as the founder of Christianity, see also "Judaism in the Church," 126. Baeck survived the concentration camp, and after the war his views on Paul softened; see "Faith of Paul."
15. Baeck, "Romantic Religion," 190, 192, 203.
16. Ibid., 198, 202.

It is a religion, moreover, that demands "the sacrifice of the intellect" and repels the social conscience because "it is at bottom a religious egoism."[17]

Hans-Joachim Schoeps, whose father died in the Theresienstadt ghetto where Baeck had been one of the chief rabbis, also approached Paul from the perspective of progressive Judaism. He was well versed in the scholarship that situated Paul in his first-century context. Paul wrestles with the right questions, says Schoeps, but arrives at the wrong answers. His apparent conviction that humans are fundamentally incapable of doing God's will evinces a basic ignorance of the Jewish belief in the power of repentance. His theology "begins with the fateful misunderstanding in consequence of which he tears asunder covenant and law" and "disregard[s] the fear of God as the existential note of the creaturely situation."[18] After the war, Schoeps turned much of his attention to dialogue that he hoped would remove the impediments to relations between Jews and Christians, impediments that he believed were inadvertently put in place by Paul himself:

> It must ever remain thought-provoking that the Christian church has received a completely distorted view of the Jewish law at the hands of a Diaspora Jew who had become alienated from the faith-ideas of the fathers. . . . And still more astounding is the fact that church theology throughout Christian history has imputed Paul's inacceptability [sic] to the Jews to Jewish insensitivity, and has never asked itself whether it might not be due to the fact that Paul could gain no audience with the Jews because from the start he misunderstood Jewish theology.[19]

Schoeps ascribes Paul's "distortions" to misunderstanding rather than to malice, which better enables him to invoke the apostle in discussion with fellow Jews who might otherwise dismiss Paul as having nothing to offer.[20]

Joseph Klausner's treatment of Paul stretches to over six hundred pages and might have been longer, he explains in his preface, had not thirty years' worth of research been destroyed in a 1929 attack by anti-Jewish rioters on his home in Palestine. Not surprisingly, his evaluation is inflected along the lines of his own Zionist commitments. He concedes that Paul is preceded by the early church in elevating Jesus—who "became all unconsciously its lawgiving prophet" and had no designs to found a new religion—to an inordinately lofty position in its worship.[21] Nevertheless, Paul the Hellenistic Jew is the

---

17. Ibid., 207, 211.
18. Schoeps, *Paul*, 218, 260.
19. Ibid., 261–62.
20. Langton, *Apostle Paul in the Jewish Imagination*, 115–18.
21. Klausner, *From Jesus to Paul*, 580–81.

"self-conscious creator and organizer of Christianity as a new religious community," responsible for making it into "a religious system different from both Judaism and paganism . . . but with an inclination toward paganism."[22] Paul is an administrative genius who is able to suppress his natural combativeness when he wants to gain followers, at which time he becomes "a compromiser, a yielder, and an appeaser." But the result is not simply non-Jewish. Paul's roots in the diaspora lead him to transform "a little Jewish sect into an anti-Jewish religion—or more correctly, a half-Jewish, half-Christian religion—that spread over the whole world."[23] Although the foundations are Jewish, his own teaching not only contradicts Judaism as a religion but moreover constitutes the *"rejection of the Jewish nation,"* a step he would never have taken had he been like the Jews of Palestine who had never been *"uprooted from their historic soil."*[24]

These and other critics are indebted to the history of religions school that, beginning in the nineteenth century, produced a library of scholarship on the religious milieu of the ancient Mediterranean that seemed to confirm many long-standing Jewish suspicions. Paul may have been Jewish, but in the diaspora he practiced a "particular sort of cheap and poor Hellenistic Judaism" that was susceptible to the temptations of gnosticism and myriad ecstatic cults.[25] This scholarship continues to trickle down and find its way into more recent works aimed at popular audiences, often mixed with less reliable sources. Orthodox authors Shmuley Boteach and David Klinghoffer, for example, rely on Hyam Maccoby's theory that Paul is not Jewish by birth and that he is lying about his Pharisaic training. Boteach, former "spiritual adviser" to Michael Jackson, believes that Paul, through "the worst kind of the-end-justifies-the-means argument," knowingly distorts Jesus's teachings to save gentile souls and in so doing becomes "the midwife—some would say, true father—of Christianity."[26] According to Klinghoffer, Jewish antipathy toward Paul has to do with his self-presentation as an "expert" in the faith when "what he really sought to do was undermine it from within," hollowing out the Hebrew Scriptures and replacing it with a new religion. Internal subversion is far more troubling than meddling by an "outsider" since an insider knows that nation's vulnerabilities and can exploit them "in a way the alien

22. Ibid., 582, 588 ("Paul, and not Jesus, was prepared to found a new church consciously and intentionally"). Klausner believes that the split between Judaism and Christianity was finalized by the time of Paul's death (598).

23. Ibid., 421, 432, 442.

24. Ibid., 355, 591 (emphasis original). On the Zionist emphases of Klausner's critique, see Langton, *Apostle Paul in the Jewish Imagination*, 106–7.

25. Montefiore, *Judaism and St. Paul*, 153.

26. Boteach, *Kosher Jesus*, 120–21.

interloper cannot."[27] But for Klinghoffer there is a relatively happy ending to this sad story. "Had the Jews embraced Jesus . . . , the Jesus movement might have remained a Jewish sect," but "because the Jews rejected Paul, there is such a thing as Christian civilization." "If you value the great achievements of Western civilization and of American society," he says, "thank the Jews" for rejecting Jesus.[28] Without Paul, history might have taken a turn for the worse.

Such popular treatments of Paul sometimes illustrate the adage that a little learning is a dangerous thing. Michael Cook chides his fellow Jews for their "amateurish" reliance on a limited range of critical scholarship and simultaneous trust in the historical reliability of the Gospels when many Christian scholars believe that such trust is not warranted.[29] This selective naïveté makes it possible to heighten any contrasts between Jesus and Paul. Academic discussions accommodate more complexity. In particular, it is now less common to find Jewish scholars drawing a hard-and-fast line between Hellenistic or diaspora Judaism and "normative" Judaism as it was lived in the land of Israel, a tendency, it should be added, that is not unique to Jewish writers. It has become increasingly clear that even Palestinian Jews had fallen under the influence of Hellenizing forces prior to the birth of Jesus and that there was a thriving Greek-speaking community of Christ believers separate from and prior to Paul's arrival.[30] This developing portrait makes it more difficult to describe the religion of Jesus and that of Paul as self-evidently at odds on account of their upbringings in radically different social contexts. It also makes it unnecessary to attribute a unique role to Paul in the formation of the church.

Paul nonetheless remains an ambiguous figure for modern Jews. By no means is it impossible to find appreciative treatments of his accomplishments. But it is more common to hear him described as a renegade Jew—if he is even acknowledged as a Jew. As flippant as it may sound, "Jesus was a good guy, Paul was a bad *goy*" expresses a view that is widely held.[31] And many who would hesitate to label Paul as an imposter when he claims to be a Jew still regard him as uncomfortably "goyish."

27. Klinghoffer, *Why the Jews Rejected Jesus*, 106–7.
28. Ibid., 7–9, 99.
29. Cook, "How Credible." In the same volume, Eugene J. Fisher ("Typical Jewish Misunderstandings," 237) observes that there is an occasional tendency among Jewish writers to attribute to Paul ideas actually belonging to spurious messianic claimants such as Shabbetai Zevi and his disciple Nathan of Gaza (e.g., the notion of the holiness of sin).
30. See esp. Heitmüller, "Zum Problem Paulus und Jesus"; M. Smith, "Palestinian Judaism"; and Hengel, *Judaism and Hellenism*.
31. Fisher, "Typical Jewish Misunderstandings," 240; cf. Brumberg-Kraus, "Jewish Ideological Perspective," 123–25.

Rehabilitating Paul?

The Holocaust inaugurated a new stage in debates over Paul's legacy and his relationship to Jesus. After 1945, one sees more Christian writers adopting views previously expressed mainly among Jews. The Nazi horrors led many to find Christianity complicit in the murder of six million Jews or at least responsible for creating the conditions that allowed it to happen. For many Christians as well as Jews, Paul's comments about the law of Moses deserve the blame for centuries of anti-Semitism that came to fruition in Auschwitz and Buchenwald. Rosemary Radford Ruether, for example, argues that the church's basic confession that Jesus is the Messiah plants a "seed of contempt" that naturally bears anti-Semitic fruit.[32] Since Paul was a follower of Jesus, however, one may wonder whether Jesus ought to share the blame. The notion that Jesus the Jew might have been anti-Semitic strikes many people as patently ridiculous, and thus they conclude that Paul must be the true source of the problem.

At the same time as one sees criticism of Paul intensifying, concerted efforts at rehabilitating or reinventing Paul also began in earnest. Rather than take aim at Paul, a growing number of scholars instead criticized traditional understandings of Paul's writings—embraced by Christians and resented by Jews—as Augustinian or Lutheran misreadings of the apostle's real message. A hint at this approach was seen already when Schoeps wonders whether "he whose theology was based on misunderstanding has himself been misunderstood by his own followers."[33] Proponents of this so-called New Perspective, who include both Jewish and Christian scholars, attempt to situate Paul within the context of a diverse first-century Jewish milieu and find that he fits more snugly than previously thought.[34] First-century Judaism was not a legalistic system of "works righteousness" devoid of the notion of divine grace, and Paul did not regard the law as null and void or find its requirements unattainable or paralyzing. When it is understood that Paul was writing exclusively to gentiles, according to the New Perspective, this portrait is revealed to be a caricature and Paul's teachings then appear to be well within the Jewish mainstream and thus not so different from those of Jesus. He does not repudiate Torah or believe that God has replaced Israel with the church. Nor does he teach that Jews will experience salvation through any means other than the

---

32. Ruether, *Faith and Fratricide*, 23; see also 104: "Paul's position was unquestionably that of anti-Judaism" in its fusing of Platonic and eschatological dualism in such a way that demonizes the Mosaic covenant as "old" and "carnal." More generally, see Hall, *Christian Anti-Semitism*.

33. Schoeps, *Paul*, 262.

34. For a general overview, see Dunn, *New Perspective on Paul*; Westerholm, *Perspectives Old and New on Paul*; Zetterholm, *Approaches to Paul*, 95–126.

covenant—including through belief in Jesus Christ. If the New Perspective provides a more faithful reading of Paul, then much of the basis for Jewish criticism of Paul would seem to melt away, as Paul is no longer understood as critical of Judaism.

Leading proponents of the New Perspective include John Gager, Stanley Stowers, N. T. Wright, Mark Nanos, and James D. G. Dunn, who built on the earlier work of Krister Stendahl and E. P. Sanders from the 1960s and 1970s. Pamela M. Eisenbaum is perhaps the most engaging of current proponents because she spells out some of the implications of the New Perspective so forthrightly in the title of her book: *Paul Was Not a Christian*.[35] This titular claim flies in the face of the traditional critique that Paul, not Jesus, founded Christianity, and that in so doing he either revealed himself not to be a Jew or ceased to be a Jew from that point forward. Not only is it wrong to say that he founded Christianity; it is wrong even to think of him as a "Christian." "Paul lived and died a Jew"—that, she says, is her central thesis—and he "became a Christian" only later, after Christianity and Judaism had gone their separate ways.[36] This process was abetted by Paul's gentile admirers who (mis)portrayed him in Acts and wrote the letters in his name that ended up in the canon.[37]

The real Paul, according to Eisenbaum, did not abandon the law, equate Jesus with God, or teach justification by faith in the form later propounded by the Reformers. Jesus did little to alter Paul's basic beliefs or practices as a Jew other than increase his sense of urgency. Jesus's death and resurrection augured the imminent end of the age and the beginning of the anticipated ingathering of the gentiles, to whom Paul was writing and about whom he was primarily concerned. In the letters, his fellow Jews are almost an afterthought because, as they possess the covenant, they do not need to be saved from their sins. Other New Perspective scholars avoid stating the conclusion so unambiguously, but not Eisenbaum: "To put it boldly, Jesus saves, but he only saves Gentiles."[38]

A major component of the New Perspective is its reluctance to label Paul a convert. This view draws on the work of Krister Stendahl's 1960 essay "The Apostle Paul and the Introspective Conscience of the West."[39] Stendahl claims that Paul possesses a quite robust conscience when he reflects on his life in

---

35. See also Eisenbaum's essay situating herself in the history of Jewish reception of Paul ("Following in the Footnotes").

36. Eisenbaum, *Paul Was Not a Christian*, 5.

37. Ibid., 32–54.

38. Eisenbaum, *Paul Was Not a Christian*, 242; see also 244: "What the Torah does for Jews," she writes, "Jesus does for Gentiles." While she is uncomfortable with the description of this position as advocating "two-ways salvation," she concedes that it is more or less accurate (251).

39. Stendahl, *Paul among Jews and Gentiles*, 78–96.

Judaism before and after coming to faith in Jesus as the Messiah (1 Cor. 4:4; 2 Cor. 1:12; Phil. 3:6). The Old Perspective, it is argued, errs when it understands Paul to be looking back on his "pre-Christian" religious experience as one attended by an unrelenting sense of inadequacy provoked by the Jewish law. Stendahl further contends that it is more appropriate to think of Paul as a prophet called to a specific task than as a convert from one religion to another.[40] In this interpretation, if Paul is unbothered by feelings of guilt, then nothing about Judaism is "broken" in Paul's eyes and thus nothing needs to be "fixed."

Reluctance to characterize the turn in Paul's spiritual career as a conversion coincides with a heightened post-Holocaust sensitivity to negative assessments of Judaism. Eisenbaum speaks for many others when she says that the portrait of Paul as the model Christian convert "has contributed to gross misrepresentations of Judaism and played no small role in the history of anti-Semitism."[41] Conversion language, many scholars contend, implies a negative evaluation of Judaism when it is applied to Paul inasmuch as it denotes a change from one religion to a different one deemed superior in the eyes of the convert. The issues involved—Paul's appraisal of his past life, the propriety of the label "convert," and the implied status of Judaism—are closely related yet technically separate, and it is important not to blur the distinctions. Were these issues not attached to the controversial figure of Paul, for instance, one could easily imagine an observant Jew in the Second Temple period deeply regretting past behavior without necessarily finding fault with the religious convictions in some measure responsible for any pangs of guilt. In resisting the label "convert" for Paul, then, the New Perspective overlooks the possibility that Paul's critics may include Paul himself.

Arthur Darby Nock's oft-cited definition of conversion as "a turning which implies a consciousness that a great change is involved, that the old was wrong and the new is right" fits Paul up to a point, though it remains a matter of considerable debate precisely which aspects of "the old" and "the new" were right and wrong, and in what particular sense.[42] It may be that, as Beverly Roberts Gaventa suggests, "transformation" is a preferable term in that it "does not require a rejection or negation of the past or of previously held values" but instead "involves a new perception, a re-cognition, of the past."[43]

---

40. Ibid., 7–23; cf. Gager, *Reinventing Paul*, 22–27, 53–54. On the history of this question, see Segal, *Paul the Convert*; B. Corley, "Interpreting Paul's Conversion"; Dunn, *New Perspective on Paul*, 347–65; and McKnight, "Was Paul a Convert?"

41. Eisenbaum, *Paul Was Not a Christian*, 3, 41–42.

42. Nock, *Conversion*, 7.

43. Gaventa, *From Darkness to Light*, 10–11, 37–40.

Whether this transformation is so sweeping that it effectively amounts to a separate religion is a question to which various participants in the debate give different answers.

Discomfort with the phenomenon of religious conversion more generally may also condition recent readings of Paul. It is tainted in popular consciousness by association with Christian fundamentalism and with "cults" such as the Mormons and Jehovah's Witnesses, whose door-to-door approach to evangelism is widely ridiculed. For many, missionary work aimed at conversion is intrusive, manipulative, and chauvinistic. It is furthermore accused of facilitating colonialism and cultural imperialism. Conversion is often understood as the unseemly corollary of proselytism. Strictly speaking, proselytism simply refers to any attempt to persuade another person to adopt a different point of view, religious or otherwise. It usually connotes the use of methods involving coercion, deceit, or excessive appeals to emotion. At the very least, it is considered bad manners, as religion in many sectors of contemporary Western society is deemed a private affair. Even many within the church "would be glad if the term conversion could be dropped from the Christian vocabulary."[44] Jewish resentment at Christian missionary activity aimed at their conversion is related to the implied notion that, as it stands, the Jewish covenant with the God of Israel is inadequate.[45]

To interpreters who argue that Paul not only remains thoroughly Jewish but also limits his message of the salvific power of Jesus's death to gentile audiences—and thus does not call for any Jewish conversion to something called Christianity—one might reasonably respond, "But what of Paul himself?" Does not Paul, a Jew, consider an existential response to Jesus as a nonnegotiable element in his own redemption? A straightforward reading of Gal. 2:15–16 suggests an affirmative answer:

> We ourselves are Jews by birth and not Gentile sinners; yet we know that a person is justified not by the works of the law but through faith in Jesus Christ. And we have come to believe in Christ Jesus, so that we might be justified by faith in Christ, and not by doing the works of the law, because no one will be justified by the works of the law.

Elsewhere Paul includes himself as well as other Jews like Peter, James, and John among those whose sins are wiped away by the death of Jesus (Rom. 5:8; 1 Cor. 15:3; 2 Cor. 5:21; Gal. 1:4; 1 Thess. 5:10). If Paul is Jewish,

44. J. G. Davies, *Dialogue with the World*, 54.
45. Kogan, *Opening the Covenant*, 138–41; cf. Eisenbaum's discomfort with conversion discourse in the anecdote she relates at the outset (*Paul Was Not a Christian*, 1–2).

then his conviction that his own life has been set right with God through Jesus seriously militates against the view that he believes "what the Torah does for Jews, Jesus does for Gentiles" or that "Jesus saves, but he only saves Gentiles."

Various attempts at "rehabilitating" Paul may thus end up overcorrecting for perceived problems in the history of interpretation in the interest of ecumenical harmony. Eisenbaum states that through a "refashioning of what constitutes Jewish and Christian identity" Paul can serve as a valuable partner in thinking about religious pluralism. Sidney Hall—notwithstanding his recognition that nonsupersessionist readings of Paul may be exercises in wishful thinking every bit as anachronistic as Luther's (mis)readings—asserts that "one must risk another misreading of Paul" if only to make audible "the silent cry of dead children in Auschwitz."[46]

Good intentions, however, do not excuse strained readings or questionable determinations about which fragments, interpolations, and even whole letters are authentically Pauline and that betray certain assumptions—some more plausible than others—about what Paul "must" have meant or what "no first-century Jew" could have believed. Attempts at explaining various idiosyncrasies in Paul's letters exemplify a similar tendency, as when John Gager remarks that "when Paul appears to say something (e.g., about the law and Jews) that is unthinkable from a Jewish perspective, it is probably true that he is not talking about Jews at all."[47] Eisenbaum senses that Paul in 1 Cor. 8:4–6 seems to put the Shema ("Hear O Israel . . .") to blasphemous use by applying it to Jesus rather than God, but dismisses this as "a misreading or perhaps simply an overreading" based on the premise that a Jew would never compromise the oneness of God.[48] Paul's stance regarding the law is said to be "one which no Jew could draw," and it is nearly impossible to fathom how "any biblically literate Jew" could have responded to Jesus or read a particular passage from the Bible after the manner of Paul.[49] Lloyd Gaston exhibits the greatest ability to divine what Paul really means from what he actually says when he claims that Paul did not believe Jesus to be the messiah, arguing that

46. Eisenbaum, *Paul Was Not a Christian*, 4; Hall, *Christian Anti-Semitism*, 58–59. E. P. Sanders, whose *Paul and Palestinian Judaism* had a major influence on the New Perspective, also wants Paul to be a solution but ultimately concludes that he remains a problem since he thinks that the only way to be saved is through Christ: "If it were to be proposed that Christians today should think the same thing, and accordingly that the Jews who have not converted should be considered cut off from God, and if such a proposal came before a body in which I had a vote, I would vote against it" ("Paul's Attitude," 185).

47. Gager, *Reinventing Paul*, 58.

48. Eisenbaum, *Paul Was Not a Christian*, 183.

49. Schoeps, *Paul*, 175; Klinghoffer, *Why the Jews Rejected Jesus*, 65.

it is not only possible to interpret Paul in this way but also "necessary to do so . . . in the post-Auschwitz situation."[50]

Whether Jesus was the messiah is properly speaking a theological rather than a historical question, and one could argue that Paul has insufficient warrant in proclaiming him to be the Lord's anointed, as he appears to do in the hundreds of instances where he refers to Jesus as Christ, the Greek rendering of the Hebrew *māšîaḥ*.[51] But in reality, authors sometimes say things they should not say or that no one would expect them to say. That Paul might say such things is precisely what makes him—depending on one's confessional stance—a genius or a heretic. (Or both. For Harold Bloom, Paul was "a great inventor" whose "genius was his powerful originality as a misreader of the Jewish Covenant with Yahweh.")[52]

What's in a Name?

On the question of whether Paul was a Christian, many writers are content to observe that he could not have thought of himself as a Christian because he never refers to himself by that term.[53] Pinchas Lapide comments that "Paul did not become a Christian, since there were no Christians in those times."[54] But this, it seems, is to beg the question, assuming the very thing that requires demonstration. It depends, of course, on what one means by "Christian." If one subscribes to a strict linguistic literalism according to which a thing cannot exist apart from a word that denotes it in a precise manner, then no, there were likely not any Christians in those times unless Acts 11:26 reflects historical conditions on the ground in Antioch during Paul's career (see below). It is furthermore true that Paul never describes his set of beliefs about Jesus as a separate religion from Judaism. But is it accurate to describe Paul as adhering to a form of Christ-believing Judaism that stood apart in key respects from all other Jewish sects of the time? Yes. And is "Christian" a fair descriptor for that form of Judaism? Yes, its use can lead to anachronistic conceptions of Paul's self-understanding, but it

50. Gaston, *Paul and the Torah*, 33–34.

51. J. J. Collins, *Scepter and the Star*, 2: "If this is not ample testimony that Paul regarded Jesus as messiah, then words have no meaning," though in reference to claims like Gaston's he comments, "The ecumenical intentions of such a claim are transparent and honorable." See also Novenson, *Christ among the Messiahs*, 24–26.

52. Bloom, *Genius*, 142.

53. On "Christianity" and "Christian" as anachronistic, see, e.g., Georgi, "Early Church"; Gager, *Reinventing Paul*, 23–25; Dunn, "Who Did Paul Think He Was?," 179; Taubes, *Political Theology of Paul*, 21.

54. Lapide and Stuhlmacher, *Paul*, 47.

is not obvious that any and all uses of "Christian" in reference to Paul are necessarily problematic.

It is unlikely that Paul intentionally set out to found a new religion. At the same time, no one denies that Judaism and Christianity now constitute separate religions. Just how early it becomes appropriate to use "Christian" to denote a member of a different religious species is a matter of great debate.[55] When and where did this linguistic turn first occur? According to Acts 11:26 (NIV), "the disciples were called Christians [*Christianous*] first at Antioch." This and the only other occurrences of the term in the NT (Acts 26:28; 1 Pet. 4:16) suggest that it originates with outsiders, very likely as a derogatory term, though it need not be seen as implying that those so designated were no longer Jews.[56] Around the turn of the century, it is used by insiders, as one sees in Ignatius of Antioch (*To the Magnesians* 10.1, 3; *To the Romans* 3.3; *To the Philadelphians* 6.1), whose own letters are among the earliest texts to quote Paul.

It is not uncommon in antiquity for outsiders to coin the name of a group that ends up sticking. It happened with the Stoics, who originally called themselves Zenonians after their founder Zeno of Citium, who taught at the Stoa Poikile (the Painted Porch) in Athens, and with the Epicureans, whose founder called his school, simply, the Garden (Diogenes Laertius, *Lives of Eminent Philosophers* 7.5; 10.10). Cynicism provides an even closer parallel. Disgusted by their utter disregard for basic social conventions, critics ridiculed Antisthenes and his disciples for their doglike (*kynikos*) behavior. Diogenes of Sinope in the fourth century CE seized on the epithet and never let go, while later Cynics emphasized every canine quality imaginable in expositions of their philosophy.[57] If "Christian" originated as a pejorative term coined by non-Christians, it would be neither the first nor the last time for members of a group to reappropriate and wear as a badge of honor an insult meant to belittle them. This phenomenon is a perennial one, even if it is easier to document with more recent instances. It happens in the arts with the Fauves and the Impressionists and in politics with the Whigs and the Tories. Yankee, Sooner, redneck, queer, and a host of other labels trace a similar semantic path, one form of a phenomenon known in historical linguistics as melioration.

55. Dunn, *Parting of the Ways*; Becker and Reed, *Ways That Never Parted*; Galambush, *Reluctant Parting*.

56. Trebilco, *Self-Designations and Group Identity*, 272–97. Harold B. Mattingly ("Origin of the Name 'Christiani,'") suggests that it was coined in imitation of *Augustiani*, the sycophantic cheerleaders at Nero's public performances.

57. Dudley, *History of Cynicism*, 5–6.

Religious history furnishes similar examples that may shed light on early Jewish-Christian relations and Paul's role in the parting of the ways. Following the practice of naming a heresy after the heretic, Johann Eck coined the term "Lutheran" in the famous Leipzig Disputation of 1519, but as soon as 1522 Martin Luther needed to dissuade his followers from using it in his "Admonition against Insurrection"—ultimately, to no effect. During the Counter-Reformation, members of the Society of Jesus adopted a term, "Jesuit," that had been used for over a century to mock anyone who too frequently invoked the name of Jesus. Brethren and Mennonite communities with origins in the Radical Reformation were mocked as Anabaptists (rebaptizers) by Catholics and many other Protestants alike because they advocated baptism after a confession of faith even if the believer had already been baptized as an infant. Classmates at Oxford in 1729 made fun of the "methodical" approach to Bible study and prayer taken by John and Charles Wesley, who thought of themselves as Anglicans rather than "Methodists." According to their founder, George Fox, members of the Religious Society of Friends became known as Quakers because they "trembled at the word of the Lord." The Shakers, an offshoot of Quakerism founded by Mother Ann Lee, were so called on account of their ecstatic forms of worship. Joseph Smith and his fellow Latter-Day Saints were called Mormons by their enemies in the 1830s to highlight their idiosyncratic belief in a new revelation purportedly originating with a fourth-century indigenous American prophet of the same name. Even "pagan," perhaps the oldest and most versatile entry in the Christian lexicon for false or depraved religiosity, has now been reappropriated by a motley assortment of twentieth-century movements claiming to revive premodern polytheistic and "nature-based" belief systems. Sometimes sooner and sometimes later, in each case the group singled out for contempt eventually embraced the language once directed against them, retaining some memory of their social history as they make that language their own. The adoption of the new moniker by the newly emergent group indicates a degree of mutual in-group, out-group recognition that something distinct has begun to crystallize.

What do these analogies suggest about Paul and his role as the putative founder of Christianity? If Paul does not "quit" Judaism to start a new religion, as most commentators assert, it may be more accurate to think of him as getting "fired." This is not to suggest that he is subjected to formal procedures that result in his expulsion from the Jewish community. But it is well established that others, later in the first century, with similar beliefs about Jesus or practices inspired by those beliefs are marginalized—in different ways and to different degrees in various locales—by Jews who did not countenance such beliefs or practices.[58] This latter group surely represents the majority of Jews in the ancient Mediterranean. To state it in a provocative manner, if anyone can be said to be responsible for the founding of Christianity as a separate religion, perhaps it should be those Jews who, quite reasonably, determined that the teachings of Paul and other "Christian" writers threatened to stretch Judaism to the breaking point and thus warranted ostracism.

Any "founding" along these lines was obviously inadvertent and would have had unintended consequences.[59] The diversity displayed by Second Temple Judaism is a testimony to its vibrancy. There had to be some limit to its elasticity, however, for a linguistically, geographically, politically, and religiously multiform Jewish community to maintain any common identity. Looking back from a post-Holocaust perspective, this may sound like "blaming the victim." But this response is partly informed by an anachronistic view of the power dynamics between Judaism and Christianity. Throughout their history, and perhaps never more so than immediately following World War II, Jews have periodically sensed that they were on the verge of extinction, often as a consequence of actions taken by the citizens of the Christian societies among which they were dispersed. Relations were different in antiquity. Estimates vary, but Jews constituted perhaps 10 percent of the population of the Roman Empire, though the true figure may be much smaller. The Jewish sect that acclaimed Jesus as Messiah was a tiny minority of that minority. In Paul's time and for several decades thereafter, Jews in the Greco-Roman world probably outnumbered messianists by a factor of fifty to one and enjoyed the (often grudging) respect that came with being seen as an ancient polity rather than a superstition newly sprung up in the aftermath of its leader's execution. For much of the past two thousand years, the church has played Goliath to Judaism's David. However, during the period when Christianity and Judaism were parting ways those roles were reversed.[60]

58. See, e.g., Forkman, *Limits of the Religious Community*; van der Horst, "Birkat ha-minim."

59. See W. Bauer, *Orthodoxy and Heresy*, 236: "It could be said that the Jewish Christians in their opposition to Paul introduced the notion of 'heresy' into the Christian consciousness. The arrow quickly flew back at the archer." Magnus Zetterholm suggests that it is James who demanded that Jesus-believing Jews and Jesus-believing gentiles maintain separate table-fellowship groups because "too close an association with Gentiles may in general have been regarded as a threat to Judaism" (*Formation of Christianity in Antioch*, 161). More speculatively, he further argues that these gentiles, once they had been segregated, sought to dissociate themselves from the Jewish Jesus movement as part of a conscious political ploy designed to secure civic benefits, a process "which eventually resulted in the emanation of a new religion" (178).

60. On the relevance of these factors for understanding the rhetoric of Paul and other early Christian authors, see L. T. Johnson, "New Testament's Anti-Jewish Slander."

Strange Bedfellows: Jews and Germans on Jesus and Paul

It is refreshing to see Paul resuming some measure of Jewishness in recent discussion. Less felicitous, perhaps, is that it comes at the expense of his Christian identity. Much of this discourse seems to posit "Christian" and "Jewish" as mutually exclusive alternatives. One oddity of this development is that it makes for some strange bedfellows on the central questions in the debate. To wit, the insistence on Paul's thorough, if occasionally atypical, Jewishness and its framing as incommensurate with traditional claims of Christian orthodoxy intersect at key points with anti-Semitic views prevalent early in the twentieth century. By no means is this observation meant to declare the New Perspective guilty by association with Nazism or to invalidate Jewish scholarship by means of what might be called a *reductio ad Hitlerum* argument. It simply highlights another of the strange twists and turns in the history of anti-Paulinism. Critics may agree in their assessment of Paul but, as in this case, for diametrically opposed reasons. In other instances, they arrive at different conclusions even when they start from shared premises.

Earlier Jewish writers like Abraham Geiger routinely set Jesus against Paul, describing a pious but not terribly original Jewish rabbi over against a deluded or apostate Jew, if not an outright pagan imposter. German writers perpetuated the dichotomy between the good Jesus and the evil Paul but radically redefined the roles these characters played (as well as the religions they practiced) in a historical narrative that struck many readers as outlandish and paranoid. Over dinner with Joseph Goebbels in December 1941, Adolf Hitler opined that "Christianity is an invention of sick brains," and of one sick brain in particular.[61] It was not Jesus; "it's certain that Jesus was not a Jew," he says, for his objective was to liberate his nation from "Jewish expression" and "Jewish capitalism."[62] If Jesus was not "the Jew who fraudulently introduced Christianity into the ancient world—in order to ruin it," who was it?[63] The answer is Paul.

The theory that the teachings of the Aryan Jesus have been undermined by the cunning Jew Paul did not originate with Hitler. Its dissemination owed much to the writings of Houston Stewart Chamberlain, the son-in-law of Richard Wagner who corresponded with Hitler while he was writing *Mein Kampf*. Chamberlain's *The Foundations of the Nineteenth Century* (1899) influenced a generation of German nationalist thinkers, including Alfred Rosenberg. In 1930, Rosenberg published *Der Mythus des zwanzigsten Jahrhunderts* (*The*

---

61. Trevor-Roper, *Hitler's Secret Conversations*, 118.
62. Ibid., 63.
63. Ibid., 255.

Myth of the Twentieth Century), which became a major source of the racial theories of the National Socialists. Intensely hostile toward Christianity in general and Catholicism in particular—Rosenberg denies the doctrines of original sin, the virgin birth, and the Trinity and barely mentions the resurrection—this long, tedious tract expounds on the alleged Jewish conspiracy to foment world revolution. This was Paul's aim "when he gave his hypnotizing sermons which were mainly attended by voluptuous women," and he was successful "thanks only to the Jewish will and the fanaticism peculiar to it."[64] Popular literature at the turn of the century had also generated slogans recommending the proper direction in which German society should gravitate: "Down with Paul! Back to Christ!" or, in the title of a 1905 book by Oskar Michel identifying Paul as "the arch-enemy of Jesus, his *Volk*, and humanity," *Forward to Christ! Away with Paul! German Religion!*[65]

Specific steps toward the realization of this objective were proposed in a 1933 rally at the Berlin Sports Palace. Reinhold Krause, a leader of the Deutsche Christen movement, declared that the NT "had to be expurgated of all perverted and superstitious passages, and the whole scapegoat and inferiority complex theology of the Rabbi Paul."[66] This "dejudaization" was to be the work of the Institute for the Study and Eradication of Jewish Influence on German Church Life (Institut zur Erforschung und Beseitigung des jüdischen Einflusses auf das deutsche kirchliche Leben), formed in 1939 under the leadership of NT scholar Walter Grundmann. German faith cannot be based on Paul, Grundmann says, "because it would then be deformed through his Jewish system of coordinates."[67] Whereas Marcion in the second century had excised everything that did not complement Paul at the core of his anti-Jewish canon, the institute deemed it unpropitious to eliminate entirely Paul's letters from its NT. The form in which they appear in the 1940 *Die Botschaft Gottes* (*The Message of God*), however, is shorn of many signature teachings.[68] The Gospel of John, with its many polemical references to "the Jews," is emphasized, while the letters are de-emphasized.

Although German writers in this period disagreed about the value of Paul's letters, they had no doubt that he was Jewish. But Jewish in what sense? There was an appreciation, however limited and malformed, of the various

---

64. Rosenberg, *Myth of the Twentieth Century*, 292. Paul "transferred this lust to rule, this lust for world domination to the overthrowing of the state" (ibid.).

65. Michel, *Vorwärts zu Christus!*, 189; see also Scholder, *Churches and the Third Reich*, 1:81–87.

66. Quoted in Bergen, *Twisted Cross*, 158. The emergence of the Confessing Church, which opposed the Nazis, was in part a response to this rally.

67. Quoted in Heschel, *Aryan Jesus*, 145–46.

68. Ibid., 92, 108, 135–36.

dimensions of Jewishness—genealogical, ethnic, cultural, political, and religious. According to Hitler, Paul was the author of a Jewish innovation that allowed Christianity to be imposed on the German *Volk* in the early dark ages:

> It's since St. Paul's time that the Jews have manifested themselves as a religious community, for until then they were only a racial community. St. Paul was the first man to take account of the possible advantages of using a religion as a means of propaganda. If the Jew has succeeded in destroying the Roman Empire, that's because St. Paul transformed a local movement of Aryan opposition to Jewry into a supra-temporal religion.[69]

Many recent scholars contend that *Ioudaios* should be understood as an exclusively ethnic or geographic category.[70] One may wonder whether Hitler would have welcomed this notion, on the grounds that "pure" Christianity would not have become so easily contaminated by Jewish religious ideas, or rejected it, as it might confute a pet theory about the mechanism by which the alleged Jewish conspiracy operates.

Paul in the Muslim Imagination

A few years ago, various media outlets began documenting a strange phenomenon taking place around the globe. Waves of Muslims were reportedly having visions of Jesus. Mystical encounters with ʿĪsā al-Masīḥ (Jesus the Messiah) were leading Fulani herdsmen in Nigeria, Turkish immigrants in Germany, even Egyptian terrorists to seek out Christians who would instruct them in the gospel. It is difficult to know exactly what to make of this phenomenon.[71] Is the explanation to be sought in social psychology? Is it an urban legend? Is it a story cooked up by missionaries, a pious fiction to boost the morale of other missionaries who have an especially difficult time gaining a hearing among potential converts from Islam? These conversion narratives often bear a striking resemblance to the story of Paul on the road to Damascus found in the Acts of the Apostles (9:1–30; 22:3–21; 26:4–23). Such parallels are hardly

---

69. Trevor-Roper, *Hitler's Secret Conversations*, 64. According to Albert Speer (*Inside the Third Reich*, 96), Hitler bemoaned the fact that Islam, a religion that believed in spreading the faith by the sword, had not been imposed on the Germans instead of the "Jewish filth and priestly twaddle" of Christianity: "You see, it's been our misfortune to have the wrong religion." Had the Arabs not lost the Battle of Tours in 732, he thought, Islamized Germans would have ruled the world.

70. On the debate about the translation of *Ioudaios*, see S. J. D. Cohen, *Beginnings of Jewishness*, 69–139; S. Mason, "Jews, Judeans, Judaizing, Judaism"; J. H. Elliott, "Jesus the Israelite"; and Miller, "Ethnicity Comes of Age."

71. Reports may be found on various internet websites and in Doyle, *Dreams and Visions*.

what one might expect given the prevalent view of Paul in the Muslim world. Interfaith dialogue has become a more common occurrence over the past century as the world has shrunk and knowledge about other religions has become more readily available. While many Muslims have contributed to this ecumenical moment, negative views of Paul have not by any means disappeared.

Many of the criticisms found as far back as the seventh century have not only persisted but also found new and wider audiences. No "official" interpretation of Paul exists, as there is nothing in Islam that functions exactly like the teaching magisterium of the Catholic Church. Broad trends may nevertheless be found. Egypt has produced a number of scholars whose works have influenced the perception of Christianity in general and Paul in particular among Muslims, including Muhammad Abū Zahrah and Ahmad Shalabī.[72] They point out that Christians enjoyed no immunity from persecution until the time of Constantine. Forced apostasy and the burning of their sacred books thus meant that there was no reliable link connecting Jesus to those who professed to be his followers. (Shalabī contends that the loss of the original "Gospel of Jesus" was a purposeful act intended to hide its similarities to the Qur'an and to make it easier to alter Jesus's original message.) Neoplatonism, a major philosophical influence in cities like Alexandria, is cited as a corrupting element in the development of Christian theology. The generally syncretistic character of Roman religion likewise made it difficult for early Christians—who did not reside in cultural ghettoes but, rather, moved about freely in the Roman world—to avoid the taint of paganism. These factors made the movement susceptible to Paul's heretical teachings.

These claims echo those of another Egyptian, Sayyid Qutb, a controversial member of the Muslim Brotherhood considered to be one of the most influential Muslim intellectuals in the twentieth century. (In a March 23, 2003, article in the *New York Times Magazine*, Paul Berman dubbed him "Al-Qaeda's philosopher.")[73] Paul's preaching "was adulterated by the residues of Roman mythology and Greek philosophy" because he was a Roman heathen convert to Christianity, and according to Qutb this state of affairs "was a catastrophe which infected Christianity since its early days in Europe, over and above its disfiguration during the early period of persecution when the prevailing circumstances did not allow for examining and authenticating its religious textual bases."[74] Constantine accelerates the subsequent "separa-

72. See Ayoub, "Muslim Views of Christianity." On the enormous popularity of Abū Zahrah, see Goddard, *Muslim Perceptions of Christianity*, 59–67.

73. See Berman, *Terror and Liberalism*, from which the article was adapted.

74. Qutb, *Islam*, 37–38. Qutb's work was first published in 1960, six years before he was executed for conspiring to assassinate Gamal Abdel Nasser.

tion of religion from the social order," which Qutb characterizes as "hideous schizophrenia."[75] Syed Muhammad Naquib al-Attas, a prominent Muslim philosopher from Malaysia, expresses similar concerns about Christianity and the way it is intertwined with a process of secularization that occurs when the various dimensions of human life become divorced from the divine will. This situation is a result of the circumstances of its origins:

> God did not charge Jesus (on whom be Peace!) with the mission of establishing a new religion called Christianity. It was some other disciple and the apostles including chiefly Paul who departed from the original revelation and true teachings based on it. . . . [It] became fixed and clarified and recognizable as the religion of a culture and civilization known to the world as Christianity.[76]

Because Christianity also has no revealed law (*shari'ah*) expressed in the teaching and personal example of Jesus as well as no coherent worldview, according to al-Attas, it had to assimilate Roman law, theology, and metaphysics. The arts and sciences therefore develop within a distinctively "Christian" worldview not shared by its presumed founder.[77] For Qutb and al-Attas, Paul's role in the origins of Christianity is viewed as integral to the so-called clash of civilizations that has been the subject of considerable debate for the last two decades.

One of the most popular proponents of this view is Muhammad 'Ata ur-Rahim, a Pakistani writer whose *Jesus, Prophet of Islam* has gone through several editions since its original publication in 1977.[78] In his reconstruction of early Christian history, he decries Paul's doctrine of redemption and atonement, which Jesus never taught because he was never crucified or resurrected. This was the first step down the road to the abominable doctrine of the Trinity, at which Christianity would never have arrived were it not for Paul's innovations.[79] Barnabas attempts to prevent this unfortunate development but to no avail, even though he had been with Jesus from the very start of his mission.[80]

Lest one treat 'Ata ur-Rahim's work as nothing more than a turgid historical treatise, it bears the imprimatur of 'Abd al-Qādir, the leader of the Darqāwī Sufi order. Al-Qādir's preface reads like a manifesto. Christianity

75. Ibid., 33, 52–57.

76. Attas, *Islām*, 25–26.

77. Ibid., 26.

78. References here are to the revised edition: 'Ata ur-Rahim and Thomson, *Jesus, Prophet of Islam*.

79. Ibid., 68, 103. 'Ata ur-Rahim lionizes Arius as one of the brave few who stood against "the Pauline church" in the fourth century (82).

80. Ibid., 4. The NT does not describe Barnabas as a companion of Jesus.

is "a historical reality based on a metaphysical fiction . . . shot through with sadism, masochism, and incest." He praises ʿAta ur-Rahim for his exposé of how this "pseudo-religion" was concocted, distinguishing it from Hinduism and Buddhism on the grounds that the latter at least retain some vestige of unitarianism, "fragments of the pure *Tawhid* [divine oneness]." True Christian teaching "was diverted, or one might say de-railed, by the powerful Pauline explosion." But Christianity's days are numbered. At the end of the day, "Christianity was, simply, Europe. And Europe is finished. Islam is the world's."[81]

Iranian-born Reza Aslan's foray into this territory has less of a polemical edge but has reached a larger English-speaking audience due to its distribution by a high-profile American publisher. In *Zealot: The Life and Times of Jesus of Nazareth*, he argues that the conventional image of Jesus as a pacifist wisdom teacher is inaccurate. It is closer to the truth to see him as a revolutionary bent on challenging the Jewish priesthood and Roman occupation on the way to establishing a theocracy in Jerusalem. Paul had little interest in this aspect of the career of the earthly Jesus, and his position carried the day. Aslan notes that while the Council of Nicaea along with the creed it promulgated in 325 was a politicized attempt to stifle dissent that resulted in a thousand years or more of unspeakable bloodshed in the name of orthodoxy, in reality it was merely codifying belief in Jesus as God that had already become de rigueur "thanks to the overwhelming popularity of the letters of Paul."[82] The canonical Gospels were influenced by Pauline teaching, and even the Gospel of John, with its emphatically incarnational Christology, is little more than Pauline theology in narrative form. "The Christ of Paul's creation," he concludes, "has utterly subsumed the Jesus of history."[83] Aslan's portrait of Jesus, though hardly original, is more surprising than his portrait of Paul in that few modern writers are inclined to paint Jesus in hues that can be described as bellicose and xenophobic. Faulting Paul for depoliticizing Jesus appears to fit with a broader trend among Muslim intellectuals on the right and the left resisting the categorization of Islam as "only" a religion.[84] In a distinctive way, then, these attacks on Paul become part of a larger critique

---

81. Ibid., xiv. It is unclear how al-Qādir's conflation of Christianity as a religious system and Europe as a geopolitical entity at this point squares with his earlier remarks faulting Christianity as the source of the concept of the secular in which the "zone of politics" is separated from the "zone of religion" (ibid., xi).

82. Aslan, *Zealot*, 214.

83. Ibid., 215–16. For a similar view of Paul and John's role in making Jesus into a deity, see the remarks of Maulana Muhammad Ali, a key figure in the pan-Islamic movement in early twentieth-century India, quoted by McDonough, "Muslims in South Asia (1857–1947)," 255.

84. Cf. Shedinger, *Was Jesus a Muslim?*, 49–71.

of perceived Western neocolonialist attempts to domesticate Islam that is not found among non-Muslim writers.

Aslan exemplifies a new aspect of Muslim interpretations of Paul, namely, the use of critical biblical scholarship produced in Europe and North America. To be sure, this scholarship is often misrepresented, misunderstood, or in some cases fabricated out of whole cloth. For example, the *Gospel of Barnabas* is frequently confused with the second-century *Epistle of Barnabas*, which makes no mention of Paul; the recipient of Paul's Letter to Titus is thought to be the Roman emperor of the same name; and there is no basis for the claim that Irenaeus repudiates Paul for injecting heretical ideas drawn from pagan religions and Platonic philosophy into Christian teaching.[85] In other instances Muslim writers invoke theories uncontroversial among biblical scholars but deploy them in novel ways to undercut traditional narratives about Christian origins. Rather than see that Paul's letters predate the writings of the four evangelists as evidence of his chronological proximity to the earliest community of believers, it is taken as proof that he is the ultimate source of the Gospels' corruption. The canonical Gospels, moreover, are seen as no more reliable than the many others written under the pseudonyms of various apostles. Sometimes Muslim writers suggest that Q, the hypothetical document consisting of Jesus's sayings that was used by Matthew and Luke, is the original "Gospel of Jesus" covered up by the likes of Paul. "Would that the church had preserved this Gospel and endeavored to protect it," writes Abū Zahrah, "so that it would be as a sharp sword against dissension."[86]

Perhaps the most popular ancient writing among Muslim critics, however, is one that biblical scholars have almost totally ignored because they do not believe it is ancient at all—the *Gospel of Barnabas*. Its resurgence was in part the unintended consequence of the publication of the first English translation, produced by Scottish missionaries in 1907. An Arabic translation was published the following year, with Urdu, Persian, and Turkish versions appearing soon thereafter. Even before the internet made it easily accessible, it could be found in virtually every library and bookstore in the Muslim world. The anti-Pauline preface and epilogue of this document and its depiction of Jesus have been almost universally accepted as historically accurate by Muslim scholars and nonspecialists alike. As a result, it is a standard component of anticolonialist literature written by Indian and Arab Muslims throughout the twentieth

85. Contra 'Ata ur-Rahim and Thomson, *Jesus, Prophet of Islam*, 78, 115. On Titus, see Reynolds, *Muslim Theologian*, 77n7.

86. Quoted in Ayoub, "Muslim Views of Christianity," 65.

century.[87] For these writers, pushback against cultural depredations abetted by Western missionaries often begins by reviving centuries-old rumors about the greatest Christian missionary of them all.

Gestures toward detente such as one sees among many Jewish writers are not yet in evidence among Muslims. This may be due to the relative dearth of literature translated from Arabic on an annual basis. Whether outsiders would hear about any newfound appreciation for Paul in the Arab-speaking world is unclear. Future initiatives may alter long-held perceptions, though it is worth noting that in the published proceedings of a recent colloquium held at Yale University devoted to the question "Do We Worship the Same God?" Paul's name occurs fewer than ten times.[88] He is regarded variously as a pagan and as a Jew, but the consensus among Muslim commentators is that any conversion undergone by Paul is best understood as the conversion of "Christianity" into a religion inimical to the proto-Islam practiced by Jesus.

The hostility of many Jews toward Paul is due in part to a projection of later circumstances onto the first century. Jewish converts to Christianity in later centuries are seen as betraying their kinsfolk by abandoning them for a more powerful community. If Paul in any sense converted—a disputed point, as noted above—he should not be seen as the prototypical Jewish turncoat because he traveled in the opposite direction, gravitating away from an established community toward a fragile one that had endured sporadic harassment during the few years it had been in existence.[89] It is likewise problematic to pose "Paul is Jewish (and ipso facto not Christian)" as the only alternative to some variation on the theme that "Paul is a Christian (and thus not, or no longer, Jewish)." In response to Hyam Maccoby's adamant articulation of the latter claim, Ellis Rivkin writes that Jewish identity can be denied only when a Jew openly rejects it. "If, however, a Jew seeks to solve a Jewish identity crisis by a solution which is believed by him or her to be Jewish," says Rivkin, "that solution must be regarded as a Jewish resolution of the

---

87. Leirvik, "History as a Literary Weapon." Leirvik notes that some Muslim scholars have suggested that the *Gospel of Barnabas* and the hypothetical Q document are the same. Most recently, it has been alleged that the unexpected resignation of Pope Benedict XVI in 2013 had to do with scandalous revelations about the origins of Christianity contained in the *Gospel of Barnabas*, a rumor repeated at a public lecture by Iranian filmmaker Nader Talebzadeh shortly after it was announced. Talebzadeh is the director of *The Messiah*, a movie based on the *Gospel of Barnabas* and funded by Islamic Republic of Iran Broadcasting (IRIB).

88. Volf, *Do We Worship the Same God?* Paul appears no more frequently in Volf, Muhammad, and Yarrington, *Common Word*, or in Volf, *Allah*.

89. Rubenstein, *My Brother Paul*, 116.

identity crisis even if the individual be the only Jew who had this crisis and resolved it this way." By this criterion, Paul did not invent a new religion but "forged a mutational Jewish identity."[90]

Rivkin puts his finger on a sensitive spot. Many of Paul's early admirers saw him as departing from Judaism and proclaiming something new. Many of his earliest Jewish detractors likewise saw him as departing from Judaism, be it in his thinking about Jesus or about the implications of gentile inclusion. Therefore, it is perhaps not unreasonable to stipulate that he was, in some crucial sense, departing from Judaism—even if he was unaware of it or would have protested at the time that he was doing nothing of the sort.[91] Paul can be understood only within the context of classical Jewish convictions about God. And yet most Jews appear to have rejected his claims about God's dealings with humanity, whether they were original to Paul or transmitted to him by the early church. These claims are at the heart of his "mutational Jewish identity." Rivkin's imagery is apt. Mutations are the primary mechanism by which genetic variation occurs, without which the formation of new species would proceed very slowly, if at all. Many mutations are harmful, many are neutral, and a few are beneficial in a way that, given the right environmental conditions, leads to the emergence of an organism that not only survives but flourishes. But it is only in retrospect that biologists can tell when this has taken place, and even then they recognize that some organisms are capable of hybridizing in a fashion that forces them to qualify the standard definition of what constitutes a separate species.[92] The same might be said concerning definitions of what constitutes Christianity and Judaism in the first century, along with determinations as to where Paul fits in the resulting taxonomy. To what extent ecumenical relations in the twenty-first century depend on a resolution of the issue remains an open question.

90. Rivkin, "Paul's Jewish Odyssey," 233. He rejects the notion that there exists "some primordial Jewish identity by which the authenticity or the non-authenticity of a Jewish identity can be measured," commenting that had there been such a standard, it would have been possible to say that the likes of Amos, Maimonides, and Theodor Herzl had forfeited their Jewishness (ibid.).

91. Scot McKnight writes, "Paul moved from one kind of Judaism to another, but even this 'other' Judaism was like new wine in old wineskins and would soon burst the boundaries" ("Was Paul a Convert?," 131). Hans Dieter Betz is more willing to acknowledge that Paul crossed (or joined others in crossing) a "line of demarcation" between being a Jew and being a Christian. In the process, "a new religion has *de facto* come into existence" (*Galatians*, 179). See also Betz, "Christianity as Religion"; and Betz, "Paul's Ideas." On Paul's "identity in flux," see Dunn, "Who Did Paul Think He Was?," 193.

92. As Charles Darwin recognized: "I look at the term species as one arbitrarily given for the sake of convenience to a set of individuals closely resembling each other." Quoted in Richards, *Species Problem*, 79, who remarks, "It is difficult to read these passages as anything other than a denial that species are real things in nature."

7

JESUS VERSUS PAUL

Spiritual but Not Religious?

Among the most striking demographic trends witnessed over the past few decades is the rising number of respondents who answer "none" when asked about their religious preference. Separate but related is another trend that sees lower levels of membership in specific religious organizations, even among those who do not identify as atheists or agnostics. Reports of religion's death issued by proponents of secularization theory appear to have been greatly exaggerated, yet the surveys on which this data is based appear to be detecting a quantifiable reaction against institutional forms of religious belief and practice. "I'm not religious but I'm spiritual" is the mantra for many individuals belonging in this group.[1]

Comparisons of Jesus and Paul bear striking rhetorical similarities to this contrast between "spirituality" and "religion." Whereas Jesus strove to spread a system of simple but universal ethical truths, it is argued, Paul is responsible for the hierarchical mentality, theological speculation, and dogmatic hairsplitting that carries the church away from its roots. These rhetorical parallels predate the emerging demographic reality documented by social scientists and articulate many of the dispositions associated with it. The entry on Paul in the classic eleventh edition of the *Encyclopedia Britannica* (1911) demonstrates that the

---

1. Cf. Fuller, *Spiritual, but Not Religious*; Niose, *Nonbeliever Nation*.

"spiritual but not religious" trope is at least a century old when the writer quotes an anonymous "modern Jew" who says, "Jesus seems to expand and spiritualize Judaism; Paul in some senses turns it upside down."[2] Efforts to rehabilitate Paul or rescue him from the role of villain likewise illustrate the negative image he conjures in many minds. A. N. Wilson, for example, wants to correct the "preconceived view of Paul as a stiff-necked reactionary who wanted the free-and-easy Jesus-religion to become a church with a set of restrictive rules and regulations" and even suggests that he is better seen as "a prophet of liberty, whose visionary sense of the importance of the inner life anticipates the Romantic poets more than the rule-books of the Inquisition."[3] Like the claim that Paul founded Christianity, "spiritual but not religious" often functions as a type of ideological shorthand. This chapter briefly considers what this antithesis signifies, where it originates, and how it sheds light on Paul and the concerns of his critics.

The Idioms of Religion and Spirituality

What does it mean to be "spiritual but not religious"? The two terms were used interchangeably until the turn of the twentieth century. They now tend to denote different sensibilities that are at odds.[4] "Spirituality" is easier to describe than to define. Its "fuzziness," in fact, is part of the appeal for the seeker who "abhors fixity in the interest of transformation."[5] Being spiritual does not necessarily entail a rejection of religion per se but of organized or institutional forms of religion, which are felt to be overly formal and lacking in vitality. Thus one finds churches advertising themselves as "church for people who don't like church." Rituals and practices are valued only insofar as they foster relationships and connections conducive to an "authentic" relationship with a "higher power." In contrast with "religion," spirituality prefers metaphor to literalism, experience to dogma, comfort and affirmation to judgment, the personal and private to the public, and pluralism to exclusivism. It is intuitive but not fideistic, and its practitioners pride themselves on being thoughtful rather than relying on blind faith.[6]

2. Bartlet, "Paul," 938.
3. A. N. Wilson, *Paul*, 14.
4. Marler and Hadaway, "'Being Religious' or 'Being Spiritual.'"
5. Roof, *Spiritual Marketplace*, 33–34; cf. Zinnbauer et al., "Religion and Spirituality"; and Fuller, *Spiritual, but Not Religious*, 5–7. Note also the disconnect between denominational affiliation and personal theological views in the case studies compiled by Gortner, *Varieties of Personal Theology*.
6. See, e.g., Besecke, *You Can't Put God in a Box*, 2–3. Besecke cites Joseph Campbell as an inspiration for herself and for many others who consider themselves "spiritual but not religious." Campbell characterizes the Middle Ages as "the reign in Europe of that order of

At the beginning of his attack on organized religion in general and Paul in particular, Thomas Paine formulates a concise motto for the "spiritual but not religious" sensibility: "My own mind is my own church."[7] Jefferson Bethke puts it in the form of an equation—"Jesus > Religion"—in the title of his book capitalizing on the popularity of his 2013 video poetry recitation "Why I Hate Religion, but Love Jesus."[8] Anne Rice, best known for her gothic novels that spawned the recent popularity of vampires in literature and film, belongs to the same chorus. In 2010, she publicly renounced the Catholic faith to which she had only recently returned while writing historical novels about Jesus, stating on her Facebook page, "I remain committed to Christ as always but not to being 'Christian' or to being part of Christianity. It's simply impossible for me to 'belong' to this quarrelsome, hostile, disputatious, and deservedly infamous group. . . . I quit Christianity and being Christian." She cites Paul's "absurdities and contradictions" as major factors contributing to her disillusionment.[9]

One need not make any ethical or existential response in order to qualify as "spiritual," and in this sense it is as much an aesthetic category as a religious one. Some commentators note that while the "spiritual but not religious" mentality rejects intolerance, its avoidance of traditional philosophical, theological, and moral questions can render it shallow and superficial.[10] Its "higher power" sometimes resembles, in the phrase of H. Richard Niebuhr, a "God without wrath [who] brought men without sin into a kingdom without judgment through the ministrations of a Christ without a cross."[11]

While it strikes a particularly modern chord, the dichotomy between religion and spirituality is not totally alien to antiquity. In book 8 of his *Confessions* Augustine tells the story of Victorinus, related to him by his friend Simplicianus. Victorinus was in the habit of saying that he was already a Christian though he had not received the sacrament of baptism. Simplicianus would respond, "I will not count you among the Christians until I see you in Christ's

---

unreason, unreasoning submission to the dicta of authority" and other "impudent idiocies" to which "Saint Paul himself had opened the door" (*Masks of God*, 4:396).

7. Paine, *Age of Reason*, 2.

8. Although their theological and political orientations may differ at many points, Bethke's rhetoric is similar to that of Meyers, *Saving Jesus*. George Orwell is the rare exception who explicitly declares, "I like the Church of England better than Our Lord," referring to the church as a bastion of quintessentially English cultural identity for which the details of one's beliefs or interior experience are largely irrelevant; see Gross, *World of George Orwell*, 156.

9. Rice regularly posts reviews of books she has purchased on Amazon.com, where she praises Hyam Maccoby's scathing description in *The Mythmaker* of Paul as the founder of Christianity as "the best [she's] ever read" (www.amazon.com/review/R36HY2VDU6UEV7?cdPage=3).

10. Sommerville, *Religion in the National Agenda*, 5–7.

11. Niebuhr, *Kingdom of God in America*, 193.

church," and Victorinus would scoff at him, asking, "It's the walls that make Christians, then?" (8.2.4). Augustine attributes Victorinus's hesitations to his fears of the opprobrium he would endure from non-Christians. Augustine was familiar with Victorinus's derisive attitude toward churchly ritualism because it was a stance he himself had adopted when he was still a Manichaean. When a close friend fell ill and was baptized without his knowledge by other friends because they believed he was on his deathbed, Augustine disapproved of the "ritual performed on an unconscious body" and teased his friend when he revived, "expecting him to join [Augustine] in making fun of the baptism he had undergone" (*Confessions* 4.4.7–8).[12]

The modern iteration of the antithesis began to take shape late in the eighteenth century. J. P. Gabler delivered an influential lecture in 1787 in which he distinguished between "religion" and "theology" in a way that paralleled the later distinction between spirituality and religion, once one accounts for shifting terminology. Gabler's "religion" closely approximates today's "spirituality." Religion, he says, "is every-day, transparently clear knowledge; but theology is subtle learned knowledge."[13] The former is more intimately involved in the lived experience of the ordinary believer, while the latter requires formal study, speculation, and investigation. Theology is an academic enterprise that aims at systematizing in a technical manner the organic "data" of religious practice. He also underscores the necessity of sifting those elements of Paul's teaching, such as the veiling of women in church, that were intended solely for his first readers from those "pure notions" meant for all times and places.

Friedrich Schleiermacher encouraged the turn inward, away from the dictates of external authorities in matters of faith, in *On Religion: Speeches to Its Cultured Despisers* (1799), one of the most important expressions of liberal Protestant thought as it developed in the nineteenth century. Like Gabler, his description of "religion" corresponds to the "spiritual but not religious" of the twentieth century rather than the merely "religious." He addresses those who see Christianity as narrow and sterile from the perspective of one who himself sensed a need "to examine the ancestral faith and to purify [his] heart of the rubble of primitive times."[14] Creeds, church attendance, and dogmas derived from Scripture do not constitute the heart of the matter: "Religion's

---

12. Augustine, *Confessions*, trans. Boulding.

13. Sandys-Wunsch and Eldredge, "J. P. Gabler," 136.

14. Schleiermacher, *On Religion*, 8. Although he was a member of the clergy, he believed that priests are untrustworthy when they speak on the subject of religion because they are "the kind of people who best like to dwell only in the dilapidated ruins of the sanctuary and who cannot live even there without disfiguring and damaging it still more" (3–4).

essence is neither thinking nor acting, but intuition and feeling."[15] The believer therefore has little need for a teacher but, rather, "should see with his own eyes and should himself make a contribution to the treasures of religion."[16] Schleiermacher tells his audience that they are right "to despise the paltry imitators who derive their religion wholly from someone else or cling to a dead document by which they swear and from which they draw proof."[17] Paul's writings, the authenticity of which Schleiermacher had been one of the very first to question in 1807, are likely among the "dead letters" he has in mind. He specifically questions the Pauline authorship of the Pastoral Epistles, the texts most commonly seen as the locus classicus for institutional rigidity and cramped dogmatism. Schleiermacher furthermore views Christianity's "cultured despisers" as more spiritual than many orthodox churchgoers. "Who hinders the vitality of religion?" he asks. Not the doubters and scoffers but, rather, it is the "prudent and practical people" who "mistreat human beings and suppress their striving for something higher."[18]

Schleiermacher's theology quickly migrated across the Atlantic and inspired transcendentalists such as Ralph Waldo Emerson, who drew on German scholarship in his rejection of Paul's instructions on celebrating the ritual of the Lord's Supper and in "sever[ing] the strained cord" that tied him to the ordained ministry at Second Church Boston.[19] Emerson was in the vanguard of thinkers who turned to non-Western religions for insight. Helena P. Blavatsky, cofounder of the Theosophical Society in New York in 1875, also belonged to this group. Theosophy, one of the more remarkable "spiritual but not religious" movements in the nineteenth century, is a form of esotericism combining elements from both Eastern and Western religions that typically fall outside the "orthodox" or institutional forms of these traditions. Adherents regard it as the primordial wisdom religion, which despite being suppressed through the centuries, has been secretly transmitted by initiates and forms the true basis for all religions. While most twentieth-century spiritualities avoid the occult aspects of Blavatsky's writings, she has been hailed as a major influence on contemporary forms of alternative religiosity.[20]

Blavatsky mentions Paul in her 1877 magnum opus, *Isis Unveiled*. Among the apostles, she says, only Paul understood the secret ideas underlying the

15. Ibid., 22.

16. Ibid., 50. In his critique of Paul and "romantic religion," Leo Baeck refers to Schleiermacher's definition of religion as "the feeling of absolute dependence" ("Romantic Religion," 192).

17. Schleiermacher, *On Religion*, 50.

18. Ibid., 59.

19. Hurth, *Between Faith and Unbelief*, 25–28; cf. Fuller, *Spiritual, but Not Religious*, 27–29.

20. Fuller, *Spiritual, but Not Religious*, 52–55, 80.

teachings of Jesus. Had Paul's writings not been corrupted, however, it would be clear that by the word "Christ" he meant nothing more than "the abstract ideal of the personal divinity indwelling in man." Missionaries to India and elsewhere have not grasped this and have, in the name of "Christ," bestowed on the natives such "blessings" as hypocrisy, practical skepticism, and atheism in addition to rum and opium. How does Paul come to possess his superior insight that "Christ is not a person, but an embodied idea"? Like Jesus, he was an initiate of the ancient Mysteries, yet "it was not Jesus, but Paul who was the real founder of Christianity."[21]

Of "Present Christianity," to be sure, she has nothing good to say. Like many of her contemporaries, Blavatsky sees "Present Christianity" as a travesty. It breeds atheism, nihilism, despair, and crime. Dedicated to opposing "theological Christianity, the chief opponent of free thought," she set her aim at "the dogmatic theologians who would enslave both history and science."[22] She also—again, like many of her contemporaries—thought of Paul as the founder. Unlike other nineteenth-century writers, she took the additional step of claiming that not only Jesus but Paul too had been smothered by churchly authorities. Blavatsky vacillates on this point, at times noting that the epistles were "disfigured . . . by dogmatic hands" before their inclusion in the canon and at other times conceding that "in the glow of his enthusiasm" Paul may have "unwittingly perverted the doctrines of Jesus."[23] This exception to the general rule—namely, that calling Paul the founder of Christianity is an accusation of betrayal—is thus a partial exception that partially proves the rule. Paul is not the founder of Christianity in its familiar form but, rather, the founder of an esoteric form of the faith that he shares with Jesus. Her use of the "true founder" trope was nonetheless guided by a desire to delegitimize tradition.

In her discussion of Paul, Blavatsky quotes liberally from Alexander Wilder, pioneer in the field of holistic medicine and author of books on alchemy and Egyptology. Wilder helped Blavatsky in completing *Isis Unveiled*, and his essay, "Paul, the Founder of Christianity," was published the same year in a weekly journal called *The Evolution*. He shows an admirable control of the latest

---

21. Blavatsky, *Isis Unveiled*, 2:574–76. These comments about Paul reappear under the heading "St. Paul, the Real Founder of Present Christianity" in the third volume of her later work *The Secret Doctrine*, 122–25, published posthumously by Annie Besant, Blavatsky's controversial successor in the Theosophical Society.

22. Blavatsky, *Isis Unveiled*, 2:iv. Blavatsky says that her work "contains not one word against the pure teachings of Jesus, but unsparingly denounces their debasement into pernicious ecclesiastical systems that are ruinous to man's faith in his immortality and his God, and subversive of all moral restraint" (ibid.).

23. Ibid., 2:241, 536.

biblical scholarship in his survey of the conflicts in the early church involving Paul before shifting to a mode of abstruse historical conjecture more typical of theosophical literature. That an essay on Paul would appear in a journal with such a title may seem peculiar. The editorial aims laid out in its maiden issue (January 6, 1877) give some sense of the disposition common to Blavatsky and to many of the spiritual movements of the twentieth century. The editors note that "there is a large class who have outgrown their political faiths, and a still larger class who have outlived their ecclesiastical creeds." But a man in this class is not an infidel.

> If he does not believe in what his fathers have taught, he does believe in something else. If he cannot accept the old faith, he has some fragments of a new faith in which he has implicit confidence, . . . a deep conviction that in time this new faith, grander, truer, and sublimer than any of its predecessors, will be completed in all its just proportions.

Writing at what they perceive to be a pivotal moment in history, the editors envision a readership "thoroughly emancipated in religion and politics" because it is "the only really earnest, faithful, constructive, hopeful, thankful portion of modern society."[24] Blavatsky's collaboration with Wilder, a frequent contributor to *The Evolution*, illustrates some of the ideological tensions that characterized discussion of religion at the turn of the century. Both viewed with great unease the scientific materialism associated with Darwinian theory that in their view rendered consciousness an illusion and the universe ultimately meaningless.[25] At the same time, the anticlerical rhetoric that regularly invoked Paul as a bogeyman was a tool deemed too useful to be laid aside.

Blavatsky's influence can be felt in two twentieth-century "spiritual but not religious" trends. One is the proliferation of ever more bizarre variations of "new age" thought. The anonymous *Urantia Book* (1955), one of the unofficial bibles of this movement, which presents itself as "the Fifth Epochal Revelation of God to this planet" by celestial beings, discusses Paul's relationship to Jesus in its concluding "paper" (§196). "Some day a reformation in the Christian church may strike deep enough to get back to the unadulterated religious teachings of Jesus," but in its present form the church "is founded almost exclusively on the personal religious experience of the Apostle Paul." He is responsible for "the greatest mistake," the founding of a religion "in which the glorified Jesus became the object of worship and the brotherhood

---

24. "Why a New Weekly," *The Evolution*, January 6, 1877, 1.
25. Hanegraaff, *New Age Religion*, 467–73.

consisted of fellow believers in the divine Christ." Paranormal writer Colin
Wilson puts an even greater distance between Jesus and Paul:

> It was St. Paul who invented the religion of Salvationism that depended on self-
> torment, and that thrived on hysteria and emotionalism. . . . It is arguable that
> St. Paul's "crosstianity" was one of the greatest disasters that has ever befallen
> the human race: a great black shadow of intolerance, a super-totalitarianism
> that makes communism seem harmless by comparison.[26]

For Wilson, Paul is one of many malefactors hindering the cultivation of
"Faculty X," a potent form of consciousness, "the power to grasp reality,"
which he says will be accompanied by telepathic abilities.[27]

The popular embrace of Eastern religion and philosophy by Westerners in
twentieth-century spirituality is the other area in which Blavatsky has achieved a
lasting legacy.[28] Ideas and practices derived from Buddhism and Hinduism such
as yoga and meditation are the most visible examples. Although dozens of books
purport to illuminate the fundamental harmony between Jesus and the Buddha,
no one has done the same for Paul. Indian authors such as Swami Vivekananda
and Swami Abhedananda frequently admire Jesus as a guru whose teachings
have been betrayed by the "churchianity" introduced by Paul and the early
church fathers. Anticolonialism often provided the context for Hindu critiques
of Christianity. This Hindu opposition took a nonviolent form—in Gandhi's
case it was informed by the Sermon on the Mount, which he so preferred to
Paul's letters.[29] Sarvepalli Radhakrishnan, former president of India (1962–67)
and prolific writer on comparative religion and philosophy, asserts that Jesus's
teachings were at odds with Judaism and more in tune with Eastern spirituality:

> The characteristics of intuitive realization, non-dogmatic toleration, as well as
> insistence on the non-aggressive virtues and universalist ethics, mark Jesus out
> as a typical Eastern seer. On the other hand, the emphasis on definite creeds
> and absolute dogmatism, with its consequences of intolerance, exclusiveness
> and confusion of piety with patriotism, are the striking features of Western
> Christianity. Jesus's religion was one of love and sympathy, tolerance and inward-
> ness. He founded no organization but only enjoined private prayer. . . . There is
> nothing in common between the simple truths taught by Jesus and the Church
> militant with its hierarchic constitution and external tests of membership.[30]

26. C. Wilson, *Occult*, 232.
27. Ibid., 48.
28. Tingay, "Madame Blavatsky's Children."
29. Gandhi, *Message of Jesus Christ*, 55.
30. Radhakrishnan, *East and West in Religion*, 57.

Radhakrishnan identifies Paul as the forerunner of a Christian fundamentalism that encourages persecution of dissidents, amplifying its native intolerance rooted in the "narrow Jewish faith" by making Jesus into a god.[31]

Institution versus Individual

Those professing to be "spiritual but not religious" often balk at the institutional aspect of religion in general. Institutions are composed of and typically aim to meet various needs of individuals, but by their bureaucratic nature they tend to compromise the personal autonomy of their members. On this score, one of Paul's greatest achievements becomes an enduring source of tension: Paul founded churches. He did not simply convert individuals to a "personal relationship with Jesus." Had he not formed his followers into communities, it is possible that Christianity would not have survived. At the very least, it is certain that it would not have survived in the same form. "Institution" may sound overly formal for the groups with whom Paul corresponds. However rudimentary they may have been in terms of structure, he likely would not have addressed them as a group if they did not possess some communal identity in which the identity of the individual was to be submerged. Over time, many groups move in the direction of higher levels of regimentation, division of labor, and routine. For the "spiritual but not religious," the results can be stultifying.

Most of Paul's letters are written to groups, not individuals. Even Philemon, ostensibly his most private letter, is addressed not only to Philemon but also to Apphia, Archippus, and the church that meets at Philemon's house (Philem. 2). His letters to Timothy and Titus, the so-called Pastoral Epistles, are addressed to trusted coworkers, yet they deal with matters of organization and administration to an extent not seen in the rest of his correspondence. It is customary for scholars to classify them as "church orders."[32] Qualifications for bishops, deacons, and elders (1 Tim. 3:1–13; Titus 1:5–9), compensation for teachers (1 Tim. 5:17–19), and requirements for enrollment on a list of "real widows" (5:3–16) are among the abiding concerns in these letters that strike many modern readers as mundane and picayune. The Pastoral Epistles, Ephesians, and Colossians also contain household codes (Eph. 5:21–6:9; Col. 3:18–4:1; 1 Tim. 6:1–2; Titus 2:1–10; 3:1–2) that govern husband-wife, parent-child, and master-slave relations. These codes

31. Radhakrishnan, *East and West: Some Reflections*, 82; Radhakrishnan, *East and West in Religion*, 62; see also Paradkar, "Hindu Interpretation of Christ," 78.

32. Schweizer, *Church Order*, 77–88; MacDonald, *Pauline Churches*, 203–24.

embed individuals within a network of relations not of their own choosing, yet they are treated as vehicles of divine grace and not as something from which one should seek to be liberated. The exalted nature of the church itself as more than a local, informal gathering of worshipers also marks these letters as examples of "early Catholicism" in the eyes of many scholars.[33] This nomenclature normally implies a negative value judgment on the part of those employing it.

All it takes to turn the frog into a prince is to take these letters away from Paul and assign them to later authors who invoke his name in support of retrogressive social agendas. Paul can do no wrong in the eyes of many scholars who divide his correspondence between seven "authentic" and six "inauthentic" letters.[34] Meanwhile, "Deutero-Paul"—the author(s) using his name as a pseudonym—has few, if any, redeeming qualities. But this solution overlooks the evidence for institutionalization in the undisputed letters such as references to "bishops and deacons" (Phil. 1:1) and the inclusion of "administrators" among those with spiritual gifts (1 Cor. 12:28 RSV). It also betrays assumptions, not supported by sociological studies, about the time required for the development of basic decision-making mechanisms and about the incompatibility of highly regimented communal life and vibrantly charismatic "spirituality."[35] Reconstructions of early church history are thus intertwined with highly fraught attempts to deal with objectionable aspects of Paul and his legacy.

The concern for "church order" was off-putting for Ludwig Wittgenstein. One does not find the same rancor as in Nietzsche, whose *Antichrist* he had read as a student. He had also read Tolstoy's *The Gospel in Brief*, which describes Paul's "metaphysico-cabalistic theory" as foreign to the spirit of Jesus.[36] His aversion to metaphysical claims in this early period was common among analytic philosophers like Bertrand Russell, with whom he had studied at Cambridge. The appeal of Jesus's proclamation in a form reduced to a concern for social justice and personal morality is evident in his appraisal of Paul: "I want to ask—and may this be no blasphemy—'What might Christ have said to Paul?' . . . In the Gospels—as it seems to me—everything is *less pretentious*, humbler, simpler. There you find huts; in Paul a church. There all men are equal and God himself is a man; in Paul there is already something

---

33. Käsemann, "Paul and Early Catholicism."

34. See, e.g., Jewett, *Paul the Apostle to America*, 15–18. For Marcus J. Borg and John Dominic Crossan (*First Paul*, 39–58), the Paul of the undisputed letters is "The Radical Paul," while the disputed letters are divided between "The Conservative Paul" and "The Reactionary Paul."

35. L. T. Johnson, *First and Second Letters to Timothy*, 75–76, 81–82.

36. Monk, *Ludwig Wittgenstein*, 121–23, 132.

like a hierarchy."[37] In Paul's letters, Wittgenstein senses "something like pride or anger, which is not in tune with the humility of the Gospels."[38]

Hierarchy and lack of humility are integrally related in the anti-Pauline complaint of Philip Pullman. They are inevitable corollaries of the power wielded by the Christian church. The corrupting influence of institutional power is a major theme in his popular *His Dark Materials* fantasy trilogy, which by Pullman's candid admission is intended as an anti-Christian response to C. S. Lewis's *Chronicles of Narnia*.[39] Publicity for a later book, *The Good Man Jesus and the Scoundrel Christ*, reveals his ideas about Paul's role in a process by which ecclesiastical authorities hijack the message of Jesus. The literary conceit of this dark retelling of the gospel story is that Mary gives birth not to one child but to two, twins named Jesus and Christ. Jesus becomes a gruff, no-nonsense teacher and performer of good deeds who enjoys the company of the godless and has little patience for theology or apologetics. Christ spends his time following Jesus and recording his deeds and words for posterity, massaging the brute facts of the story to bring out "the truth that irradiates history" under the guidance of a Svengali figure called "the stranger."[40] Together Christ and the stranger orchestrate Jesus's betrayal, death, and "resurrection" (the body is stolen in Pullman's version). The stranger persuades Christ to compile his writings into the book that becomes the NT.

Whether the stranger is an angel or a demon is unclear, but he seems to function as a muse for precisely the sort of theological chicanery Pullman associates with Paul. In interviews he consistently highlights the apostle's purported lack of interest in the historical Jesus. Pullman compliments Paul as "a literary and imaginative genius of the first order who has probably had more influence on the history of the world than any other human being, Jesus certainly included," before adding, "I believe this is a pity." Paul's administrative prowess and his view of "this entity he calls Jesus Christ, strongly skewed towards the Christ part, is what the Church has been founded on ever since."[41]

37. Wittgenstein, *Culture and Value*, 30e, emphasis original.
38. Ibid.
39. Pullman calls *The Chronicles of Narnia* "one of the most ugly, poisonous things I have ever read" ("The Dark Side of Narnia," 6).
40. Pullman, *Good Man Jesus*, 225. When Christ says that Jesus would not have recognized "that sort of truth," the stranger replies, "Which is precisely why we need you to embody it. You are the missing part of Jesus. Without you, his death will be no more than one among thousands of other public executions. But with you, the way is opened for that light of truth to strike in on the darkness of history" (ibid.).
41. O'Collins, *Philip Pullman's Jesus*, 24–27.

Experience versus Doctrine and Ritual

Discontent with Paul frequently focuses on his subordination of personal experience and privately formulated convictions to formal doctrine and ritual. He quenches the Spirit, for example, by his insistence on following protocols in worship. Here, even his most direct link to the historical Jesus—his quoting of Jesus at the Last Supper as a precedent for the Corinthian church to follow (1 Cor. 11:24–25)—is turned from a positive to a negative.[42] His emphasis on orthodoxy is furthermore felt to be not only exclusivistic and judgmental but also spiritually stifling as it inhibits the freedom to tailor beliefs and practices to suit individual preference. To ensure compliance with this orthodoxy, he adopts "a style that the officials of the Vatican can rightly claim as their own," according to Graham Shaw, "subduing critics, subjecting the faithful to his unsolicited censure, and giving firm rulings to their most intimate queries."[43]

John Toland, one of Paul's earliest modern critics, distinguishes "religion" from "true religion" in a way that parallels the later dichotomy between religion and spirituality on this score. True religion is "inward and spiritual, abstracted from all formal and outward performances." In preferring the former, Paul "wholly metamorphos'd and perverted the true Christianity."[44] Other Deists have similar complaints. Bolingbroke faults Christian writers like Paul for borrowing from Plato in establishing "Theological Christianity," which is "a religion that men have invented" and that has subverted "Genuine Christianity," which was "taught by God." Paul's letters form "a principal foundation of all that theology which has occasioned so many disputes in the world, and has rendered the Christian religion obnoxious to the cavils of infidels."[45] H. G. Wells concedes that Paul "apprehended much of the spirit of Jesus and his doctrine of a new birth,"

> but he built this into a theological system, a very subtle and ingenious system, whose appeal to this day is chiefly intellectual. And it is clear that the faith of the Nazarenes, which he found as a doctrine of motive and a way of living, he made into a doctrine of belief. He found the Nazarenes with a spirit and hope, and he left them Christians with the beginning of a creed.[46]

42. James Tabor describes Paul as "inventing" Christian baptism and the Lord's Supper (*Paul and Jesus*, 135, 178).

43. G. Shaw, *Cost of Authority*, 62.

44. Toland, *Nazarenus*, v, 24.

45. Bolingbroke, *Works of Lord Bolingbroke*, 3:442.

46. Wells, *Outline of History*, 511. Cf. Durant, *Caesar and Christ*, 588, 592: "Paul created a theology of which none but the vaguest warrants can be found in the words of Christ. . . . He had replaced conduct with creed as the test of virtue. It was a tragic change."

William Wrede also sees the systematization of Christian doctrine as an unfortunate development. "Movements in a theological direction were not unknown to the original community," but Paul "is still the real creator of a Christian theology." This shift to "theology" is perhaps a necessary evil, but an evil nonetheless, "a descent, from what is simple, immediate, natural to something complicated, secondary, reflected."[47]

Many observers find the "spiritual but not religious" sensibility to be vapid and lacking in depth, turning it on its head and declaring tongue-in-cheek, "I'm religious, but I'm not spiritual."[48] Others take what might be called a revisionist approach in attempting to reclaim Paul. Gary Wills is an example of the latter tendency. He concludes:

> Religion took over the legacy of Paul as it did that of Jesus—because they both opposed it. They said that the worship of God is a matter of interior love, not based on external observances, on temples or churches, on hierarchies or priesthoods. Both were at odds with those who impose the burdens of "religion" and punish those who try to escape them. They were radical egalitarians. . . . Paul meant what Jesus meant, that love is the only law.[49]

The project of "rehabilitating" Paul involves some measure of selective amnesia, as does vilifying him as the enemy of Jesus. Among other things, the portrait of Paul as a moralistic enforcer of orthodoxy glosses over Jesus's own announcement that he had not come to do away with Jewish law (Matt. 5:17). It also stands at odds with the older criticism that Paul allegedly rejected the law of Moses as efficacious in maintaining a relationship with God, in which case he would seem to qualify as a hero for the "spiritual but not religious" and not a scoundrel.

One might argue that these antitheses distort matters in that every "spirituality" presupposes an implicit theology or mode of religiosity and every "religion" manifests itself, minimally or maximally, in spiritual practices and dispositions. Historically, at least, it has proven more difficult to divorce the religious Paul from the spiritual Jesus than critics would have expected. For the

47. Wrede, *Paul*, 177.
48. E.g., Webster, *Dispirited*; Daniel, *When "Spiritual but Not Religious" Is Not Enough*.
49. Wills, *What Paul Meant*, 175. Elsewhere Wills argues that the Catholic emphasis on ritual creates an unnecessary and unhealthy divide between priests and the people (*Why Priests?*). Much criticism of the related doctrine of the atonement and of the system of sacraments formerly focused on Paul, but Wills deflects his attacks from Paul to the Letter to the Hebrews.

faithful, they are different, to be sure, but also complementary. Nikos Kazantzakis, who has Jesus and Paul conform to stereotypes in *The Last Temptation
of Christ*, nevertheless allows Mary Magdalene to express the difference in
a way that may have the ring of historical truth. "He is all sweetness; you all
fire," she tells Paul. "Together, you will conquer the world."[50]

50. Kazantzakis, *Last Temptation of Christ*, 454.

8

A WORLD WITHOUT PAUL?

Christian History in Counterfactual Perspective

"I wish I'd never been born!" The Christmas classic *It's a Wonderful Life* turns on this line, spoken in despair by the protagonist, George Bailey. A guardian angel proceeds to show George, played by Jimmy Stewart, what life in Bedford Falls would have been like had he never been born. Needless to say, things are very different but not quite what George expects.

Many of Paul's critics wish he had never been born. Others are less harsh, perhaps, but nonetheless agree that the world would be a better place without him and the legacy of his writings. To arrive at this view, one assumes certain social, cultural, and theological trajectories if Paul were deleted from history. What would a world without Paul look like? This, in broadest strokes, is the hypothetical question at the heart of much criticism leveled at the apostle. Naming him as the founder implies that but for Paul, Christianity would have never come into existence or, had it managed to survive a messy birth, would not have grown into anything resembling the religion practiced by hundreds of millions of people today.

In formal terms, this type of argument or assertion is known as a counterfactual conditional. Philosophers have devoted a great deal of attention to the counterfactual, as it is more commonly if less precisely known. It may be defined as a subjunctive conditional statement whose first clause (the antecedent) describes a circumstance that is known to be false in the real world and whose second clause (the consequent) describes how matters would have been if the antecedent were true.[1] Technical definitions, however, are hardly needed to characterize a common mode of reasoning that, according to many psychologists, forms a fundamental aspect of human experience.[2] More than philosophers and psychologists, historians have engaged in counterfactual analysis in a form that is readily recognizable to the average reader. Would this event have occurred if that one had not? What would have happened if history had zigged instead of zagged at that point? Nevertheless, counterfactual approaches to historical causality are not uncontroversial. How do responses to Paul look when viewed against the backdrop of these debates—responses not simply to Paul as a theologian in comparison with other thinkers but, in particular, hostile responses to his life and legacy that lament his putative role in the history of Christianity.

Counterfactual History in Context

Consideration of counterfactual historical claims has a long and distinguished pedigree. Livy goes on a famous digression in his *Ab Urbe Condita* (9.17–19) in which he wonders whether Alexander the Great at the height of his power could have defeated the Roman legions.[3] In his *City of God*, Augustine responds at great length to the charge that Rome would not have fallen into decline had the empire remained true to its ancestral religion rather than embracing Christianity. In the *Pensées* (§162) Pascal mused that "the whole face of the world would have changed" had Cleopatra's nose been a little shorter.[4] And Winston Churchill spawned a virtual cottage industry when he wrote a story framed as an essay by a historian living in a world where the Confederacy had won the Civil War.[5]

Recent decades have witnessed the spread of explicitly counterfactual thinking to a wide variety of disciplines. Military history is one field that has proven especially fertile.[6] What if the weather had been different at Waterloo or on

1. The most influential philosophical analyses, out of the enormous body of secondary literature, are Goodman, *Fact, Fiction, and Forecast*; and Lewis, *Counterfactuals*.

2. Byrne, *Rational Imagination*.

3. Probably not, he concludes. Famed British historian Arnold Toynbee similarly wondered about what might have happened if Alexander had lived longer, playfully speculating that he would have realized his dream of creating a brotherhood of man in a cosmopolitan world that would last up to the present, when a united humanity would flourish under the reign of Alexander LXXXVI! (*Some Problems in Greek History*, 441–86).

4. Pascal, *Pensées*, trans. Levi, 10.

5. Churchill, "If Lee Had Not Won."

6. E.g., Cowley, *What If?* In addition to the Civil War, World War II remains by far the most common object of study by English-speaking historians taking a counterfactual approach.

D-Day or on the night Washington crossed the Delaware? Could the Spanish army under Cortés have conquered the Aztecs if the local population had not been weakened by a smallpox epidemic during the siege of Tenochtitlán? Would the Confederacy have emerged victorious at Gettysburg if Robert E. Lee had not committed the Army of Northern Virginia to Pickett's Charge? In such affairs it is easy to see how seemingly insignificant decisions and chance events can have a disproportionate effect.

The consequences of these and other wartime contingencies are hardly confined to the battlefield. They often have an enormous ripple effect that spans centuries and touches elements of culture and society far removed from any combat. Fifth-century Greece likely would not have witnessed the same glory had the Persians prevailed at Salamis or Plataea, and Western civilization would have followed a more easterly trajectory. Similarly, the very idea of Europe would be very different had Arab and Ottoman forces not been turned away at Tours in 732, Lepanto in 1571, and Vienna in 1683. Politics and international relations likewise provide plenty of material for hypothetical conjectures by scholars and pundits of all stripes.[7] Whether the Soviet Union would have survived were it not for Gorbachev's reforms, whether Reagan would have turned to politics had he been a better actor, whether an older Martin Luther King Jr. would have altered the priorities or tactics of the civil rights movement in the 1970s—these and many other questions in the same vein continue to captivate large audiences.

Sports offer perhaps the most popular arena for counterfactual analysis. A staple of barroom arguments is the "what if" involving contests that never took place. Who would win a series between the 1927 New York Yankees and the 1975 Cincinnati Reds? Had Tiger Woods played a few decades earlier, would he have been a better golfer than Jack Nicklaus? Questions like these are, of course, impossible to answer. Less fanciful are debates about the potential consequences of events that actually or very easily could have transpired. Fans still wonder what would have happened if the Portland Trailblazers had picked Michael Jordan in the 1984 draft instead of injury-prone Sam Bowie, or how many home runs would Barry Bonds have hit had he not played during "the steroids era." The most recent trend is the use of advanced metrics for evaluating a player's worth that aim to arrive at an "objective" calculation of how a team would have performed had a player been replaced by an "average" player.

These statistical models are borrowed from economists, who have attempted to bring some measure of scientific rigor to the use of counterfactual

---

7. Tetlock and Belkin, *Counterfactual Thought Experiments*; Lebow, *Forbidden Fruit*; Greenfield, *Then Everything Changed.*

arguments.[8] They employ methods such as regression analysis to investigate the causal relationships between multiple variables in a given system and to estimate the degree of confidence warranted by the results. Their analyses often influence real-world affairs more than those of historians and political scientists. Conclusions about New Deal programs, for instance, and whether they prolonged the Great Depression or kept it from getting worse inform policy debates in the present. Will higher taxes stimulate or retard economic growth? Answers to such questions about what will happen are based on determinations about what would have happened in similar situations in the past, all other things being equal. Aspirations to scientific precision and reliability in such matters are often mocked, as in the old joke about economists having predicted ten of the last five recessions.

Physicists may not influence daily affairs to the same degree as economists, but the counterfactual scenarios they ponder could hardly be more sweeping in scope. What would the universe look like if the cosmological constant or any of a wide array of other variables were other than what they are? Would it lack the remarkable "fine tuning" that appears to be a necessary condition for supporting "life as we know it"? The "many-worlds interpretation" of quantum mechanics attempts to answer the latter question, postulating that the present universe is one of a vast number of alternate universes that together compose the "multiverse."[9] This theory posits the actuality of all possible alternative pasts and futures. In other words, everything that could have happened in the past but did not happen has actually happened in the past of some other "parallel" universe. Worlds in which the apostle Paul was never born—or was born but never stopped persecuting Christ followers, or died before traveling to Damascus, or never wrote letters that were included in the NT canon—thus exist. Unfortunately, it will be impossible to describe these worlds since the parallel universes in which these eventualities unfold are noncommunicating. By no means do all physicists embrace this theory. The casual reader may be inclined to agree with those who feel that "with the multiverse we seem to have taken leave of our senses and entered into wild speculation."[10]

With or without parallel universes, counterfactual analyses sometimes resemble a species of science fiction. It should come as no surprise, then, that this approach has proven immensely popular as a subgenre of fantasy literature usually labeled "alternate history." Harry Turtledove is the acknowledged

8. McClelland, *Causal Explanation*; McCloskey, "Counterfactuals."
9. J. A. Barrett, *Quantum Mechanics*, 149–84.
10. Impey, *How It Began*, 351.

master of the genre, but mainstream novelists such as Philip Roth, Kingsley Amis, and Michael Chabon have also tried their hand at it. Scholars too have begun to study the genealogy and the poetics of alternate history, sometimes as manifestations of a postmodern sensibility.[11]

The Damascus Road Not Taken

Although there is little overlap with these areas of inquiry in terms of substance, the rhetorical similarities with the study of Paul and his place vis-à-vis Jesus in the history of Christianity are instructive. Popular writers occasionally take an explicitly counterfactual approach.[12] Scholars are less apt to do so. A few such essays appear in a volume devoted to "virtual history" and the Bible, including one by Richard Bauckham considering a hypothetical detour in Paul's missionary travels.[13] Much would have been different, Bauckham concludes, but the gospel would still have spread across the empire had Paul worked in the eastern diaspora instead of in the west. In the same volume Loveday Alexander and John Dominic Crossan consider other factors that could have drastically altered the received version of the movement's infancy or smothered it in the crib, with or without Paul—such as systematic rather than sporadic imperial persecution or the return of Jesus's followers to the countryside after his death.[14] Carlos M. N. Eire elsewhere notes that the canonical Gospels suggest an inflection point where history might have curved in a different direction: What if Pilate had pardoned Jesus?[15] A scenario in which Jesus avoids crucifixion is, because it involves far fewer contingent variables, more plausible than one in which the early Christian movement is stillborn

11. Hellekson, "Toward a Taxonomy"; Winthrop-Young, "Fallacies and Thresholds"; Doležel, *Possible Worlds.*

12. E.g., Kennedy and Newcombe, *What If Jesus Had Never Been Born?* A much less conventional approach is taken in many of the stories collected in Bishop, *Cross of Centuries.* There are numerous novelistic treatments of Paul's life, but they rarely take the form of alternate histories.

13. Bauckham, "What If Paul Had Travelled East rather than West?" John Gillies works with the same premise, but rather than using the counterfactual as a means of exploring Paul's legacy, he constructs an allegory intended to tweak American sensibilities as they relate to foreign missionary work ("Sending Parable").

14. Alexander, "What If Luke Had Never Met Theophilus?," and Crossan, "Earliest Christianity."

15. Eire, "Quest for a Counterfactual Jesus." On the basis of statements in the Qur'an (e.g., 4.157–58), it is widely believed among Muslims that Jesus did not die on the cross but, unbeknownst to most onlookers, was replaced by Simon of Cyrene or Judas Iscariot. Jesus does not embark on a post-Calvary career in Muslim tradition, however, having been taken up into heaven immediately following his supposed death.

in Paul's absence. (Of course, a secondary effect of a Christ without a cross would be a gospel very different from what Paul preaches.)

It is much more common to find approaches to Paul that are implicitly rather than explicitly counterfactual in orientation. This is unexceptional given that counterfactual arguments almost always presuppose certain ideas about causality. Causality in this connection may refer to Paul's particular purpose or motivation in pursuing a missionary strategy or instructing his readers to believe specific doctrines, or it may refer more generally to the social, cultural, and historical milieu in which Paul operates. In the former sense, asking "Why did Paul do this or teach that?" means "What did Paul hope or intend to accomplish?" In the latter sense, the question entails asking "What circumstances prompted or set the stage for Paul to teach this or that?"

Answers to these questions almost always imply a hypothetical. With this in mind, it becomes possible to "translate" standard scholarly descriptions of Paul into counterfactual claims: If Paul had not written his letters in Greek, his influence on the history of Western civilization would have been negligible. If Paul had not been such an avid letter writer, the letter would not have become a standard literary genre in early Christianity. If gentiles had never expressed so much unexpected enthusiasm for the gospel, Paul would not have formulated his signature doctrine, justification by faith. If Paul had not so adamantly insisted on gentile inclusion, he would not have been such a controversial figure among his contemporaries. If Paul had not relied on the Septuagint translation of Isaiah, his argument in Romans would be less persuasive. If Paul had been acquainted with loving, monogamous relationships between partners of the same sex instead of the pederasty that was rampant in ancient Greece, his treatment of homosexuality would not have been so strident and censorious. If the Gospels had been written earlier than 70 CE, Paul would have quoted them. If the Letter to the Hebrews had not been attributed to Paul, it would not have been included in the NT canon. If the system of Roman roads had not been so extensive, Christianity would never have spread very far beyond Palestine through the efforts of Paul or anyone else. If slavery had not been so deeply ingrained in the fabric of Greek and Roman society, Paul would have called unambiguously for its abolition. If Paul had not been worried about the perceptions of outsiders, he would not have discouraged the Corinthian women from prophesying. If Paul had not expected the imminent return of Jesus to establish God's reign on earth, his advice on matters pertaining to sex and marriage would not have had such a strongly ascetic cast. If Paul had not misrepresented Jewish attitudes about Mosaic law, the doleful history of anti-Semitism could have been avoided.

Each of these statements simply takes a position that is widely, though by no means universally, accepted in the field of Pauline studies and reformulates it as a counterfactual, with nothing of substance added or subtracted. Many more could have been listed, and some are more plausible than others. But the point here is not to argue for or against the claims they make. It is simply to highlight how firmly embedded counterfactual thinking is among scholars who study Paul.

Prevailing views about the authorship, dating, and theological orientation of the deutero-Pauline letters are tangled up with assumptions about "what Paul (would have) thought." Many scholars, for example, emphasize the differences between "Pauline" letters like Philemon and Galatians and "non-Pauline" letters like the Pastoral Epistles when it comes to concerns about church organization. Since Paul did not dwell on such matters as job descriptions for elders and deacons in Corinth, it is assumed, he would not have done so in Ephesus or Crete. What if circumstances had arisen calling for a more intentional effort at ordering affairs among a local body of disciples? This appears to have occurred not long after Paul's death. There is no reason it could not have occurred a few years earlier, while he was still alive. How might Paul have responded? (If such situations did in fact arise, as many scholars would argue, the proper question is "How *did* Paul respond?") It may be impossible to answer this question, but it is likewise impossible to avoid it if one wants to establish the basic parameters of Paul's thought world and the range of options at his disposal in meeting the practical and ideological challenges confronting him in his ministry. Neither those scholars who limit the label "Pauline" to the seven undisputed letters nor those who want to apply it to all thirteen canonical letters are exempt on this score. Wondering what Paul would have or could have done is a hard habit to break. And when his critics are the ones wondering, "would have" and "could have" not infrequently sound a lot like "should have."

The Peril and Promise of Counterfactual History

Historians are supposed to describe the past "as it actually happened," not "as it might have happened." For this reason, counterfactual approaches have stimulated considerable debate about theory and method.[16] Critics are more

16. Murphy, "On Counterfactual Propositions"; Demandt, *History That Never Happened*; Ferguson, "Virtual History"; Bulhof, "What If?"; Tetlock and Parker, "Counterfactual Thought Experiments"; R. Collins, "Turning Points"; Nolan, "Why Historians (and Everyone Else) Should Care."

vocal than supporters. In the first place, counterfactual approaches to historical inquiry are arbitrary in scope and in the selection of variables deemed relevant. Out of the infinite number of individuals and events on which history hinges, why highlight one and not another? Why examine a sequence of causes and effects starting at this point in time and not that? It is not self-evident that Paul was indispensable to the development of Christianity when other strong candidates such as John the Baptist, Peter, and Mary Magdalene might be chosen. The plausibility of a given reconstruction depends in part on a myopic focus on a preferred sequence and a simultaneous disregard of other potential starting points. Simplifying matters in this way is human nature, but human nature and responsible historical method do not always go hand in hand.

Critics of counterfactual history also cite its speculative character. It amounts to little more than a parlor game with few, if any, controls or criteria for determining what qualifies as evidence. Any "evidence" for what might have happened in a world where Paul did not spread the good news is drawn from a world in which he did.[17] Moreover, the approach overlooks the multiplication of contingencies with each new counterfactual scenario. Piling inference on top of inference about what would or could or might have happened in a proposed sequence of historical causes and effects exponentially stacks the odds against the expected outcome in very short order.[18] Hindsight, it would seem, provides the only reliable method for distinguishing significant from insignificant factors in history.

Most damning may be the contention that counterfactual history does not deserve to be called history. Political philosopher Michael Oakeshott cites Paul's putative role in the founding of Christianity as a case in point. To claim that, for example, Christianity would not have become the center of Western civilization without Paul's escape from Damascus in a basket is "not merely bad or doubtful history, but the complete rejection of history" in that it presupposes a prior and privileged knowledge of what is essential and what is incidental.[19] The eminent Marxist historian E. H. Carr shares Oakeshott's low opinion of counterfactual arguments even though their respective political sympathies could not have been further apart. According to Carr, "History is a record of what people did, not of what they failed to do," and thus playing games with might-have-beens is "a purely emotional and

17. D. Fischer, *Historians' Fallacies*, 16.
18. Fischer contends that limiting one's speculations to a shorter time horizon does not solve this problem: "The only difference between long-run and short-run counterfactuals is that the absurdity of the former is more glaringly apparent" (ibid., 19).
19. Oakeshott, *Experience and Its Modes*, 128–29.

unhistorical reaction."[20] Put more bluntly, counterfactual history is for losers, and sore losers at that, as "theories that stress the role of chance or accident . . . will be found to prevail" among those riding in the trough of history rather than on the crest.[21] This is not to say that history ought to be written by the "winners," but it ought not to be rewritten by self-serving losers engaged in a frivolous exercise in wistful thinking.

Defenders of the approach counter these objections by pointing out that, like it or not, everyone practices counterfactual history all the time. Insofar as historians seek to do more than drily chronicle sequences of events, it is unavoidable. History is not just an account of what happened; it is also an attempt to understand why it happened. So long as historians seek to discern the cause-and-effect relationships that guide events, hypotheticals are essential because every statement about causation implies a counterfactual claim. Causal inferences by their very nature involve assumptions about how events would have unfolded in the absence of one condition or another. Positing an alternative outcome is one way to weigh the relative significance of various factors. The heuristic function of counterfactual reasoning is so fundamental that historians take it for granted without realizing it.

Much more than an effective rhetorical device that makes for good story-telling, these approaches also help to counteract hindsight bias, that is, the tendency to view events as more predictable or less subject to contingency than they really are. Uncertainty when it comes to the future is the norm, but once the end of one chapter of history is known, it is easy to forget how uncertain that "future" seemed at the time. In the same vein, many see in counterfactual history a much-needed antidote to deterministic theories that emphasize impersonal forces as the engine of world history to the exclusion of chance and human agency.[22]

A World without Paul?

Historical determinism, however, can take other forms than those associated with Marx and Hegel. Statements having a deterministic ring to them can be found throughout the Bible, including Paul's letters (Prov. 16:4; Isa. 14:27; Acts 13:48; Rom. 8:29–30; 9:10–13; Eph. 1:4–5; 2 Thess. 2:13; 2 Tim. 1:9). If God had an "eternal purpose which he has realized in Christ Jesus" (Eph. 3:11 RSV), it may strike some as blasphemous to suggest that it is possible

20. Carr, *What Is History?*, 98, 167.
21. Ibid., 132.
22. On this tendency in Marxist historiography, see Ferguson, "Virtual History," 38–41, 52–56.

to thwart his will, in this or in any parallel universe. It may be that Paul was destined to act and write as he did, with the result that Christianity developed as it has, no more free than Jeremiah to resist God's call in a hypothetical past (Jer. 1:4–10). Paul tells the Galatians that his role as apostle to the gentiles was ordained by God, never considering what other life he might have possibly led (Gal. 1:15–16; cf. Rom. 1:1–2; 1 Cor. 1:1).

For their part, proponents of counterfactual approaches to early Christianity can also cite weighty precedents. Paul himself makes frequent use of counterfactual arguments. Believers possess a wisdom decreed before all ages, which none of the rulers of this age understood, "for if they had, they would not have crucified the Lord of glory" (1 Cor. 2:7–8). He also reminds the Corinthians that, if Christ had not been raised from the dead, they would still be in their sins (15:17). Some scholars see the third-century *Gospel of Judas* taking this logic back a few days earlier than Easter. "Without the betrayal," Bart Ehrman writes, "there would be no arrest, without the arrest there would be no trial, without the trial there would be no crucifixion, without the crucifixion there would be no resurrection—and in short, we still wouldn't be saved from our sins. So why were Judas's actions such a bad thing?"[23] Jesus, commenting in the form of a counterfactual, stops far short of hailing Judas as a hero of salvation history: "Woe to that man by whom the Son of man is betrayed! It would have been better for that man if he had not been born" (Matt. 26:24 RSV).

But most people who make counterfactual arguments about Paul and his role in early Christian history seem unaware that they are doing so. For this reason they fail to put in place the kinds of "quality control" measures found in the work of historians operating with a methodological awareness of the pitfalls that attend such approaches. Is it theoretically possible that Paul was the indispensable man who kept Christianity from becoming whatever it might have otherwise become in the wake of Jesus's death? Perhaps, but to admit its possibility is a far cry from saying that it is probable. Contemplating the contours of a hypothetical world without Paul can generate a productive research agenda. Bauckham and Crossan, for example, show how the milieu of early Christianity can be fleshed out in a creative yet disciplined manner, but they are atypical in this regard. Formulating questions that can be answered with some degree of certainty is a key ingredient in any such endeavor. Otherwise, the result is little more than a series of claims that may sound plausible but,

---

23. Ehrman, "Christianity Turned on Its Head," 93. In the years since the *Gospel of Judas* was first made public, many scholars have disputed the interpretation that has Judas playing a positive role in the story.

as they are unfalsifiable, can never be proved. Just as important, neither can they be definitively disproved. This quality helps to explain the staying power that many arguments about Paul exhibit.

This longevity may also have something to do with the way in which claims about Paul resonate at an emotional level. Both Jesus and Paul provoked strong feelings during their lifetimes. With Jesus, the negative responses have mostly subsided. Not so with Paul. The whimsy one finds in many examples of counterfactual history is totally missing from the study of Paul. Perhaps this is to be expected given the role his writings have played in shaping norms in such matters as gender and sexuality. Jesus's teachings are no less counter-cultural from a modern perspective, and yet he is loved and admired, if not always worshiped. Why the difference? Had narratives about Paul suffering a grisly death—beheading, according to early church tradition—on account of his convictions been canonized, would his legacy be different? Would fewer people look back in anger? That is yet another hypothetical question that, alas, cannot be answered. It is worth noting that counterfactual thought experiments are typically attended by strong emotions, such as regret, remorse, indignation, and nostalgia.[24] Rarely are they matters of indifference to those who conduct them. Outcomes that are perceived in a dim negative light more commonly prompt such reflection. Furthermore, according to social psychologists, dwelling on what might have been has a powerful capacity to amplify those emotions. For many of his critics Paul is like a scab that, when picked at, makes the wound hurt more than it did in the first place.

The emotional element of such thought experiments is in part a function of their presentist character.[25] Framed as analyses of the past, they nevertheless express feelings about and provide commentary on the present. Broadly speaking, these feelings are manifested in counterfactual speculation that comes in two forms.[26] Fantasy scenarios describe a past that is preferable to the present. Discontent with the status quo correlates with a desire to change it. Nightmare scenarios lean in the opposite direction, envisioning a suboptimal past and thus viewing the present with a higher degree of satisfaction.

Paul's foes generally fall into the former camp and his friends into the latter. The latter are less inclined to consider the consequences of a world without Paul, and when they do, they are less likely to make him uniquely responsible for how Christianity developed even as they celebrate his contribution and recognize its outsized significance. The former more readily reimagine the

---

24. Landman, "Through a Glass Darkly," 250–51.
25. Rosenfeld, "Why Do We Ask 'What If?'"
26. Ibid., 92–94.

past, and when they do, it is a past that was on track before Paul caused it to go off the rails. Might it have been still worse? The thought hardly ever occurs. Nor do other, less nebulous questions: If more of his letters were extant, would his thinking come into clearer focus or cohere more perfectly than it appears to on the basis of the woefully small sample of the thirteen letters attributed to him? Or, what if he had lived longer? Despite the dearth of information about his movements between various jail stints, many scholars will not countenance the possibility that Paul may have survived a first trial and imprisonment in Rome and was thus able to engage in further travel and teaching than is depicted in Acts. Five or six more years and he would have witnessed, or heard about, the destruction of the temple in Jerusalem as a consequence of the Judean revolt against Rome. Would an event of this magnitude have altered his worldview? Would he have evolved subtly or more dramatically with the advance of age or other developments in his ministry such as failures, successes, or increasing estrangement from his fellow Jews after the fall of Jerusalem? It seems arbitrary to entertain the notion of an early movement of Christ followers with Paul totally subtracted from the equation but not these other scenarios with the same level of prima facie plausibility, in that they require a lesser degree of extrapolation from the known data.

Selectivity of the sort one sees when it comes to the Pauline counterfactuals deemed worthy of consideration is seen in the case of Jesus as well. This is relevant to an evaluation of Paul because the terms of the debate about the founding of Christianity almost inevitably include an unfavorable comparison with Jesus. Right or wrong, these comparisons seem to assume unwittingly that Jesus had essentially completed his ministry at the time of his death. New Testament texts like Matt. 16:21 and Heb. 10:5–10 suggest that it was Jesus's conscious plan to sacrifice himself in Jerusalem, but most scholars are hesitant to accept this notion. What might a longer career have looked like? Just more of the same—more miracles, more sermons, more parables, more arguments with Pharisees—with no "development"? Would he have ventured out into the diaspora, to Tyre and Sidon and beyond, to preach not only to the lost sheep of Israel but also to the "dogs," his mind having been changed by the Canaanite woman in Matt. 15:21–28? Would he have found it expeditious to adapt his message in the same way that it is claimed Paul did, in such a way that other Jews would have accused him of distorting or abandoning Torah? The NT and early rabbinic literature indicate that many Jewish leaders leveled this charge against Jesus even without imagining a longer career. Would Jesus have ended up founding a different "Christianity" after not founding it in his early thirties? Again, it is impossible to know, but one could argue that hypothetical comparisons of an older Jesus to a younger Jesus are of no less heuristic validity than comparisons of Jesus with Paul implicitly taking the form of "Jesus would never have taught what Paul taught concerning _____."[27]

Robert Wright is one of the very few writers to compare Paul favorably to Jesus, and he argues that a key difference between them is instrumental in the ultimate success of Christianity. Why did Christianity survive antiquity, he asks, when so many other religions fell into the dustbin of history? Constantine plays a role, but Charles Darwin is the real key to answering this question. Natural selection favors systems of belief and moral behavior that promote "interethnic amity" because they foster the peaceful relations that lead to human flourishing. Much more so even than Jesus, Wright argues, Paul was the most important carrier of this beneficial "mutation," as seen in his emphasis on love in 1 Cor. 13 and elsewhere.[28] It was Paul's vision of a universal brotherhood that enabled Christianity to outlast its competitors. Constantine's endorsement did little more than put the imperial seal of approval on a process that was already moving forward with inexorable force. Even if Paul had never been born or taken that fateful trip to Damascus, natural selection would have eventually produced similar results because "any religion that came to dominate the Roman Empire would have been conducive to interethnic amity."[29] Without Paul—or Jesus, for that matter, if Wright is correct—the world might not look so different from the way it looks now. Pity Paul: no sooner does he emerge as a sympathetic protagonist than he gets relegated to a bit part or written out of the script entirely.

Exercises in writing alternate histories of Christianity call to mind lines from T. S. Eliot's *Four Quartets* about "what might have been." It is "an abstraction," he writes in the opening stanza, "Remaining a perpetual possibility/ Only in a world of speculation."[30] Consensus will likely remain elusive when it comes to Paul's role in the birth of Christianity because the debate tends to revolve around ceteris paribus arguments at almost every turn. In other

27. Nikos Kazantzakis weaves these two threads together when he has an older Jesus encounter Paul in the concluding dream sequence of *The Last Temptation of Christ*, 477–78.

28. R. Wright, *Evolution of God*, 265, 285.

29. Ibid., 296–97. Wright sees the popularity of Marcionite Christianity in the second century as evidence that some other version of Christianity would have prevailed if the Pauline version had not. Even if Jesus had never been born or had died in obscurity, "some other vehicle for the meme of transethnic amity might well have surfaced" (295). Wright describes himself as an agnostic, and so the Whiggish character of this narrative, with its emphasis on congenial values that are relevant to present-day concerns, is not a function of any Christian triumphalism on his part.

30. Eliot, *Four Quartets*, lines 7–8 of "Burnt Norton" (p. 13).

words, it is impossible to know whether Christianity would have emerged and developed as it did without Paul but "all other things being equal," since "all other things" are never quite the same in the ebb and flow of history. Statisticians study various factors and use regression analysis to help differentiate between causation and correlation, but those who study the history of ideas have no such instrument at their disposal. Historians can do little more than speculate about the specifics of a world without Paul. Was he unique? Is it conceivable that others could have arrived at similar insights and achieved similar missionary results in his absence? Hypothetical questions of this sort are captivating in part precisely because there can be no closure, but they also serve as salutary reminders of the contingency of history.

9

NOT BY PAUL ALONE

Other "Founders" of Christianity

After Jesus, Paul appears to be the leading candidate for the title "founder of Christianity." His is not, however, the only hat to have been thrown into the ring. A number of other names have been put forward as worthy of the title. To appreciate the various claims made for and about Paul and his peculiar legacy, it will be helpful to put him in perspective by looking at these other putative founders. Some are household names, while others are much less familiar. Although they may be fringe candidates, their cases deserve consideration for what the similarities and differences reveal about Paul's role in Christian history and about those dissatisfied with traditional narratives that trace Christian origins back to Jesus.

John the Baptist

Few traditions about Jesus have as firm a historical foundation as his relationship with John the Baptist. That they had some sort of relationship is certain even if the precise nature of that relationship is obscure. He is traditionally regarded as the "forerunner" of Jesus as well as his cousin.[1] Insofar as Christianity is defined by special beliefs about the identity of Jesus, John the Baptist

1. Wink, *John the Baptist*, 58–82.

has a strong claim to the title of founder. So prescient and precocious is he that he proclaims the good news in utero. At the Visitation (Luke 1:39–45), an otherwise unremarkable meeting of relatives takes a dramatic turn when the child in Elizabeth's womb leaps at the sound of Mary's voice (1:41). To paraphrase Freud, sometimes a baby kicking is just a baby kicking. But John's mother interprets his prenatal gymnastics, which the narrator ascribes to the agency of the Holy Spirit, as a recognition of Jesus's exalted status: "And why has this happened to me, that the mother of my Lord comes to me?" (1:43). Christian readers are so accustomed to calling Jesus "Lord" that the audacity of this statement may at first elude them.

Thirty years later, John's public ministry is similarly dedicated to shining the spotlight on his relative. He tells the Judeans who come to him to be baptized in the Jordan, "The one who is more powerful than I is coming after me; I am not worthy to stoop down and untie the thong of his sandals. I have baptized you with water; but he will baptize you with the Holy Spirit" (Mark 1:7–8). In the Fourth Gospel, it is John who first declares Jesus to be "the Lamb of God who takes away the sin of the world" (John 1:29) and the very "Son of God" (1:34). His own role as the one who prepares "the way of the Lord" is itself a fulfillment of OT prophecy (Matt. 3:3; Luke 3:4–6; John 1:19–23; cf. Isa. 40:3–5).

Were it not for this proclivity for self-deprecation, it is not difficult to imagine a place of honor for John in the church even more exalted than he already enjoys. Teachings and practices associated with John show up in the preaching of Jesus and become central to the new faith: not only his novel insight that Jesus was the Messiah, but also the emphasis on repentance, the announcement of the imminent arrival of God's reign, the ritual of water baptism, and the metaphor of rebirth for redemption.[2] In fact, there are grounds for believing that John had a higher profile than Jesus during their brief, overlapping earthly careers. One possible conclusion to draw from Jesus's submitting to the baptism of John is that the former is the disciple and the latter is the master, an awkward implication that the Gospels (Matt. 3:13–15) take great pains to address. Some scholars even believe that messianic claims on John's behalf may have been made during or shortly after his lifetime.[3] (His emphatic protestation in John 1:20—"I am not the Messiah"—when no one in the narrative has suggested anything to the contrary is curious.) All

2. Ernest William Parsons demonstrates how pervasive these elements are in the Letters of Paul, Hebrews, 2 Peter, and Acts, as well as in the Gospels ("Significance of John the Baptist," 2–6).

3. Raymond E. Brown notes that the author of the Fourth Gospel may have had followers of John the Baptist in view when writing his prologue (*Gospel according to John*, 1:lxvii–lxx).

in all, this is a magnificent resumé for someone whose ministry was shorter than Jesus's and who left behind no writings.

While there is little indication of personal rivalry between the historical John and the historical Jesus, in the second century and later it appears that their respective followers could view one another with mutual suspicion (Justin Martyr, *Dialogue with Trypho* 80). Such sectarian groups may be the same circles from which the Mandaeans emerged, perhaps as early as the mid-second century. Mandaeism is a gnostic religious movement that originated as a heterodox form of Judaism and still survives today, though fewer than ten thousand adherents remain in the Mandaean heartland of Iraq and Iran. John the Baptist is the most highly honored of their prophets. Among their principle scriptures, composed in a dialect of Eastern Aramaic, is the *Book of John*, likely set down in writing in the seventh or eighth century in part to gain toleration from Muslim authorities as a "People of the Book." This text includes combative dialogues between John and Jesus, who is presented as an apostate aiming to create a new religion by relaxing the strict Mandaean moral code that aids the soul in its ascent into the World of Light.[4] In the same way, then, that Paul is sometimes accused of displacing Jesus, devotees of John the Baptist label Jesus a usurper and false messiah who perverted the teachings of their master.[5]

Mary

The Virgin Mary recognized Jesus as much more than a prophet and therefore possesses the same basic qualifications as the other candidates included in this chapter. In fact, according to the NT she perceives it before anyone else. Her acquiescence to Gabriel's announcement that she will bear a child who will be called the Son of God—"let it be with me according to your word" (Luke 1:38)—has frequently been treated as the pivotal moment in the history of the salvation that the church offers to the world. Had Mary said no, according to a popular appropriation of this text that dates back at least to Irenaeus in the second century (*Adversus haereses* 3.22.4), there would be no Christianity

---

4. Buckley, *Mandaeans*, 24–25.

5. J. Ramsey Michaels and Robert Eisenman offer two very different ways of looking at the relationship between John the Baptist, Jesus, and Paul. While no one would argue that John the Baptist was a major influence on Paul, says Michaels, John seems to have been "a more appropriate role model than Jesus precisely because he was not Jesus, but (like Paul) someone who called people to believe in Jesus" ("Paul and John the Baptist," 259). Eisenman not only believes that any such similarities between Paul and John are forced, but he also suggests that Paul may have had a hand in the execution of the Baptist by Herod (*James*, 654–55).

and no hope for the human race. In the story of the wedding at Cana, Mary wants Jesus to assume a role with which he appears uncomfortable (John 2:3–5). Jesus hesitates but later solves the problem of the wine shortage. Mary's maternal nudging, then, leads to the first revelation of Jesus's glory and to the disciples' faith in him (2:11).

"All generations will call [her] blessed" (Luke 1:48), yet it is exceedingly rare to hear Mary called the founder of Christianity.[6] Sexism may be the reason for this, but this seems unlikely given that the title is not usually intended as praise. Perhaps it is her reticence in the Gospel accounts; unlike Peter and John the Baptist, who preach and proselytize in public, Mary tends to keep things to herself (Luke 2:51). More customary is the title "first Christian."[7] Applied to Mary, this title has a positive connotation, unlike Nietzsche's application of it to Paul as a corrupter of the teachings of Jesus. As the first Christian, she is also the model Christian, and it is in this capacity that even the Reformers held her in high esteem despite any qualms over Catholic devotional practices and doctrines connected to her person.[8]

Peter

A special regard for Jesus as the Christ, the Jewish Messiah, is a defining element of Christianity. Not long after his death, "Christ" begins to function almost like a proper name, either in combination with "Jesus" or by itself (Acts 2:38; 8:12; 1 Cor. 1:2; 6:11; 1 Pet. 4:14). But who was the first to bring the name and the title together in such a way as to mark the beginning of something new? Mark credits Simon Peter with this seminal insight. After the Twelve report a number of popular but apparently mistaken notions about his identity, it is Peter who gives the correct answer when Jesus asks, "But who do you say that I am?" Peter replies, "You are the Messiah" (Mark 8:29). Yes, he conveniently forgets who Jesus is once Jesus is arrested, but his confession at Caesarea Philippi, according to F. J. Foakes-Jackson, "literally founded the Christian religion" by supplying, in essence, "the first creed of the Church."[9]

---

6. Mary plays an apostolic role, according to Max Thurian, "not in the sense that like the apostles she was one of the founders and leaders of the Church" but in the sense that she was an eyewitness to the life of Jesus and a proclaimer of the saving events she had seen (*Mary*, 12). Nōni Tyent's short story presents a very different Mary who, after delivering Jesus stillborn, embarks on a three-year career as the messiah and suffers crucifixion with eleven of her female disciples. But the message of "Miriamism" spreads far and wide, and "much in the world that was stupid, arbitrary, and cruel inevitably, albeit gradually, lost its foothold" ("Miriam," 34).

7. De Satge, *Mary and the Christian Gospel*, 74.

8. Pelikan, *Mary through the Centuries*, 153–63.

9. Foakes-Jackson, *Peter*, 60.

Matthew presents a slightly longer version of this exchange that significantly augments Peter's credentials. Jesus blesses him and adds, "You are Peter [*Petros*], and on this rock [*petra*] I will build my church, and the gates of Hades will not prevail against it. I will give you the keys of the kingdom of heaven, and whatever you bind on earth will be bound in heaven, and whatever you loose on earth will be loosed in heaven" (Matt. 16:18–19). Jesus's response, involving a pun on Peter's name that is even clearer in Aramaic than it is in the Greek, has been regarded by Roman Catholics as the clearest biblical basis for the institution of the papacy. Protestants, naturally, demur on this point, preferring to interpret the "rock" on which the church is built not as Peter himself but the faith made manifest in his confession of Jesus as the Messiah.[10] Both camps would likely agree on a subtle but important grammatical point, if nothing else: in whatever sense the church may have been founded *on Peter*, it was not founded *by Peter*.

Acts likewise portrays Peter as the primary human catalyst for the birth of Christianity. His Pentecost sermon, shortly after the descent of the Holy Spirit, results in the conversion of three thousand Jews (Acts 2:14–42). For this reason Pentecost is widely celebrated by Christians as the "birthday" of the church.[11] Not only is Peter the first and foremost missionary to the Jews in Acts; he is also given credit as the first to bring a non-Jew into the fold, a point that is easy to forget given the spotlight shone on Paul throughout the narrative as the apostle to the gentiles. Peter's encounter with the Roman centurion Cornelius is so pivotal an episode in the expansion of Christianity according to Acts that it takes up nearly two entire chapters (Acts 10:1–11:18).

The *Sepher Toledot Yeshu* ("Book of the Generations of Jesus"), a popular legend among medieval Jews, presents a distinctive way of thinking of Peter as the founder.[12] It relates scurrilous tales about Jesus's birth, his feats of sorcery, his death, and his followers' attempts to burnish his messianic credentials by stealing his body. To quash the movement that springs up after his death, the rabbis recruit Peter (here called Simeon Kepha) as a Manchurian candidate. Posing as a disciple of Jesus, Peter teaches Jesus's followers to abandon Jewish feasts, dietary laws, and circumcision. Peter's true aim in inventing Christianity according to the *Toledot Yeshu* was to bring an end to intra-Jewish strife by

10. Bigane, *Faith, Christ, or Peter*; Caragounis, *Peter and the Rock*; Kling, *Bible in History*, 45–82.

11. Orthodox Christians, however, do not hold this view, citing ancient sources that describe the church as existing before the creation of the world (*Shepherd of Hermas, Vision* 2.4.1; *2 Clement* 14.1–2).

12. See the analysis of Gager, "Simon Peter," 221–25.

showing Christians the door. Intriguingly, the last line states that Peter was known as Paul among the Nazarenes.

That Peter is not mentioned as the founder of Christianity more often is somewhat surprising given his splendid dossier. It is likely due to the peculiar place he occupies in intramural debates among various Christian communions. Attributing the founding of Christianity to anyone other than Jesus is usually intended as a backhanded compliment, a way to assign responsibility for any number of perceived defects and deviations from the truth. This rhetorical strategy works, however, only on the assumption that particular Roman Catholic claims about Peter's historical preeminence have merit. "Blaming" Peter in this manner would seem to undercut any arguments to the effect that Peter's role in the history of the church has been greatly exaggerated by the papists.

Mary Magdalene

In each of the Synoptic Gospels, Mary Magdalene is among the women who first witness the empty tomb and hear the good news that Jesus had risen from the dead (Matt. 28:1–10; Mark 16:1–8; Luke 24:1–12; Mary is singled out as the first witness in Mark's longer ending). They are instructed to spread the word to the disciples, who initially disbelieve their report. The criterion of embarrassment—it is highly improbable that early Christians would have concocted such a story since many contemporaries would have dismissed their beliefs as the delusions of a silly woman—leads many historians to conclude that she is the earliest source of the Easter faith. For this reason, Mary is often called the apostle to the apostles, a title that was especially popular during the Middle Ages and is usually traced back to Hippolytus in the third century.[13]

Mary has an even more prominent role in the Gospel of John (20:1–18). Not only is she the first witness to the resurrection; rightly understood, according to Jane Schaberg and others, John shows that she is also the first to grasp its full meaning. "The threatening thought" to which this fact gives rise is "that Mary Magdalene can be considered a—or the—founder of Christianity."[14] Dan Brown's 2003 best seller *The Da Vinci Code* popularized the conspiracy

13. On the pagan critique of Christianity as based on the testimony of a "hysterical woman," see Origen, *Contra Celsum* 2.55. Howard Brenton's play *Paul* turns this trope on its head by having Mary Magdalene participate in the plot to dupe Paul into believing that Jesus had risen from the dead.

14. Schaberg, *Resurrection of Mary Magdalene*, 303. See also Ehrman, *Peter, Paul, and Mary Magdalene*, 229: "It is not at all farfetched to claim that Mary was the founder of Christianity . . . [and thus] the most important person in the early history of Christianity." Thecla Schreuders

theory that Mary and Jesus were married and produced a royal bloodline in France that lasted for centuries, and that this history was covered up on account of the challenge posed to the institutional church by "the sacred feminine." Few scholars put any stock in the outlandish particulars of this theory, but the identification of the Beloved Disciple as Mary Magdalene is not original with Brown.[15] Nor is the notion of a "Magdalene Christianity" to which "the struggle for egalitarianism was central," until its suppression by "Petrine Christianity" and other androcentric expressions of the faith.[16] Mary's candidacy for the title of founder is thus an exception to the general rule by which it functions as a reproach.

James

James, the Anglicized form of the Hebrew Jacob, is a popular name in the NT. Two of the twelve apostles share this name, as does one of Jesus's brothers (Matt. 10:2–4; Mark 6:3). Zebedee's son was one of Jesus's first followers (Mark 1:19–20), but it is James, "the Lord's brother" (Gal. 1:19), who assumes a larger role in early Christianity. He is one of only three persons connected to early Christianity mentioned by Josephus in his voluminous writings on affairs in first-century Palestine (*Jewish Antiquities* 20.9; the others are Jesus and John the Baptist). Along with Peter and John, he was a "pillar" of the church in Jerusalem (Acts 12:17; Gal. 2:9; Eusebius, *Hist. eccl.* 2.23.4), and he presides over the Council of Jerusalem described in Acts 15, which culminates with a compromise between those who would impose all of Torah's demands on gentile converts and those who would do away entirely with the require-ments of Jewish law. In issuing the first so-called apostolic decree, then, he sets the new faith on a course that will eventually diverge from mainstream Judaism in such a way that a new religion is the result.[17]

Some scholars believe that James played an even larger role in history than one finds in Acts, which gives a skewed picture of the early church. In this

likewise makes the claim that Mary should be considered the founder of Christianity in her 2004 BBC documentary *The Real Mary Magdalene*.

15. E.g., De Boer, *Gospel of Mary*, 178–90. Raymond Brown notes the difficulty in discern-ing who was the first to "believe" in Jesus's resurrection in John 20:8 but does not endorse the theory that Mary Magdalene is the Beloved Disciple (*Gospel according to John*, 2:987).

16. Schaberg, *Resurrection of Mary Magdalene*, 347–49; cf. Schüssler Fiorenza, *In Memory of Her*, 332.

17. On the historical questions raised by the account of this event in Acts, see Dibelius, "Apostolic Council"; and Hengel, *Acts*, 111–26. It is a commonplace for this meeting to be described as a "watershed" in the history of Christianity; see Wall, "Israel and the Gentile Mission," 441; Just, "Apostolic Councils," 261.

view, the *Gospel of Thomas* is closer to the truth when it depicts the disciples asking Jesus whom they should follow when he departs and Jesus telling them to follow James the Just, "for whose sake heaven and earth came into being."[18] Robert Eisenman, who calls James "the missing link" between the Judaism of his day and Christianity, is the most vigorous and vocal proponent of this perspective. James, and not Peter, was "the true heir and successor of his more famous brother Jesus and the leader at the time of whatever the movement was we now call 'Christianity.'"[19] The NT gives a distorted portrait of both James and Jesus, who in reality were ethnically, politically, and religiously Jewish to the core in a way that does not typically appeal to contemporary sensibilities: "zealous for the Law, xenophobic, rejecting of foreigners and polluted persons generally, and apocalyptic."[20] Eisenman's reconstruction takes a surprising turn when he asserts that James and the shadowy Teacher of Righteousness mentioned in some of the Dead Sea Scrolls are one and the same. Even more provocative (and idiosyncratic) is his further claim that the Spouter of Lies who appears as the Teacher of Righteousness's nemesis in the Damascus Document and Pesher Habakkuk is a code name for Paul.[21] As the legitimate successor to Jesus in this telling, James is the founder of what might be termed "proto-Christianity." The movement that subsequently expropriates the title "Christianity" is an anti-Semitic "Pauline or Overseas Christianity," led by a man who is not really the Jew he claims to be.[22]

John the Evangelist

John was likewise a common name among Jews in the first century and, hence, among Christians as well. After John the Baptist, the best known may be John the son of Zebedee and brother of James. This John was one of the twelve apostles—the so-called Beloved Disciple (John 13:23; 19:26; 20:2; 21:7,

18. *Gos. Thom.* 12, trans. Lambdin.
19. Eisenman, *James*, xvii, xx. James D. Tabor says that "rather than being the founder of a church, Jesus was a claimant to a throne" (*Jesus Dynasty*, 4). On the related idea that James was the first "pope" or "caliph," see Hengel, "Jakobus der Herrenbruder"; and Stauffer, "Zum Kalifat des Jakobus."
20. Eisenman, *James*, xxiii.
21. Eisenman (ibid., 529) further suggests that Paul provided intelligence to Nero during the Jewish revolt of 66–70, a war that may have been triggered by the assassination of James.
22. Ibid., 58–59. In commenting on Paul's description of Moses in 2 Cor. 3, Eisenman states that "no more scurrilous accusation has ever been recorded by the founder of one major world religion against that of another" (650). As expressions of this spurious Pauline Christianity, Eisenman would also include most of the parables and "the most oft-quoted and highly prized sayings of Jesus" (59).

20)—and is the personality associated with the Fourth Gospel. To the extent that Christianity emerges as a form of devotion to Jesus in response to the story of his life, death, and resurrection, perhaps the authors of the Gospels have a claim on the title of founder. Yet most scholars believe that Mark, not John, is the earliest Gospel. Where, then, does this leave John?

According to Louis A. Ruprecht Jr., the eventual emergence of Christianity as a new and separate religion corresponds to a fatal shift in the meaning of Christian compassion brought about by John. Whereas Mark invented a new genre, "a marvelously supple literary tapestry" that helped to turn Christianity into a religion that was independent of Judaism, John wrote "a very different kind of story," intending "not so much to supplement what the other gospel writers had done as to replace them and to subvert their claims to authority."[23] By the early third century, an all-inclusive faith "gave way to a much harsher movement increasingly defined by a line-drawing, border-defining, heresy-hunting religiosity that became ever more violent when it attained imperial power in Rome." How does this happen? John, in this view, deliberately turns Mark's understanding of Jesus upside down, especially at the point where Jesus prays in Gethsemane to have the cup of suffering pass from his lips. Ruprecht claims that John presents a Jesus who actually mocks this prayer, and in the process "Mark's tragedy was slowly turned into a comedy of Christian error."[24] This dramatic reinterpretation paves the way for a very different Christianity, which becomes even more dominant after the Protestant Reformation. Victorian sexual codes, opposition to evolutionary theory, literalist interpretation of the Bible, "a surprisingly unreflective version of patriotism"—Ruprecht believes that these and other stances usually associated with the "Religious Right" can be traced all the way back to John.[25]

To these elements, one may add the exclusivism that offended Greek and Roman religious sensibilities, which finds its most succinct expression in the mouth of the Johannine Jesus: "I am the way, and the truth, and the life. No one comes to the Father except through me" (John 14:6). An even greater stumbling block to interreligious dialogue is the purported role of the Fourth Gospel in laying the groundwork, or at least providing a pretext, for anti-Semitism, which in the eyes of many is inherent in Christianity and not a mere aberration.[26] Although his name is rarely mentioned as the founder, it is clear that negative evaluations of John mirror those of Paul at several points. If Benjamin W. Bacon was correct a century ago, this is no coincidence. Bacon

23. Ruprecht, *This Tragic Gospel*, 5–6, 185–86.
24. Ibid., 4, 9.
25. Ibid., 187: "John might have argued this way, and did so."
26. See Leibig, "John and 'the Jews.'"

speculated that the unnamed Beloved Disciple in the Fourth Gospel was none other than the apostle Paul.[27]

Isaiah

Chronologically speaking, one of the more surprising names put forward is that of the prophet Isaiah. Arthur Drews, better known as an advocate of the Christ-myth theory, makes the suggestion in the course of attacking the historical reliability of the Gospels:

> Have not our inquiries shown that in the long run the contents of the gospels may be traced to the prophet Isaiah, whose "predictions," sayings, penitential appeals, and promises reappear in the gospels, in the form of a narrative? *Hence Isaiah, not Jesus, would be the powerful personality to whom Christianity would owe its existence.* . . . The *ideal Christ*, not the historical Jesus of modern liberal theology, was the founder of the Christian movement, and made it victorious over its opponents. It is more probable that Jesus and Isaiah are one and the same person than that the Jesus of liberal theology brought Christianity into existence.[28]

He regards the well-known Song of the Suffering Servant in Isa. 53 as "the real germ-cell of Christianity."[29]

Others have demonstrated, albeit in a less provocative and polemical mode, the pervasive influence of Isaiah on Christianity in its formative stage and in every period of its existence. Texts from Isaiah have played a particularly significant role in the early church's understanding of its separation from Judaism and in the spread of the faith among gentiles.[30] Paul himself illustrates this process in his frequent references to Isaiah (Rom. 9:27–29; 10:11; 11:8, 26–27, 34; 15:12; 1 Cor. 2:9; 14:21; 15:32, 54; 2 Cor. 6:17–18; 9:10). When Drews speaks of Isaiah, however, he appears to have the canonical text in mind instead of the flesh-and-blood figure of the late eighth century BCE. Apart from the desire to disprove the historical existence of Jesus of Nazareth, he is also interested in disputing the notion "that only a great individual personality

27. Bacon, "Disciple Whom Jesus Loved." James Tabor contends that the Beloved Disciple is actually James, the brother of Jesus (*Jesus Dynasty*, 81, 165, 258, et al.). Few scholars have found either theory persuasive.

28. Drews, *Historicity of Jesus*, 296–97, emphasis original. Unlike many other writers, Drews also transfers to Isaiah various positive qualities usually associated with Jesus, such as solidarity with the poor (244).

29. Ibid., 69; cf. 179.

30. Sawyer, *Fifth Gospel*, 32–41.

can bring about a spiritual movement, and that such a movement must in all circumstances be traced to a single outstanding personality."[31] Would Paul, perhaps, be comfortable with this perspective? Very likely so, according to those scholars who contend that Paul betrays little knowledge and evinces little interest in the biography or personality of Jesus. Others argue that this is, at best, an argument from silence.[32]

Philo, Seneca, and Mark

Friedrich Engels relays the theory of Bruno Bauer in his 1882 obituary for the man who had been the student of Hegel and the teacher of Marx. According to Engels, Bauer had shown that the prolific first-century Jewish writer Philo of Alexandria was "the real father of Christianity, and that the Roman Stoic Seneca was, so to speak, its uncle."[33] Set forth most fully in his *Christus und die Cäsaren* (*Christ and the Caesars*), Bauer's theories about the founding of Christianity were intertwined with his anti-Semitism and with his belief that Jesus never existed.[34] Judaism lent little more than the outward form of Christian teaching. Only Philo's thoroughly hellenized form of the ancestral faith made a seminal contribution, while Seneca's Roman Stoicism had an even more profound impact.[35]

Neither Philo nor Seneca, however, was aware of his familial relations to the new religion, because the gestation period lasted well into the second century. Without Mark, the birth of Christianity might not have come about when it did during the reign of Hadrian. Bauer was an early advocate of the idea that Mark was the earliest of the Synoptic Gospels, though he dated it much later than did other scholars and believed the history and characters it contained to be entirely fictional. "Mark," whoever he may have been, put literary flesh

---

31. Drews, *Historicity of Jesus*, 293.

32. See the contrasting evaluations of Rudolf Bultmann: "The personality of Jesus has no importance for the kerygma either of Paul or of John or for the New Testament in general" (*Theology of the New Testament*, 1:35; cf. Bultmann, *Jesus and the Word*, 8); and W. D. Davies: "Paul is steeped in the mind and words of his Lord" (*Paul and Rabbinic Judaism*, 140, cf. 147–49).

33. Engels, "Bruno Bauer," 196. Engels was fond of this formulation; see also his 1883 essay "The Book of Revelation," where he calls Philo "the doctrinal father of Christianity" (207).

34. He also doubts the historicity of Rabbi Hillel, one of the most important figures in ancient Judaism (B. Bauer, *Christus und die Cäsaren*, 301). On Bauer's anti-Semitism, see Leopold, "Hegelian Antisemitism."

35. Only the "skeleton" (*Knochengerüst*) derives from Judaism, not the soul (*Gemüth*); see Bauer, *Christus und die Cäsaren*, 302. Bauer traces many key ideas found in the NT back to Seneca (47–61). Lactantius (*Divinarum institutionum* 6.24.13–14) early in the fourth century speculates less provocatively that Seneca would have become a Christian if he had only received proper instruction.

on philosophical ideas appearing in Seneca and elsewhere in a manner that resembles the synthesis of Hegelian dialectic. For Bauer, then, Christianity is "the invention of a single original evangelist" whose fictive "Jesus" satisfies the longings of the Greco-Roman world by reconciling the antithesis between God and man in his person.[36] History consists of humanity's progress toward self-consciousness. The birth of Christianity was a critical part of this process, but insofar as Christianity has fixated on past formulations, it is a hindrance to the ultimate goal toward which history inexorably moves. As it turns out, Bauer's radical historical skepticism keeps him from identifying Paul as the founder. Not only does he reject all thirteen of the Pauline Letters as second-century forgeries, but he also believes that, like Jesus, "Paul" is a fabrication as well.

Apollonius of Tyana

Few cases are more curious than that of Apollonius of Tyana, a first-century Neopythagorean ascetic from Asia Minor "whose true history and persona," in the apt phrase of the *Oxford Classical Dictionary*, "it is scarcely possible to grasp."[37] Philostratus wrote a third-century biography of dubious historical value that describes Apollonius's itinerant preaching and wonder working as well as his sojourns in India and assumption into heaven at death. Eusebius and Sossanius Hierocles sparred over the miraculous deeds attributed to Apollonius in the early fourth century, starting a long tradition of comparing him to his older contemporary, Jesus, for a variety of polemical and apologetic purposes that continues to this day.[38] The ingenuity of his admirers in finding parallels between the two figures is impressive.

Alice Winston takes the observations of such luminaries as Helena Blavatsky and Ezra Pound a step further when she claims for Apollonius the title of founder of Christianity. Apollonius deserves this title because, in addition to being an incarnation of Krishna and the Buddha, he and Jesus were actually the same person, a fact that would be more widely known had the fire at the

---

36. See Pfleiderer, *Development of Theology*, 226; see also B. Bauer, *Christus und die Cäsaren*, 43–46.

37. Rose and Spawforth, "Apollonius of Tyana," 128.

38. See Barnes, *Constantine and Eusebius*, 164–67. Scholarly treatment of the parallels is discussed by Koskenniemi, "Apollonius of Tyana." Perhaps the most notorious participant in this debate is the Marquis de Sade, who makes the comparison in the course of characterizing all religion as fraudulent. In his 1782 *Dialogue entre un prêtre et un moribund*, the dying man is no more impressed with the miracles of Jesus than with those of Apollonius and tells the priest that, founder of Christianity or not, "Jesus is no better than Mohammed, Mohammed no better than Moses, and the three of them combined no better than Confucius" (*Dialogue between a Priest and a Dying Man*, 46).

great library of Alexandria not destroyed the supporting documentation.[39] The NT conceals the true biography of Jesus/Apollonius, who was not crucified in his thirties but, rather, taught and traveled until shedding his "physical garment" at the age of ninety. The "so-called Christian religion," which no longer emphasizes astrology or vegetarianism, was thus founded on an untruth. Paul, however, escapes blame for this betrayal: "Had it not been for Paul the world would have had none of the actual esoteric Teachings. It is regrettable that humanity does not possess them pure and intact, for Paul was a mental giant, as well as a deep occultist."[40] Few scholars put any stock in these bizarre speculations, yet they are worthy of notice because they have found a large audience with the advent of the internet and because they reflect the concerns about uniqueness, innovation, and transparency that often lurk near the surface when religious foundings are under discussion.

Whatever elements of historical and theological insight all these theories may contain, it should be obvious that they cannot all be true. It is more than a little likely, moreover, that none of them is true in its entirety. As a group, perhaps the only thing they have in common is that none of these figures claims responsibility for starting a new religion. Differences are easier to find. Many are authors or ascribed authors of documents that have survived from antiquity. Others (Mary, John the Baptist, Mary Magdalene, Apollonius) are the subjects of books or even lend their names to books for which claims of authorship are nowhere made on their behalf. On this score, the former are more like Paul and the latter are more like Jesus.

The varied subtexts constitute the more intriguing differences among the cases surveyed in this chapter. While they are all dark horses, not all are bêtes noires. Institutionalization and hierarchy are matters of concern in certain narratives (Peter, John), especially as the interests of the church and of imperial Rome converge.[41] Personality and character traits come into play on other occasions (Mary, Peter). Christianity's perceived departure from or betrayal of its Jewish roots is not infrequently the subject of critique (James, John

39. Winston, *Apollonius of Tyana*, xv. Winston's source for the information in these documents, she says, is a "Venusian" with whom she communicated via "clairaudience" (vi–vii).

40. Ibid., xvi. Herbert J. Muller speculates that the only reason Christianity triumphs and not a mystery religion like that practiced by Apollonius is that "Jesus alone attracted an extraordinary missionary, unsurpassed in religious history for his devotions, his fervor, and his genius," that is, Paul (*Uses of the Past*, 156–57).

41. See also Eisenman's reference to Eusebius as "Constantine's confidant and a principal founder of High Church Christianity as we know it" (*James*, 317).

the Baptist). This last theme often takes the form of a more thoroughgoing attack on traditional Christianity as a morally bankrupt farce or the result of an elaborate fiction (John, Isaiah, Seneca, Apollonius).

No single individual embodies or encompasses as many of these concerns as the apostle Paul. He is a prolific author, with additional books written about him and in his name. These writings project a forceful personality that, variously, inspires or offends those who encounter it. His letters have provided rationales for organizational structures that have both united and divided the church for centuries. From the beginning, his relationship with Judaism has been fraught, to say the least. And because Jesus is a cultural icon, almost universally admired even by those with little affinity for the religion of his followers, criticism of Christianity is usually deflected elsewhere. Someone has to bear the brunt, and Paul has proven uniquely capable of doing so.

10

FROM JESUS TO PAUL

An Experiment in Comparative Religion

Religious controversy frequently focuses, sooner or later, on questions of origins. Whether Paul deserves the credit—or, for Nietzsche and others, the blame—for founding a religion centered on Jesus is the form such debates often assume in the case of Christianity. But Christianity is not the only religion to witness controversy over the circumstances of its birth. Questions about whether or in what sense it is appropriate to think of Confucius as the founder of Confucianism or Muhammad as the founder of Mohammedanism (as Islam was still called well into the twentieth century) provide parallels that are useful in considering what is at stake in certain critiques of Paul. Who asks such questions? When and to whom are they most pressing? What is the relationship between "development" and "deviation"? What do they reveal about the ways in which the past is remembered and authority negotiated in the present? What do the differences and similarities between the various religions reveal about the character of Christianity? Do intra-Christian debates at the denominational level replicate rhetorical patterns commonly on display in discussions of Paul's role vis-à-vis that of Jesus? A survey of the landscape shaped by these concerns within other traditions provides an opportunity to map their contours with respect to Paul and Jesus from a different perspective.

Asian Religions

It has been argued that any comparison of religious founders is problematic in that it imposes Western categories covertly derived from Christianity onto variegated realities. The concept of religion as a generic entity arose in the nineteenth century when one of the "nearly requisite means of identifying an individual religious tradition as distinct, unique, and irreducible to any other" was the naming of an extraordinary historical personage as the initiator of the tradition.[1] But it is possible to overcorrect for this bias. The phenomenon of preeminent individuals playing decisive roles in the birth and propagation of various religions is not purely a figment of the Western imagination. It predates the European engagement with Eastern religions by several centuries, as one finds in the speculation that Confucius, Laozi, and the Buddha may have been the same individual and that disagreements among "his" followers are what ultimately led to the establishment of three separate religions.[2]

Daoism

According to tradition, the founder of Daoism in the sixth century BCE was Laozi, the reputed author of the classic *Daodejing*. A preliminary question about Laozi's status as founder is one that has been posed with respect to Jesus: Did he exist, or does he belong exclusively to the realm of legend? Chinese historians wonder whether Laozi was simply a mythical figure already in the second century BCE.

There are fewer questions surrounding the historicity of Zhuangzi, the fourth-century BCE teacher who is sometimes hailed as the true founder of philosophical Daoism, even though the eponymous work ascribed to him was critical in establishing Laozi as the founder. It has been suggested that Zhuangzi essentially uses Laozi as a character in a fictional dialogue that allows him to demonstrate the superiority of his teachings to those of Confucius.[3] This earlier "philosophical" Daoism (*Daojia*) is frequently contrasted with "religious" Daoism (*Daojiao*), which is usually dated from the manifestation of the divine form of Laozi in Sichuan to Zhang Daoling in 142 CE and the rise of the Celestial Master school. This theophany and subsequent revelations in later centuries are seen as superseding Zhuangzi's own "original" teachings, and there are lineages within the Daoist tradition that do not trace their roots

1. Masuzawa, *Invention of World Religions*, 132.
2. Yao, *Introduction to Confucianism*, 226.
3. Graham, "Origins of the Legend of Lao Tan."

back to Laozi.[4] Yet the dichotomy between the religion and the philosophy, a false one in the eyes of many observers, does not seem to correspond to any rivalry between Zhuangzi and Laozi in the way that Paul has been accused of contaminating the simple piety of Jesus with abstract Greek concepts. To what extent would either sage countenance, among other things, moral relativism, political anarchism, alchemy, divination, or t'ai chi martial arts as legitimate developments of the ideas propounded in his works? Oddly, Western scholars who specialize in Daoism often show more scruples in adjudicating this type of question than do practicing Daoists themselves.

Confucianism

Two issues attend any consideration of Confucius's status as the founder of Confucianism. First, not everyone agrees that Confucianism is a religion since it lacks deities, doctrines about the afterlife, and other "standard" religious elements. Most Chinese today do not think of it as a religion.[5] It is better understood as a system of ethics or perhaps a civil religion, especially given the role of the *Analects* in the curriculum for the civil service examinations over many centuries. Some scholars go so far as to claim that Confucianism did not exist until Jesuit missionaries invented it in the sixteenth century as a counterpart to Christianity or that Chinese scholars early in the twentieth century such as Kang Youwei reinvented it as a response to Western influences.[6]

Second, even if one classifies Confucianism as a religion, it is not clear that Confucius is the person who started it. "I transmit but do not innovate," he declares (*Analects* 7.1).[7] What did he aim to transmit? The answer: *ru*, a multivalent term that denotes a body of political, religious, and cultural tradition that was shared by all the elite in preimperial China.[8] But if it predates Confucius, it is obviously problematic to see him as its founder. He came to be regarded as such soon after his death in part because all schools of thought needed a forebear and rival schools needed a specific target for their attacks. In the Warring States period, Mencius (fourth century BCE) and Xunzi (third century BCE) both claimed to be the true heirs of Confucius despite their disagreement on the fundamental question of whether human nature was good or evil. After Confucius, they are the two most important thinkers

---

4. In fact, some medieval texts ridicule the notion that either Laozi or Zhuangzi founded Daoism; see Raz, *Emergence of Daoism*, 21–26, 210–12.

5. Sun, *Confucianism as a World Religion*, 110–19.

6. L. M. Jensen, *Manufacturing Confucianism*, 3–28; Chen, *Confucianism as Religion*, 45–58.

7. Confucius, *Analects*, trans. Lau.

8. Zufferey, *To the Origins of Confucianism*, 165–375.

in the Confucian tradition. Criticism of one school by the other, however, never involves an accusation, as one sees with Paul, that Mencius or Xunzi "founded" a separate religion from that of Confucius or that contemporary Confucianism is bankrupt due to its deviation from the master's authentic teachings. Consideration of Confucius as a specifically religious founder appears to have begun with the arrival of Buddhism in China in the first century CE. Later, Communist writers who saw religion as antithetical to the scientific spirit of modernity sometimes portrayed Confucius as a cultural reformer rather than as a religious founder, though others cast him as a religious figure as part of an effort to criticize "reactionary" elements of traditional Chinese society, as one sees with the use of "Criticize Confucius!" as a propaganda slogan during the Cultural Revolution. Korea, Japan, and Vietnam have also been heavily influenced by Confucian thought, but the notion of Confucius as the founder of a religion is not as politically fraught in those countries as it is in his native land.

Buddhism

Siddhartha Gautama's teachings form the foundation of Buddhism. Doubts about the historicity of the Buddha have been expressed by some scholars, but the consensus is that he did exist even if little can be confirmed about his biography. He is believed to have founded the *sangha*, the community of Buddhist monks and nuns committed to preserving the master's teachings, though neither he nor any of his disciples wrote down his teachings until the first century BCE. A peculiar complication when it comes to understanding the relationship between the founder and founding is that the Shakyamuni, as Siddhartha Gautama is often called, is variously regarded as the fourth (or the sixth or the twenty-fifth) "awakened one." Buddhas through the ages periodically appear, discover the Dharma, and establish communities for the purpose of propagating this message. When the Dharma is forgotten or becomes corrupted, a new Buddha emerges and the process repeats itself. The cyclical aspect of revelation may explain why Buddhists are relatively uninterested in any quest for the historical Buddha, as the individual who lived in India over two thousand years ago is only one link in a chain that stretches backward and forward for eternity. For Buddhists, the fact that the Shakyamuni is not unique is, paradoxically, central to his status as a founder.[9]

The particular image of the Buddha as the founder of a religion is in no small part the product of European scholarship in the late nineteenth

---

9. R. S. Cohen, "Shakyamuni," 133.

century. The earliest Western interpreters of the Buddha had difficulty distinguishing him from the Hinduism of his native India. It is a commonplace to hear the Buddha called the Luther of India and described as a religious reformer who challenged the Vedic priesthood. Narratives of Buddhist origins are reminiscent of the Protestant Reformation, perhaps no coincidence given the anti-Catholic climate in which the English and German pioneers of comparative religion were writing. The Protestant inclination to locate the most authentic form of a religion in its earliest stages and in written scriptures likewise coincided with the prioritization of India over forms of Buddhism found in Tibet and elsewhere in Asia and with the denigration of various devotional practices of living adherents, which were deemed to have been corrupted by sutra-chanting, relic-venerating monks.[10] Much like the Quest for the Historical Jesus sought to strip away Pauline accretions that had supposedly obscured the pure faith, returning to the historical Buddha was a way to recapture Buddhism's true essence. In this process, however, Western scholars of Buddhism often presumed to know Buddhism better than Buddhists themselves.[11] They selectively ignored the "superstitious" elements found in the earliest writings attributed to the Buddha and highlighted such Enlightenment themes as empiricism, universalism, individualism, and open-mindedness, even though Buddhists in South and East Asia seemed to have little need for such a Buddha.[12]

Sewn into the fabric of the tradition is the idea that "the decline of the Dharma" is inevitable as it becomes increasingly difficult to follow the Noble Eightfold Path, and only the arrival of the next Buddha, Maitreya, can set things right. No individual—such as Tapussa or Bhallika, the Buddha's first followers, or the companions who heard his first sermon at the Deer Park in Benares—is responsible for this process of degeneration, and no attempts are made to place blame by "elevating" another individual to the position of founder. The traditional Buddhist belief from as early as the second century BCE is that during this age the true teachings of the Buddha will remain in circulation but that, due to widespread moral depravity, it will become impossible to attain nirvana. Sectarian rivalry, carelessness in passing on the Dharma, an overemphasis on intellectual disputation, secularism, excessive state control, and the appearance of counterfeit teachings are also cited as

10. Almond, *British Discovery of Buddhism*, 24–28, 37–40, 73–76.

11. This phenomenon can also be seen in such contemporary writers as New Atheist Sam Harris, who writes that "to turn the Buddha into a religious fetish is to miss the essence of what he taught," and that the wisdom of the Buddha "is currently trapped within the religion of Buddhism" ("Killing the Buddha," 73).

12. D. S. Lopez, *Scientific Buddha*, 21–46.

causes of corruption and decline.[13] Worries about this decline in the Buddhist world sometimes function to maintain the status quo so as to prevent further decline, while in other settings there arise new schools, such as Pure Land and Nichiren Buddhism, that insist on innovation as appropriate for different dispensations.

Hinduism

Hinduism is unusual in that it claims no founder in the normal sense. This vacuum has been cited as one reason for the astonishing variety found within Hinduism, as there is no clear-cut hierarchy or source of authority.[14] Far from perceiving it as a weakness, many gurus cite the fact that Hinduism's origins cannot be fixed in time and space to a single individual as a strength when compared with other religions that are constrained by the circumstances of their foundings. Disputes about authority thus tend to focus on texts such as the Upanishads rather than on the precedent of any specific individual standing at the font of the tradition.

Judaism and Islam

Geographically, chronologically, and theologically, Judaism and Islam stand closer to Christianity than do the religions of Asia. Does this proximity translate into more similar theories of origins, conceptions of the founder, or critical assessments of any innovation introduced by subsequent representatives of the tradition?

Judaism

Three names emerge as serious contenders for the title "founder of Judaism."
1. In Genesis, it is Abraham who is first called to leave his home and kinsfolk and become the ancestor of a new people with a special relationship with the God of Israel. The biblical account says nothing about his fitness for this role, though extrabiblical texts such as the *Apocalypse of Abraham* speculate that his precocious monotheistic sensitivities elicited God's favor. He takes on circumcision as the sign of the covenant and passes the test when God commands him to sacrifice his son Isaac. God takes the initiative, but

13. Nattier, *Once upon a Future Time*, 120–32, 136–39. According to the *Saṃyutta Nikāya*, the Buddha also predicted that the true Dharma would last only five hundred years on account of the admission of women into the *sangha*.
14. Flood, *Introduction to Hinduism*, 6.

Abraham's obedient response makes him "father of the faithful." When he is cast in the role of founder, Judaism is understood primarily as an ethnic or social category and as a religion in a secondary sense. Jewishness is defined more in terms of descent than a decision made by the individual.

In the modern period, Abraham scores a hat trick of sorts by becoming the father of not one but three faiths, the so-called Abrahamic religions.[15] It is a curious honor in that, while each traces its lineage back to the patriarch, neither Jews nor Christians nor Muslims refer to themselves as practitioners of "Abrahamic religions." Gotthold Lessing's 1779 play *Nathan the Wise* is one of the earliest and most influential expressions of "Abrahamic" thinking. As a plea for tolerance among these three faiths, united by genealogy and by monotheistic conviction, Lessing's play anticipates the post–World War II preference for "Abrahamic" over the more exclusive "Judeo-Christian." This vaguely defined rubric tends to gloss over or ignore entirely the marked differences between the three Abrahams, such as the Pauline portrait of Abraham as a prototype of righteousness apart from the law and the Muslim notion that he is an exemplar of the pristine, pre-Jewish faith restored by Muhammad.[16] However noble the ecumenical desire to promote harmony among the peoples of the world may be, to treat Abraham as an empty vessel into which one can pour any ideological content that contemporary circumstances demand—as so frequently happens to Jesus, at Paul's expense—nonetheless fails to do full justice to historical realities.

2. Insofar as Judaism emphasizes orthopraxy over orthodoxy, it is natural that Moses is credited by Jews and non-Jews alike with founding Judaism. According to Exodus, he convenes Israel to affirm its role as "a priestly kingdom and a holy nation" (19:6), and it is through Moses at Sinai that they receive the law that defines their polity. When, during the golden calf episode, God threatens to destroy Israel and start anew by making Moses into a great nation—in place of Abraham(!)—Moses persuades him to reconsider (32:7–14). No figure looms as large in the Jewish tradition, and "never since has there arisen a prophet in Israel like Moses" (Deut. 34:10). Moses's flaws, however, are on full display in the Bible, indicating that moral perfection is not a requisite quality for assuming the role of founder. But neither in the Bible nor in later Jewish tradition is he accused of betraying Abraham. Rather, he is portrayed as bringing God's promises to the patriarch one step closer to fruition.

15. E.g., Kritzeck, *Sons of Abraham*; F. E. Peters, *Children of Abraham*; Harries, Solomon, and Winter, *Abraham's Children*; and K. J. Clark, *Abraham's Children*.

16. Levenson, *Inheriting Abraham*, 173–214; and A. W. Hughes, *Abrahamic Religions*.

Rabbinic tradition sees Moses as standing at the head of a long chain of tradents who have preserved the Torah received at Sinai. Nevertheless, it is evident that the faith practiced in ancient Israel and that of later times are not identical. That ancient readers were aware of this is apparent from the talmudic story of Moses being transported from his seat in heaven to the academy of Rabbi Akiba late in the first century CE and understanding nothing the rabbi says (*b. Menaḥot* 29b). When a student asks about his reasoning in a contentious ruling, Akiba replies that it came from the law received by Moses. Shocked but then pleased, Moses returns to heaven with the assurance that the eternal Torah remains alive in the world even as it bears little obvious resemblance to its original form.

Criticism of Moses in antiquity functions as criticism of Judaism as a whole, as few other Jews enjoyed any name recognition at all among non-Jews.[17] Sometimes this criticism, as when Quintilian mentions Moses as the "founder of the Jewish superstition" (3.7.21),[18] expresses political as well as ethnic or religious enmity. A much later commentator on Moses as a religious founder, albeit with an ambivalent relationship to Judaism, is Sigmund Freud.[19] In *Moses and Monotheism*, he claims that Moses is an Egyptian who learns about the one God from the pharaoh Akhenaten but is later murdered by the Hebrews whom he has led out of bondage. Wracked by Oedipal guilt and remorse, they later become loyal sons of the father they have slain by zealously clinging to the law he had bequeathed to them. Freud's theory constitutes a psychoanalytic history of Judaism that fits with his broader ideas about religion as a symptom of underlying neuroses. (Daniel Langton contends that Freud's work is almost as much about the apostle Paul as about Moses in that it attempts to explain how the former midwifed the birth of Christianity by processing the Jewish guilt that had accumulated from the death of the latter.)[20]

3. The Babylonian Talmud says that "had Moses not preceded him, Ezra would have been worthy of receiving the Torah."[21] Given the paucity of historical data about Abraham and Moses, many modern writers are inclined to agree that the fifth-century BCE scribe is the true founder of Judaism.[22] Study of Torah in the synagogues built during and after the Babylonian exile took

17. Charges against Moses, such as charlatanism and deception, include many of those leveled at Paul in antiquity. See Gager, *Moses in Greco-Roman Paganism*.

18. Quintilian, *Institutio Oratoria*, trans. Butler.

19. Yerushalmi, *Freud's Moses*; and Bernstein, *Freud and the Legacy of Moses*.

20. Langton, *Apostle Paul in the Jewish Imagination*, 264–70.

21. *Sanhedrin* 21b, trans. Epstein.

22. Kratz, "Ezra—Priest and Scribe."

on a heightened role after the destruction of the temple in 586 BCE. Scribes gained influence in this context, when many of the books later included in the Jewish canon were written and edited. Ezra guided the community as it faced the erosion of its identity through intermarriage with foreigners. In this role, Ezra was the forerunner of the rabbis of the Mishnah and the Talmud, whose interpretation of Torah has shaped normative Judaism up to the present day. Timing matters too, since it was in Ezra's day that Judaism emerged as distinct from the older Israelite institutions attested in the Bible that did not survive the Assyrian and Babylonian conquests.[23]

Ezra has a higher profile among Jews than among non-Jews, but some scholars wonder about the correlation between the portrait of Ezra as the founder of a legalistic, ethnically exclusive religion and the anti-Semitism endemic to the eighteenth- and nineteenth-century British and German context of the biblical criticism that gave the notion a wider circulation.[24] In his 1885 Bampton Lectures delivered at Oxford, Frederic W. Farrar identified Ezra as the founder of Judaism "as distinct from Mosaism":

> And yet by what a gulf of inferiority is Ezra separated from the mighty Prophets of his race! It is a gulf like that which separates the Bible from the Talmud; the Decalogue from the halakha; the religion of righteousness from the religiosity of Tradition; the freedom of spiritual enlightenment from the pettiness of ceremonialism; the holiness of the heart from the outward holiness of Levitic purifications.[25]

Farrar's characterization of Ezra and his accomplishment is consistent with the habit of labeling the Judaism of the time of Jesus *Spätjudentum,* "late Judaism," carrying the connotation that Judaism reached its zenith with the lofty ethical idealism of the classical prophets and has declined ever after. It was God's will that Jesus play his part "in a decadent epoch, and for a degenerate people."[26] Needless to say, Jews and non-Jews are likely to disagree on whether his role is that of the hero or the villain.

---

23. See Brettler, "Judaism in the Hebrew Bible?"; Kratz, "Ezra—Priest and Scribe," 164. After the construction of the second temple in 515 BCE, Levitical priests sometimes appeal to King David alongside, or even in place of, Moses to legitimate their authority; see De Vries, "Moses and David."

24. Becking, *Ezra, Nehemiah,* 22–23. According to Leora Batnitzky, the German Jewish philosopher Moses Mendelssohn "invents the modern idea that Judaism is a religion" in this period as part of a process that anticipates later debates about cultural assimilation, separation of church and state, and the scope of religious tolerance (*How Judaism Became a Religion,* 13).

25. Farrar, *History of Interpretation,* 51, 53–54; "The Judaism which he established was far inferior to the true Hebraic spirit" (56).

26. Ibid., 56.

Islam

"Muhammad is not the founder of Islam." This statement is a regular refrain in English-language literature about Islam. Non-Muslims who say that Muhammad founded a religion called Islam generally mean no offense, but Muslims find it necessary to correct what they see as a serious misconception. Muhammad was a prophet with a message to deliver, and that message marks him as a reformer seeking to restore a religion that had been lost or corrupted. Because this religion is as old as creation, properly speaking its founder is God. It is inappropriate to conceive of Muhammad as a founder because he did not add anything to Islam, the path of submission to which the Qur'an calls all of humanity. He is the last of the prophets, not the first. And while Muhammad is called the first "submitter" or "devoted one" (*muslim*: 6:14; 39:12), the Qur'an also refers to earlier individuals such as Noah, Abraham, Ishmael, Moses, and the disciples of Jesus as "Muslims" (2:128, 131; 3:52, 67; 5:111; 7:143).

Muhammad's status as founder raises questions beyond those of chronology: Did he establish a religion, or something more comprehensive like a culture or a civilization? "Islam is not a religion" is another refrain one often hears from both Muslims and critics of Islam alike, albeit for very different reasons.[27] For Muslims, it is a *din*, a "way of life" that is pursued in obedience to divine law (Qur'an 1:4; 4:46; 9:11; 22:78). Religion cannot and must not be restricted to a discrete sphere in society or in the life of the individual. Any attempt to separate the sacred from the secular is not in keeping with the designs of the prophet. (This illegitimate way of thinking is sometimes traced back to Paul.)[28] For this reason it does not trouble Muslims, as it does some non-Muslims, that Muhammad acts variously as prophet, lawgiver, statesman, and military leader.

The Qur'an constantly reminds the reader that Muhammad is only a messenger and as such should not be confused with the message (3:144). He is not presented as a perfect human being. Yet the first pillar of Islam, the *Shahāda*, declares not simply that there is only one God but that Muhammad is his prophet as well. Moreover, in later Islamic tradition one finds the image of Muhammad as "exemplar of humanity par excellence."[29] Is this a necessary function of his position at the origins of Islam in the early seventh century, or is it incidental, appearing only later as part of Muslim efforts to present Muhammad as a prophet comparable or superior to Jesus? Does it preclude

---

27. See Ernst, *Following Muhammad*, 67–69; and Shedinger, *Radically Open*, 76–77.
28. Attas, *Islām*, 25–26.
29. Schimmel, *And Muhammad Is His Messenger*, 235.

the possibility that he made errors that had to be "corrected" later, either by his followers or already within the pages of the Qur'an through the process of abrogation? For example, did Jesus and Muhammad believe the world would end in their lifetimes, and are the true foundings of Christianity and Islam thus to be located in the attempts of their respective followers to come to terms with their "mistakes"?[30] Is the importance of the prophet's example (*sunnah*) limited to matters of behavior, or does it include any and all matters of theological substance such that any "development" is forbidden?[31]

The authority of the prophet's *sunnah* and the manner in which it is transmitted have proved to be especially thorny issues. In fact, divergent understandings of what forms the basis for fidelity to the vision of Muhammad inform one of the most momentous divisions in the history of Islam. Upon his death, Muhammad had no male offspring to whom he might pass on the mantle of leadership. Abū Bakr had been appointed to lead communal prayer in Muhammad's absence and was chosen as the first caliph soon after the prophet's death. The notion that there should be a successor to Muhammad and that he should be drawn from the circle of Muhammad's companions did not go unchallenged by Muhammad's relatives, "the people of the house," who believed that succession should be based on heredity. The latter group claimed that Muhammad had designated 'Alī, Muhammad's cousin and son-in-law by marriage to his daughter Fāṭima, as the rightful successor. 'Alī's supporters—who add "and 'Alī is the saint of God" when reciting the *Shahāda*—form the Shī'ite sect of Islam. Their beliefs about the spiritual endowments of the murdered 'Alī are sometimes deemed *ghulūw* (exaggeration) by the Sunni majority.

As a result of this political conflict, Sunnis and Shī'ites regard different texts as forging a trustworthy link to the prophet. Both groups rely on the hadith literature, containing volumes of tradition relating to non-Qur'anic deeds and sayings of the prophet. A critical component of the hadith material is the *isnād*, the chain of authorities attesting to the tradition's authenticity. Shī'ites do not trust a chain of attestors that goes back to Abū Bakr. By far the most prolific narrator of hadith traditions is Abū Hurayrah, a companion of Muhammad with an allegedly infallible memory. Shī'ite commentators regard the honor accorded him by Sunni Muslims as evidence of how far they have veered from the right path because Abū Hurayrah was an enemy of 'Alī and

---

30. Shoemaker, *Death of a Prophet*, 118–96. When the end failed to arrive on schedule, according to Shoemaker, "the meaning of Muhammad's message and the faith that he established had to be fundamentally rethought by his early followers" (267).

31. On the differences between the Christian concept of *imitatio Christi* and the Islamic idea of the prophet's *sunnah* and its use in criticizing Paul, see Reynolds, *Muslim Theologian*, 112–17.

a convert from sun worship who spent only a few years in the prophet's company. In popular sectarian discourse he is regularly and explicitly compared to the apostle Paul as an example of one who has superseded in influence those who were closer to the prophet and has thereby corrupted the religion.[32]

Christianity

Most Christian denominations recognize a founding figure to whom members pay varying degrees of honor and respect. Intra-Christian arguments about origins in connection with denominational theology and policy tend to hinge less on the invocation of these founders themselves than on certain foundational principles. Methodism is a case in point. Traveling preacher George Whitefield was called the founder of Methodism by his contemporaries as often as John Wesley.[33] The two fell out over the doctrine of predestination, with Whitefield following Calvinist teachings and Wesley remaining staunchly Arminian. They healed the breach before they died, however, and it is exceedingly rare to hear modern Methodists appeal to one over against the other in settling denominational disputes.

Issues of a different sort arise when a leader, whose status as founder is not contested, is responsible for views or actions that later followers find objectionable or embarrassing. Even the proudest Lutheran, for example, would squirm at some of the things Luther says in his voluminous writings, no matter how dedicated one might be to the principle of *sola scriptura* or the doctrine of justification by faith. To what extent do Lutherans feel obliged to mount a defense? It is a delicate matter to disavow the founder's words or deeds and still claim him as one's own. Is it possible to reject Luther on "Lutheran" or more broadly Protestant principles? Do his flaws in some measure delegitimize the movement he started, or is the movement independent of the prime mover? Would it be convenient to have an alternate authority whose precedents the faithful might consult in order to meet the perceived exigencies of the present while maintaining continuity with the past? Or does this only complicate matters, a case of too many cooks spoiling the proverbial broth?

Mormon history features controversies that illustrate a number of these issues. Joseph Smith is universally recognized as the founder of the Church of Jesus Christ of Latter-Day Saints (LDS)—except by members of smaller groups like the Strangites and the Reorganized Church of Jesus Christ of Latter-Day Saints, which regard the mainstream church headquartered in

32. Juynboll, *Authenticity of the Tradition Literature*, 62–99.
33. Lawson, "Who Founded Methodism?," 45–48.

Utah as the product of Brigham Young's usurpation of the position rightfully belonging to Smith's son. Apart from the allegations of immorality that have been made about both Smith and Young, their positions on polygamy and on racial equality have been the source of considerable conflict both within the Mormon world and with the rest of American society, which saw the distinctive Mormon practices in these areas as, respectively, bizarre and discriminatory. Plural marriage was officially repudiated in 1890 as part of Utah's campaign for statehood, a decision seen by many Mormon groups as an assimilationist act of apostasy on the part of Smith's supposed successors. Black males were finally admitted to the Aaronic priesthood in 1978, and only recently has the LDS hierarchy publicly disavowed Young's policy and his justifications for it.[34] Not only is this an admission, however muted, of a break in the continuity between the founder and a towering figure of the church, but it is unusual in that it takes the form of an official statement.

Few denominations feature the same vitriol as one sees in some corners of Mormonism. The ferocity of any debates revolving around the status of a denomination's founders is usually tempered somewhat by the tacit agreement among all parties that Jesus is the only "founder" that ultimately matters. This is not to say that the disputants are not eager to align their own construal of their founder's teachings with those of Jesus. But the rhetoric of such debates is different from many others in that originality is subordinated to fidelity, and any innovation is couched in terms of restoration.

As this survey demonstrates, Paul and Jesus are not alone in being placed at odds, either by their coreligionists or by those looking on from the outside. Nor is Christianity the only religion whose beginnings are entangled with later questions about ethnic identity or political conflict. Other traditions have their villains, though none perhaps who have had to shoulder more of the blame for supposedly destroying the foundation laid by one's predecessor. When Paul is singled out for his role in any process of perceived decline, he is portrayed more often as an active agent than as a helpless pawn in some cosmic scheme.

The dynamics at play in these debates are not quite unique to religion. Certain philosophers have founded schools with members anxious to protect the legacy of their teachers with a quasi-religious zeal from those who would traduce or misappropriate it. Almost from the moment of his execution, different schools staked their claim to most faithfully embody the spirit of Socrates, the father of Western philosophy. Plato emerged as his most

---

34. D. V. Mason, *Brigham Young*, 142.

influential interpreter, but critics abounded in his own lifetime. Antisthenes, Aristippus, and Diogenes the Cynic accused Plato of distorting Socrates's ideas (Diogenes Laertius, *Lives of Eminent Philosophers* 3.35–36). In the aftermath of World War II, Karl Popper declared that Plato had betrayed his teacher by attributing to him in *The Republic* Plato's own totalitarian theories, "and he had no difficulty in succeeding, for Socrates was dead."[35] The Young Hegelians in the nineteenth century engaged in similarly acrimonious debate about the sense in which Hegel believed that the dialectic of history had reached its conclusion. (It seems not to have occurred that, by the terms of his own system, whatever thesis Hegel might have formulated would inevitably generate its own antithesis, resulting in a synthesis that would by necessity differ from what Hegel originally taught.) Karl Marx was one of these Young Hegelians whose own followers would later fight among themselves as to whether Marxism was viable in its original form and who was most qualified to defend or adapt his philosophy to new situations.[36]

A key difference between such secular examples and debates that have religious founders as their focal point has to do with age and accessibility. By and large, the putative founders of the major religions are ancient history. So far back in the hoary past are Abraham, Laozi, and the Buddha that there are reasonable doubts about whether they ever lived. At the very least, the great distance separating them from the present makes it difficult to know what they taught with any certainty. On this score, Christianity and Islam are closer to each other than to any of the other religions. Conspiracy theories to the contrary notwithstanding, it is not only certain that Jesus, Paul, and Muhammad were real historical figures, but it is also possible to date their careers with relative precision. Scholars who study early Christianity and Islam are the envy of those who study other religions for the quantity and quality of the primary sources available. The state of the sources may engender an unwarranted degree of confidence that the histories of early Christianity and Islam can be reconstructed in minute detail and then used to locate various ideas and events with respect to the trajectory established by scholars. It is therefore more common to hear accusations to the effect that Paul or one of the early caliphs deviated from the narrow path mapped out by Jesus or Muhammad.

This misplaced confidence partly explains the vituperativeness of Paul's critics. If we can so clearly see the vast difference between what Jesus and

---

35. Popper, *Open Society*, 1:194.

36. McLellan, *Young Hegelians*. Most recently, see Eagleton, *Why Marx Was Right*. Paul Lafargue, Marx's own son-in-law, propounded a version of Marxism that led Marx to proclaim, "If anything is certain it is that I am not a Marxist" (quoted in an 1882 letter from Friedrich Engels to Eduard Bernstein). See Balibar, *Philosophy of Marx*, 116.

Paul taught (so the argument seems to go), then surely Paul was aware of it too. And if Paul was aware of it and yet persisted in his error, then the only explanation must be hypocrisy, dishonesty, self-interest, or some other ethical defect. For these critics, to grant that Paul was sincere but mistaken is not an option. To justify their views, they also lay claim to the support of various participants in the "succession" struggles of early Christianity and Islam such as James or Barnabas or one of Muhammad's widows. Critics who maintain that Paul unknowingly transmogrified the message of Jesus do not pass moral judgment yet still assume—oblivious to the effects of confirmation bias—that the existing body of knowledge about Jesus is sufficiently complete as to permit authoritative and incontrovertible repudiations of Pauline teaching.

In Christianity, as in Islam, divine revelation tends to be mediated through discrete events and identifiable personages. General theological principles occupy an important place, but historical particularities play a proportionately larger role, at least in comparison with the other major religious traditions. This holds true even though the "scandal of particularity" makes Christian claims appear irrational in the eyes of Christianity's opponents. Human history is of greater metaphysical consequence for Christians than it is for Daoists and Buddhists. This ineluctably historical character in part accounts for the vigor with which Paul's place in that history is contested. From the earliest period, Christian writers cite the chain of witnesses going back to the time of Jesus who authenticate the church's teaching. That Paul himself is the earliest known writer to pursue this strategy—telling the Corinthians that he is delivering to them what he had received from Peter and the other apostles (1 Cor. 11:23–26; 15:1–11)—has eluded some of his latter-day detractors. Others recognize his role in shaping this form of Christian discourse but either (a) distrust him as a participant in it or (b) believe that he is simultaneously devious enough to hijack the nascent movement by manipulating its official narrative yet too slow to anticipate that later historians would be able to deconstruct that narrative and hoist him by his own petard. Do these critics spurn the message because of the one who bears it, or do they shoot the messenger because of their distaste for the news he brings? Is it possible that Paul's critics themselves are unsure of the answer?

CONCLUSION

What We Talk about When We Talk about Paul

After listening to the many voices in this admittedly one-sided survey, one may come down on the side of Paul's critics, suspecting that where there is so much smoke, there must be fire. Or one may conclude that Paul is a truth speaker who escapes Jesus's condemnation: "Woe unto you, when all men shall speak well of you, for so did their fathers to the false prophets" (Luke 6:26 KJV). In any event, if he is to be spit out, it will not be because he has provoked only lukewarm reactions (Rev. 3:16). Judging from his remarks in 1 Cor. 1:18–25, Paul would not be terribly surprised to learn that he had made his share of enemies. By preaching "Christ crucified," a "stumbling block to Jews and foolishness to Gentiles" (1 Cor. 1:23), Paul proclaimed a message that struck a sour note with every imaginable demographic since every human being falls into one group or the other. In 2 Cor. 2:15–16 he expresses the same point by means of an olfactory metaphor: "For we are the aroma of Christ to God among those who are being saved and among those who are perishing; to the one a fragrance from death to death, to the other a fragrance from life to life." Paul knows that his message puts him in bad odor with many of the very people he wants to reach.

It scarcely seems possible to organize these voices into a harmonious choir inasmuch as they so often sing from such different hymnals. A more suitable coda might be to construct a provisional taxonomy of anti-Paulinism. Any such taxonomy might sort Paul's critics into the following categories.

Paul the pagan. This is one of the earliest attacks and turns one of Paul's supposed strengths back against him. His success in attracting non-Jews to the messianist movement is perceived as coming at the expense of his fidelity to Torah. In its strong form, found among medieval and contemporary Muslims, Jewish-Christian groups in the second century, and some modern Jewish scholars such as Hyam Maccoby, this critique alleges that Paul is lying when he claims to be a Jew or that he intends to "Romanize" the gospel of Jesus the Jewish messiah by converting it into a polytheistic cult. In its softer form, as one sees at various points in Jewish history, Paul is not an anti-Jewish schemer; he simply, but disastrously, "goes native" in his overly enthusiastic outreach to the gentiles.

Paul the Judaizer. These critics seem to be talking about someone other than the Paul described by those in the previous category. Here Paul is faulted for taking the message of universal salvation proclaimed by Jesus and "re-Judaizing" it. This stance was also assumed by many Muslim writers in the medieval period as well as by modern writers such as Friedrich Nietzsche. Sundry anti-Semites, most notoriously Adolf Hitler, also leveled this charge, frequently combining it with abstruse racial theories asserting that Jesus was not Jewish.

Paul the libertine. Early Jewish interlocutors criticized Paul's attitude toward the Mosaic law partly on the grounds that it does away with the law's ethical obligations and thus encourages immorality, highlighting the contrast with Jesus's heightening of its moral demands in the Sermon on the Mount. Non-Jewish critics often took up this charge as well, characterizing his cavalier dismissal of behavioral criteria for salvation as a form of cheap grace. Modern observers are far more likely to fall into the next category.

Paul the moralizer. He denigrates the pleasures of the flesh, especially those related to sexuality. Hardly a libertine, Paul is a prude of the highest order. It would be one thing if Paul restricted his puritanical code to his own affairs, but he has to impose it on others. He is not just a moralist; he is moralistic. The touchstone for this anti-Paulinism also happens to come from the Sermon on the Mount: "Judge not, that ye be not judged" (Matt. 7:1 KJV). (So off-putting is this perceived judgmentalism that, when discussing Paul's prescription for the man "living with his father's wife" in 1 Cor. 5:1–13, many students are willing to overlook the near-universal taboo on incest because Paul is unwilling to offer the forgiveness they believe Jesus would demand.)

Paul the propagandist. For some critics, Paul has been the source of misery on a vast scale by urging his readers to "be subject to the governing authorities" (Rom. 13:1) and thus lending support to the imperialist state in its exercise of hegemony over the spiritual realm. Others see him as depoliticizing the radical message of Jesus and substituting for it an otherworldly faith that neuters the gospel.

Paul the misogynist. An educated guess: today, roughly half of Paul's readers in the West will listen to nothing he says because of his attitude toward women. Although the thought probably occurred earlier, it went virtually unexpressed—in writing, at any rate—until the nineteenth century.

Paul the neurotic. Paul's views on sex, women, and many other matters are frequently attributed to some form of mental illness. His propensity to experience visions, along with his willingness to stake his authority on their validity, has been regarded by many as confirmation that he was in the grips of psychosis or some other derangement. The heightened sensitivity to and sympathy for those afflicted by personality disorders, however, is rarely extended to Paul.

Paul the teacher. Specific doctrines traced to Paul's letters are the bane of many commentators. Among these are original sin, the Trinity, the atonement, and his obsession with the death and resurrection of Jesus to the near exclusion of his earthly ministry of teaching and healing. His lack of patience and charity with those who would disagree with him demonstrates a reprehensible exclusivism in doctrinal matters, leading many in an age that values pluralism to concur with Will Durant when he states that "Fundamentalism is the triumph of Paul over Christ."[1] The heavy emphasis he places on theological rectitude also squelches the freedom desired by those who describe themselves as "spiritual but not religious."

Paul the hypocrite. That Paul contradicts himself repeatedly in his letters is bad enough.[2] More exasperating is the inconsistency many sense between his words and his deeds. His chameleon-like flexibility in becoming "all things to all men" (1 Cor. 9:22 RSV), which results in egregious instances of hypocrisy, is not excused by his critics on the grounds that he thereby saves some of his listeners. "For all his talk of weakness and identification with the cross," according to Graham Shaw, "it is by no means clear that he stands with the crucified. There is a horrid suspicion that he ultimately stands with those prepared to crucify in order to defend and preserve their position."[3]

While this list is by no means exhaustive, it covers the main lines of the anti-Pauline argument over the centuries. Much of the case against Paul is argued cogently and merits serious consideration. At the same time, more

1. Durant, *Caesar and Christ*, 592.
2. J. C. Beker ("Paul's Theology") attempts to defend Paul by distinguishing between the coherent themes of his letters and their contingent applications, though one wonders whether Paul would balk at which elements are classified as merely "contingent." Heikki Räisänen (*Paul and the Law*) argues that Paul's comments on the law are full of contradictory statements that cannot be reconciled.
3. G. Shaw, *Cost of Authority*, 213–14.

than a little of it is shrill and over the top when it is not oversimplified and incoherent. And it is not only to the work of the nonscholars that this applies. When one hears NT scholar Gerd Lüdemann liken Jesus to Paul as superstar to supernova and propose that "Christianity as we know it began in the empty center of a red supergiant that imploded somewhere along the hot, dusty road to Damascus," or French philosopher Michel Onfray assert that Jesus was little more than an "invisible ectoplasm" or a "concept" fleshed out according to "the ravings of a hysteric" with a "hatred of intelligence" who created the world in his own image, "a deplorable image, fanatical, . . . sick, misogynistic, masochistic," one may be pardoned for asking: With enemies like these, who needs friends?[4]

Toward a Solution?

There is a substantial convergence between those who are critical of Paul's legacy and those who consider him to be the founder of Christianity. Rarely is he granted this title in a positive or even a neutral sense. It normally signals the idea that his "founding" was an illicit accomplishment and that historic Christianity in its traditional forms is corrupt to a lesser or greater degree. Many others find fault with his teachings without suggesting that he is the founder, though these critics tend to have much less in common with others who explicitly reject the role of founder for Paul. "Founder" is as much a theological category as it is a purely descriptive term for historical realities. Implicit in its application to any one person, whether Jesus or Paul, is the claim—still a matter of dispute in this case—that something new has begun. Taking that title away from Jesus and giving it to Paul understandably upsets many Christians. And yet the classic creeds of the church, quintessentially theological documents even when they make claims about history, nowhere refer to Jesus as founder.

The range of options available for settling the matter is somewhat limited. One option is to endorse the view of the many writers appearing in the preceding chapters that Paul, and not Jesus, is the founder of Christianity. To sustain this position, one must overlook the fact that there is ample evidence for the early spread of Christianity to Rome, North Africa, Syria, Cyprus, and other areas untouched by the Pauline mission network. It is also inconvenient that the author of Luke-Acts, usually assumed to be Paul's chief publicist, not only testifies to the existence of non-Pauline forms of the faith among gentiles but

4. Lüdemann, *Paul*, 246; Onfray, *Atheist Manifesto*, 131–39.

also provides more information about the family of Jesus—including James, Paul's main rival according to second-century anti-Pauline documents—than do the other Gospels. Furthermore, differences between the Gospels and Paul's letters are taken as proof that Paul has deviated from Jesus's teachings, but when the two bodies of literature are found to be in fundamental harmony, it is often explained away by positing Pauline influence on one or more of the Gospels. Nullifying evidence contrary to the hypothesis that Paul founded Christianity in this manner begins to resemble a game of "heads I win, tails you lose."

This solution, moreover, tends to gloss too lightly over the many jarring statements Jesus makes. He describes with great relish, for example, the fate of those who will be cast into the outer darkness where "there will be weeping and gnashing of teeth" (Matt. 8:12; 13:42, 50; 22:13; 24:51; 25:30; Luke 13:28). He talks about hell more than anyone else in the Bible. He refers to a gentile woman as a "dog" and to Peter as "Satan" (Matt. 15:26; 16:23). He speaks in parables despite—or, on account of (Mark 4:11–12)—their incomprehensibility to outsiders. He declares certain sins unforgivable (Luke 12:10). In the meantime, Paul is never given the benefit of the doubt when he says something harsh or appears to contradict Jesus. When one examines the long list of discrepancies that David Wenham and others feel compelled to address in order to defend Paul against charges of perfidy, it boggles the mind.[5] Yes, Jesus and Paul were reared in different settings, but they also had a lot in common.[6] It strains credulity that Paul's teachings could have been so antithetical to those of Jesus on so many matters both great and small unless he were deliberately trying to contradict him, auditioning, in a manner of speaking, for the role of the antichrist. After all, if it had been Paul's intention to found a new religion, Jacques Ellul wonders, "why, among so many thaumaturges, prophets, and rebels, did he select a defeated wretch of twenty-five years back, and then, instead of echoing his teaching, make of it something totally different?"[7] It is one thing to be skeptical of efforts to align Paul with Jesus. It is quite another to willfully misunderstand him. Such comparisons throw Paul into sharper relief and thus produce an effective foil, but these selectively drawn portraits may be a function of confirmation bias to which even the most conscientious interpreters are susceptible.

5. Wenham, *Paul*; Wenham, *Did St. Paul Get Jesus Right?* See also Dodd, *Problem with Paul*. Wenham provides the most thorough analysis of the exegetical dimension of the problem in English.

6. On the biographical parallels, see Murphy-O'Connor, *Jesus and Paul*. On the methodological and theological ramifications, see Wedderburn, "Paul and Jesus."

7. Ellul, *Subversion of Christianity*, 119.

Also noteworthy is the common ground this approach shares with certain strands of Protestantism that place the doctrine of justification at the center of the faith. Martin Luther's "canon within the canon" consisted of Paul's letters, and any compromise of his theology threatens doom for Christendom, as Paul and apparently Paul alone resisted the call for imposing the obligations of Torah on the gentiles. On this score, Christianity stands or falls with Paul under the terms of this tacit consensus affirmed by his admirers as well as his detractors. Unnoticed by both sides is the way in which this manner of framing the issue implicitly affirms the Great Man theory of history. Thomas Carlyle's aphorism that "the history of the world is but the biography of great men" concisely expresses the theory's operating principle.[8] Proponents of *nouvelle histoire*, "People's History," and "history from below" view this approach, which held sway in the nineteenth century, as elitist and oversimplified.[9] Whatever the merits of these newer schools of thought, it is peculiar to find writers who on other grounds may be inclined to reject the Great Man theory making an apparent exception in the case of Paul.[10]

A second option is to think of Paul as the "accidental" founder. In this scenario, he would not be unique in the history of religions.[11] Were it not for the ascendency of the Pharisees after the destruction of the temple in 70 CE, coupled with the decline of the Sadducees and of the militant nationalism associated with the Zealots that had sparked the Jewish revolt, it is conceivable that Paul, who had died only a few years earlier, would never have assumed such a central place in Christian thinking. The Pharisaic emphasis on the interpretation of Torah, unlike the more priestly and political orientations of other Jewish groups, translated into greater adaptability and relevance in the post-70 situation and pitted the Pharisees against the other sectarian

---

8. Carlyle, *On Heroes*, 21. "Universal History, the history of what man has accomplished in this world, is at bottom the History of the Great Men who have worked here . . . ; all things that we see standing accomplished in the world are properly the outer material result, the practical realisation and embodiment, of Thoughts that dwelt in the Great Men sent into the world" (ibid., 1). Carlyle discusses Muhammad but makes only one passing reference to Jesus and omits Paul entirely.

9. Cf. Burke, *New Perspectives on Historical Writing*; and Horsley, "Unearthing a People's History."

10. Leo Tolstoy is perhaps the most famous example. Throughout book 10 of *War and Peace* Tolstoy criticizes the Great Man theory in his comments on the Napoleonic Wars. Men like Napoleon imagine that they are the prime movers in history, but they are all "involuntary tools of history." To believe that Russia and France have been "shaped by the will of one man" is "not merely untrue and irrational, but contrary to all human reality" (*War and Peace*, 761, 874–75). A few years later, however, he places the blame for the corruption of Jesus's teachings squarely on Paul (*My Religion*, 219).

11. Hans Dieter Betz further notes that in most cases where there is evidence of conscious planning to start a new religion, the "founder" failed ("Paul's Ideas," 274–75).

group that survived the destruction of Jerusalem—the messianists. A recurring feature of Paul's writings is theoretical reflection on the status of the law. The survival of so many of his letters relative to other Christian writers may be incidental, a function of the increased relevance they were thought to possess late in the first century when they and the Pharisees were the fierce rivals in their respective claims to represent fidelity to Torah.

A variation of the "accidental founder" solution is to describe Paul as an innovator who, in his formation of local groups of worshipers, came up with a successful "franchise" or "business model" that eventually dominated a key sector of the market.[12] Pauline faith communities thus became "Christianity" in this view, though by no design of his own. Or one might extend the analogy suggested by Margaret M. Mitchell's incisive portrayal of Paul's relationship with the Corinthians and its role in "the birth of Christian hermeneutics" and decide that "father" (or "mother"?) is more fitting than "founder"—in which case Christianity is, figuratively speaking, the result of an unplanned pregnancy that many wish had been terminated. Absent the conflict and misunderstandings their correspondence reflected and engendered, she argues, the ideas about Jesus that coalesce into Christian doctrine might never have come to expression.[13]

A third option is to deny the claim that Paul should be considered the founder. This denial can assume multiple forms. Following the cue of New Perspective scholars like John Gager and Pamela Eisenbaum (see chap. 6), one can reclaim Paul as a Jew and reject the label "Christian" as not simply anachronistic but as an insidious distortion of his true values and beliefs. This reading attempts to salvage Paul by absolving him of anti-Judaism. But to an extent it also intersects with the anti-Paulinism that serves as a proxy critique of Christianity insofar as it appears to presuppose or insinuate that Christianity, as it has been typically understood by its adherents, is indeed anti-Jewish at a fundamental level and that it is illegitimate to invoke Paul in support of its central tenets.

This strategy inevitably entails distinguishing Paul from the "Paul" of the six disputed letters. The evidence against their Pauline authorship may in some cases be slightly overstated, and the certitude of the broad consensus that Paul wrote only the seven undisputed letters is not entirely warranted given the range of unknown factors at work in their composition. Many

12. For an interpretation of Paul's missionary activity along the lines of an organizer of civic or cultic associations, see Hanges, *Paul, Founder of Churches*.

13. M. M. Mitchell, *Birth of Christian Hermeneutics*, 5: For Paul, Jesus Christ is the foundation, but "the foundation itself is set in words; it lies on a scriptural subfloor without which Jesus Christ crucified would be an unmarked grave under an undeveloped plot."

scholars—though virtually no other readers until Schleiermacher at the beginning of the nineteenth century—find it hard to believe that the same person who wrote Romans and Galatians also wrote the more quotidian dispatches that come down to posterity as 1 Timothy and 2 Thessalonians.[14] It is as much an aesthetic or even a theological observation as it is a literary one, as if there were an unwritten but immutable law of nature that genius will always make itself known and can never be suppressed. Students of literature know better. Odd as it may seem, the same person responsible for such exercises in mediocrity as *Henry VI, Part III* and *Titus Andronicus* also wrote *Hamlet* and *Macbeth*. Critics who cannot fathom that Paul was capable of the profound insights into human nature that one finds in Rom. 7 and also the bourgeois platitudes of the household codes in Colossians, or the exquisite poetry of 1 Cor. 13 and also the tangled syntax of Galatians (2:3–5; 4:14; 5:11), too quickly forget that unevenness plagues even the very best thinkers and writers.

The charged tone of many "reclamations" of the historical Paul belies their self-presentation as sober historical analysis.[15] It is customary to speak of reclaiming something only when it has been illegitimately expropriated. Couching the scholarly task in these terms signals a recognition that Paul is too important to be left on the sideline in the cultural contests of the day. Either he is for us or he is against us. Neither side can let go of him for fear of the mischief he might make on behalf of the other. Paul's despisers often start from a stance of antipathy toward established Christian tradition and then labor to assign the deficiencies to him instead of to Jesus. "There is usually even in the most emancipated minds a feeling that Jesus was probably right," Henry J. Cadbury says of modern portraits of Jesus, to which many would add, "and that Paul was wrong." "We so easily assume our own approach is the right one, and therefore that a person of Jesus's insight must have shared it," he continues, and as with the widespread admiration for Jesus, one has reason to infer that the attendant disapproval of Paul "contains so often a quite unintentional self-flattery."[16] However tempting it is to compare the reception of Paul to the reception of Jesus and observe that, just as readers tend to project their most cherished ideals onto Jesus, they project their worst grievances onto Paul, the antiparallel is not quite so precise. Nevertheless, sure knowledge about the aims and assumptions of Jesus and Paul is sufficiently scarce that

14. "Never was a writer more unequal," writes Ernst Renan. "One may seek in vain throughout the realm of literature for a phenomenon as bizarre as that of a sublime passage like the thirteenth chapter of the First Epistle to the Corinthians by the side of feeble arguments, laborious repetitions, and fastidious subtleties" (*Apostles*, 164).

15. E.g., Borg and Crossan, *First Paul*.

16. Cadbury, *Peril of Modernizing Jesus*, 37–38.

both figures become free-floating signifiers, and that as a consequence, the reactions they provoke are sometimes reminiscent of a Rorschach test.

In contradistinction to this construal, one may resist the "founder" label and argue that Paul, though different from Jesus in many respects, maintains a creative fidelity to his person and to the proclamation of the early church. This position is more commonly held by thinkers on the traditionalist end of the theological spectrum. There are noteworthy exceptions, however, such as self-described Christian anarchist Jacques Ellul and Rudolf Bultmann, NT scholar and great bugbear of conservative theologians.[17] Here one sees a range of opinion on the degree of material correspondence between Jesus and Paul. Differences are plentiful, especially when they are highlighted in isolation rather than in context. But the level of continuity is likewise impressive. Whether the differences are so great as to constitute flat-out contradictions, once historical-cultural context and rhetorical strategy are taken into account, remains a matter of ongoing debate, as does the question of whether such differences and discontinuities rise to a threshold at which Paul becomes the true founder of Christianity.

N. T. Wright can tolerate more disparity than many other defenders of Paul because, he explains, Jesus and Paul saw themselves as called to play special, but not identical, roles in an eschatological drama.

> If Paul had simply trotted out, parrot-fashion, every line of Jesus's teaching—if he had repeated the parables, if he had tried to do again what Jesus did in announcing and inaugurating the kingdom—he would not have been endorsing Jesus, as an appropriate and loyal follower should. He would have been denying him. Someone who copies exactly what a would-be Messiah does is himself trying to be a Messiah.[18]

Although he would put it differently, it seems that Bultmann would assent, as would more conservative writers like J. Gresham Machen. Paul regards Jesus as a redeemer who succeeded in completing his mission; therefore, if Jesus was not in fact a redeemer, "then Paul was no true follower of Jesus, but the follower of a new religion."[19] This cohort candidly faces the fact that any resolution of the "Jesus-Paul debate" is, perhaps inextricably, linked to one's estimation—acceptance or rejection—of Paul's message concerning Jesus. Adjudication of the interpretive disputes is to some degree an inherently

17. Ellul, *Subversion of Christianity*, 5–6, 117–20. On Bultmann, see Furnish, "Jesus-Paul Debate," 37–39.

18. N. T. Wright, *What Saint Paul Really Said*, 180–81.

19. Machen, *Origin of Paul's Religion*, 167–68.

subjective affair, and it may be that the most crucial questions are unanswerable, all the more so in light of shifting scholarly judgments over time.[20]

Notwithstanding the many claims that he acts out of ignorance or bad faith, Paul consistently emphasizes his continuity with Jesus. He is building on the "foundation" that is Jesus Christ rather than laying a separate one (1 Cor. 3:10–11). Continuity, however, need not preclude any and all development or adaptation of Jesus's teachings. Before "What would Jesus do?" it appears that Paul's instinct was to ask, "What would Jesus have his disciples do in light of his death and glorious resurrection?" Had Paul been more specific when he advised the Corinthians, "Be imitators of me, as I am of Christ" (1 Cor. 11:1), it might be easier to discern how closely the answers to these two questions are connected. To insist that Paul fundamentally misunderstood or misrepresented Jesus in a way that eluded most (though not all) readers much closer to the sources in terms of language, culture, and worldview is to employ a hermeneutics of suspicion that may on occasion require more faith than Paul's critics realize.

Settling the matter of Paul's relationship with Jesus has absorbed the time, energy, and emotion of countless thinkers over the centuries. Like the Manhattan Project, which produced the atomic bomb, or the Apollo program, which put a man on the moon, this undertaking has provided many ancillary benefits for the church and the academy. At times, it has also proceeded from misplaced priorities and generated collateral damage of a sort that has not always been unanticipated or unwelcomed. There is much to be learned by listening to Paul's critics, even if it is not always what his gainsayers think.

---

20. S. G. Wilson, "From Jesus to Paul," 17–21. Wilson comments that the issues have been debated most thoroughly in the academy, "which is probably just as well for it would not do to have people's beliefs subject to the vagaries of scholarly fashion" (19).

BIBLIOGRAPHY

Aaronovitch, David. *Voodoo Histories: The Role of the Conspiracy Theory in Shaping Modern History*. New York: Riverhead, 2010.

Adams, Dickinson W. *Jefferson's Extracts from the Gospels: The Philosophy of Jesus and the Life and Morals of Jesus*. Princeton: Princeton University Press, 1983.

Agnew, Francis H. "The Origin of the NT Apostle-Concept: A Review of Research." *Journal of Biblical Literature* 105 (1986): 75–96.

Alexander, Loveday C. A. "What If Luke Had Never Met Theophilus?" In Exum, *Virtual History and the Bible*, 161–70.

Allison, Dale C., Jr. "James 2:14–26: Polemic against Paul, Apology for James." In *Ancient Perspectives on Paul*, edited by Tobias Nicklas, Andreas Merkt, and Joseph Verheyden, 123–49. Göttingen: Vandenhoeck & Ruprecht, 2013.

Almog, Shmuel. "The Racial Motif in Renan's Attitude toward Judaism and the Jews." *Zion* 32 (1967): 175–200.

Almond, Philip C. *The British Discovery of Buddhism*. Cambridge: Cambridge University Press, 1988.

Annet, Peter. *The History and Character of St. Paul, Examined*. London: F. Page, n.d.

Anthony, Sean W. "The Composition of Sayf b. 'Umar's Account of King Paul and His Corruption of Ancient Christianity." *Der Islam* 85, no. 1 (2008): 164–202.

Antonakes, Michael. "Christ, Kazantzakis, and Controversy in Greece." In *God's Struggler: Religion in the Writings of Nikos Kazantzakis*, edited by Darren J. N. Middleton and Peter Bien, 23–35. Macon, GA: Mercer University Press, 1996.

Ariel, Yaakov. "Christianity through Reform Eyes: Kaufmann Kohler's Scholarship on Christianity." *American Jewish History* 89 (2001): 181–91.

Aslan, Reza. *Zealot: The Life and Times of Jesus of Nazareth*. New York: Random House, 2013.

211

'Ata ur-Rahim, Muhammad, and Ahmad Thomson. *Jesus, Prophet of Islam*. London: Ta-Ha, 1996.

Attas, Syed Muhammad Naquib al-. *Islām, Secularism and the Philosophy of the Future*. London: Mansell, 1985.

Augustine, Saint. *The Confessions*. Translated by Maria Boulding. Hyde Park, NY: New City, 1997.

Aune, David E., ed. *Rereading Paul Together: Protestant and Catholic Perspectives on Justification*. Grand Rapids: Baker Academic, 2006.

Ayoub, Mahmoud. "Muslim Views of Christianity." *Islamochristiana* 10 (1984): 49–70.

Bacon, Benjamin W. "The Disciple Whom Jesus Loved and His Relation to the Author." In *The Fourth Gospel in Research and Debate*, 310–31. London: T. Fisher Unwin, 1910.

Baeck, Leo. "The Faith of Paul." *Journal of Jewish Studies* 3 (1952): 93–110.

———. "Judaism in the Church." *Hebrew Union College Annual* 2 (1925): 125–44.

———. "Romantic Religion." In *Judaism and Christianity*, translated by W. Kaufmann, 189–292. Philadelphia: Jewish Publication Society of America, 1960.

Bagley, Paul J. "Spinoza, Philosophic Communication, and the Practice of Esotericism." In *Piety, Peace, and the Freedom to Philosophize*, edited by P. J. Bagley, 233–69. Dordrecht: Kluwer Academic, 1999.

Bainton, Roland H. *Here I Stand: A Life of Martin Luther*. Nashville: Abingdon, 1950.

Baird, William. *History of New Testament Research*. Vol. 1, *From Deism to Tübingen*. Minneapolis: Fortress, 1992.

———. *History of New Testament Research*. Vol. 2, *From Jonathan Edwards to Rudolf Bultmann*. Minneapolis: Fortress, 2003.

Baldwin, James. *The Devil Finds Work*. New York: Dial, 1976.

———. *The Fire Next Time*. New York: Delta, 1963.

———. "White Racism or World Community?" *Ecumenical Review* 20 (1968): 371–76.

Balibar, Etienne. *The Philosophy of Marx*. Translated by C. Turner. London: Verso, 1995.

Barker, Gregory A., and Stephen E. Gregg, eds. *Jesus beyond Christianity*. Oxford: Oxford University Press, 2010.

Barkun, Michael. *A Culture of Conspiracy: Apocalyptic Visions in Contemporary America*. Berkeley: University of California Press, 2003.

Barnes, T. D. *Constantine and Eusebius*. Cambridge, MA: Harvard University Press, 1981.

———. "Porphyry *Against the Christians*: Date and the Attribution of the Fragments." *Journal of Theological Studies*, n.s., 24 (1973): 424–42.

———. "Sossianus Hierocles and the Antecedents of the 'Great Persecution.'" *Harvard Studies in Classical Philology* 80 (1976): 239–52.

Barrett, C. K. "The Apostles in and after the New Testament." *Svensk exegetisk årsbok* 21 (1956): 30–49.

———. "Paul's Opponents in II Corinthians." In *Essays on Paul*, 60–82. London: SPCK, 1982.

Barrett, Jeffrey A. *The Quantum Mechanics of Minds and Worlds*. Oxford: Oxford University Press, 1999.

Bartlet, James Vernon. "Paul." In *Encyclopedia Britannica*, edited by H. Chisholm, 11th ed., 20:938–55. New York: Encyclopedia Britannica, 1911.

Barzegar, Abbas. "The Persistence of Heresy: Paul of Tarsus, Ibn Saba', and Historical Narrative in Sunni Identity Formation." *Numen* 58 (2011): 207–31.

Batnitzky, Leora. *How Judaism Became a Religion*. Princeton: Princeton University Press, 2011.

Bauckham, Richard. "The Origin of the Ebionites." In *The Image of the Judaeo-Christians in Ancient Jewish and Christian Literature*, edited by Peter J. Tomson and Doris Lambers-Petry, 162–81. Wissenschaftliche Untersuchungen zum Neuen Testament 158. Tübingen: Mohr Siebeck, 2003.

———. "What If Paul Had Travelled East Rather Than West?" In Exum, *Virtual History and the Bible*, 171–84.

Bauer, Bruno. *Christ and the Caesars: The Origin of Christianity from Romanized Greek Culture*. Translated by Frank E. Schacht. Charleston, SC: Charleston House, 1998.

———. *Christus und die Cäsaren: Der Ursprung des Christenthums aus dem rö-mischen Griechenthum*. 2nd ed. Berlin: Eugen Grosser, 1879.

Bauer, Walter. *Orthodoxy and Heresy in Earliest Christianity*. Translated and edited by R. A. Kraft and G. Krodel. Philadelphia: Fortress, 1971.

Baugh, Lloyd. *Imaging the Divine: Jesus and Christ-Figures in Film*. Kansas City: Sheed & Ward, 1997.

———. "Martin Scorsese's *The Last Temptation of Christ*: A Critical Reassessment of Its Sources, Its Theological Problems, and Its Impact on the Public." In *Scandalizing Jesus? Kazantzakis's* The Last Temptation of Christ *Fifty Years On*, edited by Darren J. N. Middleton, 173–92. New York: Continuum, 2005.

Baur, F. C. "Die Christuspartei in der korinthischen Gemeinde, der Gegensatz des paulinischen und petrinischen Christentums in der ältesten Kirche, der Apostel Petrus in Rom." *Tübinger Zeitschrift für Theologie* 4 (1831): 61–206.

———. *The Church History of the First Three Centuries*. Translated by Allan Menzies. Vol. 1. London: Williams & Norgate, 1878.

———. *Die sogenannten Pastoralbriefe des Apostels Paulus*. Stuttgart: J. G. Cotta, 1835.

Beard, Charles. *Martin Luther and the Reformation in Germany until the Close of the Diet of Worms*. London: Philip Green, 1896.

Beauvoir, Simone de. *The Second Sex*. Translated by H. M. Parshley. New York: Knopf, 1953.

Becker, Adam H., and Annette Yoshiko Reed, eds. *The Ways That Never Parted: Jews and Christians in Late Antiquity and the Early Middle Ages*. Texts and Studies in Ancient Judaism 95. Tübingen: Mohr Siebeck, 2003.

Becking, Bob. *Ezra, Nehemiah, and the Construction of Early Jewish Identity*. Tübingen: Mohr Siebeck, 2011.

Beker, J. C. "Paul's Theology: Consistent or Inconsistent?" *New Testament Studies* 34 (1988): 364–77.

Bekkum, Wout van. "The Poetical Qualities of the Apostle Peter in Jewish Folktale." *Zutot: Perspectives on Jewish Culture* 3 (2005): 16–25.

Ben-Gurion, David. *Israel: A Personal History*. Tel Aviv: Funk & Wagnalls, 1971.

Bennett, D. M. *The Champions of the Church: Their Crimes and Persecutions*. New York: Liberal and Scientific Publishing House, 1878.

Bentham, Jeremy. *Not Paul, but Jesus*. London: John Hunt, 1823.

———. *Not Paul, but Jesus*. Vol. 3, *Doctrine*. London: Bentham Project/UCL, 2013.

———. *Of Sexual Irregularities, and Other Writings on Sexual Morality*. Edited by Philip Schofield, Catherine Pease-Watkin, and Michael Quinn. Oxford: Oxford University Press, 2014.

Berchman, Robert M. *Porphyry "Against the Christians."* Studies in Platonism, Neoplatonism, and the Platonic Tradition 1. Leiden: Brill, 2005.

Bergen, Doris L. *Twisted Cross: The German Christian Movement and the Third Reich*. Chapel Hill: University of North Carolina Press, 1996.

Berger, David. *The Jewish-Christian Debate in the High Middle Ages: A Critical Edition of the "Nizzahon Vetus" with an Introduction, Translation, and Commentary*. Philadelphia: Jewish Publication Society of America, 1979.

Berman, Paul. *Terror and Liberalism*. New York: Norton, 2003.

Bernstein, Richard J. *Freud and the Legacy of Moses*. Cambridge: Cambridge University Press, 1998.

Besecke, Kelly. *You Can't Put God in a Box: Thoughtful Spirituality in a Rational Age*. New York: Oxford University Press, 2013.

Bethke, Jefferson. *Jesus > Religion: Why He Is So Much Better Than Trying Harder, Doing More, and Being Good Enough*. Nashville: Nelson, 2013.

Betz, Hans Dieter. "Christianity as Religion: Paul's Attempt at Definition in Romans." *Journal of Religion* 71 (1991): 315–44.

———. *Galatians*. Hermeneia. Philadelphia: Fortress, 1979.

———. "Paul's Ideas about the Origins of Christianity." In *Paulinische Studien: Gesammelte Aufsätze III*, 272–88. Tübingen: Mohr Siebeck, 1994.

Bigane, John E. *Faith, Christ, or Peter: Matthew 16:18 in Sixteenth Century Roman Catholic Exegesis*. Washington, DC: University Press of America, 1981.

Bird, Michael F., and Preston M. Sprinkle. "Jewish Interpretation of Paul in the Last Thirty Years." *Currents in Biblical Research* 6 (2008): 355–76.

Bishop, Michael, ed. *A Cross of Centuries: Twenty-Five Imaginative Tales about the Christ*. New York: Thunder's Mouth, 2007.

Blavatsky, H. P. *Isis Unveiled: A Master-Key to the Mysteries of Ancient and Modern Science and Theology*. Vol. 2. Pasadena, CA: Theosophical University Press, 1950.

———. *The Secret Doctrine: The Synthesis of Science, Religion, and Philosophy*. Vol. 3. London: Theosophical Publishing House, 1897.

Bloom, Harold. *Genius: A Mosaic of One Hundred Exemplary Creative Minds*. New York: Warner Books, 2003.

Blumenfeld, Bruno. *The Political Paul: Justice, Democracy and Kingship in a Hellenistic Framework*. Journal for the Study of the New Testament Supplement Series 210. London: Sheffield Academic Press, 2001.

Bockmuehl, Markus. *The Remembered Peter: In Ancient Reception and Modern Debate*. Wissenschaftliche Untersuchungen zum Neuen Testament 262. Tübingen: Mohr Siebeck, 2010.

Bolingbroke, Henry St. John (Viscount). *The Works of Lord Bolingbroke*. Vol. 3. Philadelphia: Carey & Hart, 1841.

Boman, Thorleif. "'Paulus abortivus': (1. Kor. 15,8)." *Studia theologica* 18 (1964): 46–50.

Borg, Marcus J., and John Dominic Crossan. *The First Paul: Reclaiming the Radical Visionary behind the Church's Conservative Icon*. San Francisco: HarperOne, 2009.

Boteach, Shmuley. *Kosher Jesus*. Jerusalem: Gefen, 2012.

Brandes, Georg. *Jesus: A Myth*. Translated by E. Björkman. New York: Boni, 1926.

Brandon, S. G. F. *The Fall of Jerusalem and the Christian Church: A Study of the Effects of the Jewish Overthrow of A.D. 70 on Christianity*. 2nd ed. London: SPCK, 1957.

Brandt, Lori Unger. "Paul: Herald of Grace and Paradigm of Christian Living." In *Kierkegaard and the Bible*, edited by Lee C. Barrett and Jon Stewart, 189–208. Aldershot, UK: Ashgate, 2010.

Brenton, Howard. *Paul*. London: Nick Hern, 2006.

Brettler, Marc Zvi. "Judaism in the Hebrew Bible? The Transition from Ancient Israelite Religion to Judaism." *Catholic Biblical Quarterly* 61 (1999): 429–47.

Brodie, Thomas L. *Beyond the Quest for the Historical Jesus: Memoir of a Discovery*. Sheffield: Sheffield Phoenix, 2012.

Brown, Raymond E. *The Gospel according to John*. 2 vols. Anchor Bible 29–29A. Garden City, NY: Doubleday, 1966–70.

———. "Not Jewish Christianity and Gentile Christianity, but Types of Jewish/Gentile Christianity." *Catholic Biblical Quarterly* 45 (1983): 74–79.

Brumberg-Kraus, Jonathan D. "A Jewish Ideological Perspective on the Study of Christian Scripture." *Jewish Social Studies* 4 (1997): 121–52.

Buber, Martin. "The Holy Way." In *On Judaism*, edited by Nahum N. Glatzer, 108–48. New York: Schocken, 1967.

———. *Two Types of Faith*. Translated by N. P. Goldhawk. New York: Macmillan, 1951.

Buckley, J. J. *The Mandaeans: Ancient Texts and Modern People*. New York: Oxford University Press, 2002.

Bulhof, Johannes. "What If? Modality and History." *History and Theory* 38, no. 2 (1999): 145–68.

Bultmann, Rudolf. "Jesus and Paul." In *Existence and Faith: Shorter Writings of Rudolf Bultmann*, translated by S. M. Ogden, 183–201. New York: Meridian, 1960.

———. *Jesus and the Word*. Translated by L. P. Smith and E. H. Lantero. New York: Charles Scribner's Sons, 1958.

———. "The Significance of the Historical Jesus for the Theology of Paul." In *Faith and Understanding*, translated by L. P. Smith, 220–46. London: SCM, 1969.

———. *Theology of the New Testament*. Translated by K. Grobel. 2 vols. New York: Scribners, 1951–55.

———. "Zur Geschichte der Paulus-Forschung." *Theologische Rundschau* 1 (1929): 26–59.

Burke, Peter, ed. *New Perspectives on Historical Writing*. University Park: Pennsylvania State University Press, 1992.

Burns, David. *The Life and Death of the Radical Historical Jesus*. Oxford: Oxford University Press, 2013.

Bush, M. L. *What Is Love? Richard Carlile's Philosophy of Sex*. London: Verso, 1998.

Bütz, Jeffrey. *The Brother of Jesus and the Lost Teachings of Christianity*. Rochester, VT: Inner Traditions, 2005.

———. *The Secret Legacy of Jesus*. Rochester, VT: Inner Traditions, 2010.

Byrne, Ruth M. J. *The Rational Imagination: How People Create Alternatives to Reality*. Cambridge, MA: MIT Press, 2005.

Cadbury, Henry J. *The Peril of Modernizing Jesus*. New York: Macmillan, 1937.

Callahan, Allen Dwight. "'Brother Saul': An Ambivalent Witness to Freedom." *Semeia* 83/84 (2004): 235–50.

Callan, Terrance. *Psychological Perspectives on the Life of Paul*. Studies in the Bible and Early Christianity 22. Lewiston, NY: Edwin Mellen, 1990.

Campbell, Joseph. *The Masks of God*. Vol. 4, *Creative Mythology*. New York: Viking, 1968.

Canales, Isaac J. "Paul's Accusers in Romans 3:8 and 6:1." *Evangelical Quarterly* 57 (1985): 237–45.

Caragounis, C. C. *Peter and the Rock*. Beihefte zur Zeitschrift für die neutestamentliche Wissenschaft 58. Berlin: de Gruyter, 1990.

Carlile, Richard. "To the Christian Judge Bailey (Letter XXV)." *The Republican* 10 (1824): 673–98.

———. "What Is Love?" *The Republican* 11 (1825): 545–69.

Carlyle, Thomas. *On Heroes, Hero Worship, and the Heroic in History.* London: James Fraser, 1841.

Carr, E. H. *What Is History?* London: Penguin, 1961.

Cartwright, Steven R., ed. *A Companion to St. Paul in the Middle Ages.* Leiden: Brill, 2013.

Chadwick, Henry, trans. *Lessing's Theological Writings: Selections in Translation with an Introductory Essay.* Stanford, CA: Stanford University Press, 1957.

———, ed. and trans. *Origen: Contra Celsum.* Cambridge: Cambridge University Press, 1953.

Champion, Justin. "'I Remember a Mahometan Story of Ahmed Ben Edris': Freethinking Uses of Islam from Stubbe to Toland." *Al-Qanṭara* 31 (2010): 443–80.

Chen, Yong. *Confucianism as Religion: Controversies and Consequences.* Leiden: Brill, 2013.

Chiesa, Bruno, and Wilfrid Lockwood. *Ya'cūb al-Qirqisānī on Jewish Sects and Christianity: A Translation of Kitāb al-Anwār, Book I, with Two Introductory Essays.* Frankfurt am Main: Peter Lang, 1984.

Chubb, Thomas. *The True Gospel of Jesus Christ Asserted.* London: T. Cox, 1738.

Churchill, Winston. "If Lee Had Not Won the Battle of Gettysburg." *Scribner's Magazine* (December 1930): 587–97.

Clark, Elizabeth A. *Founding the Fathers: Early Church History and Protestant Professors in Nineteenth-Century America.* Philadelphia: University of Pennsylvania Press, 2011.

Clark, Kelly James, ed. *Abraham's Children: Liberty and Tolerance in an Age of Religious Conflict.* New Haven: Yale University Press, 2012.

Cleage, Albert B. *The Black Messiah.* New York: Sheed & Ward, 1968.

Cohen, Richard S. "Shakyamuni: Buddhism's Founder in Ten Acts." In *The Rivers of Paradise: Moses, Buddha, Confucius, Jesus, and Muhammad as Religious Founders*, edited by D. N. Freedman and M. J. McClymond, 121–232. Grand Rapids: Eerdmans, 2001.

Cohen, Shaye J. D. *The Beginnings of Jewishness: Boundaries, Varieties, Uncertainties.* Hellenistic Culture and Society 31. Berkeley: University of California Press, 1999.

Coker, K. J. "Nativism in James 2:14–26: A Post-colonial Reading." In *Reading James with New Eyes: Methodological Reassessments of the Letter of James*, edited by Robert L. Webb and John S. Kloppenborg, 27–48. London: T&T Clark, 2007.

Collins, John J. *The Scepter and the Star: The Messiahs of the Dead Sea Scrolls and Other Ancient Literature.* New York: Doubleday, 1995.

Collins, Randall. "Turning Points, Bottlenecks, and the Fallacies of Counterfactual History." *Sociological Forum* 22 (2007): 247–69.

Confucius. *The Analects*. Translated by D. C. Lau. Hong Kong: Chinese University Press, 1983.

Conybeare, F. C. *The Life of Apollonius of Tyana, the Epistles of Apollonius and the Treatise of Eusebius*. Loeb Classical Library. London: Heinemann; New York: Macmillan, 1912.

Conzelmann, Hans. *1 Corinthians: A Commentary on the First Epistle to the Corinthians*. Translated by James W. Leitch. Hermeneia. Philadelphia: Fortress, 1975.

Cook, Michael J. "How Credible Is Jewish Scholarship on Jesus?" In Garber, *Jewish Jesus*, 251–70.

Corley, Bruce. "Interpreting Paul's Conversion—Then and Now." In *The Road from Damascus: The Impact of Paul's Conversion on His Life, Thought, and Ministry*, edited by R. N. Longenecker, 1–17. Grand Rapids: Eerdmans, 1997.

Corley, Kathleen. *Women and the Historical Jesus: Feminist Myths of Christian Origins*. Santa Rosa, CA: Polebridge, 2002.

Cowley, Robert, ed. *What If? The World's Foremost Military Historians Imagine What Might Have Been*. New York: G. P. Putnam's Sons, 1999.

Crafer, T. W. *The Apocriticus of Macarius Magnes*. London: SPCK, 1919.

Crossan, John Dominic. "Earliest Christianity in Counterfactual Focus." In Exum, *Virtual History and the Bible*, 185–93.

Crowley, Aleister. *The Gospel according to St. Bernard Shaw*. Edited by Karl Germer. Barstow, CA: Thelema, 1953.

Csikszentmihalyi, Mark. "Confucius." In *The Rivers of Paradise: Moses, Buddha, Confucius, Jesus, and Muhammad as Religious Founders*, edited by D. N. Freedman and M. J. McClymond, 233–308. Grand Rapids: Eerdmans, 2001.

Daly, Mary. *Pure Lust: Elemental Feminist Philosophy*. Boston: Beacon, 1984.

Danby, Herbert. *The Mishnah: Translated from the Hebrew with Introduction and Brief Explanatory Notes*. Oxford: Oxford University Press, 1933.

Daniel, Lillian. *When "Spiritual but Not Religious" Is Not Enough: Seeing God in Surprising Places, Even the Church*. New York: Jericho, 2013.

Dassmann, Ernst. *Der Stachel im Fleisch: Paulus in der frühchristlichen Literatur bis Irenäus*. Münster: Aschendorff, 1979.

Davidson, Edward H., and William J. Scheick. *Paine, Scripture, and Authority: "The Age of Reason" as Religious and Political Idea*. Bethlehem, PA: Lehigh University Press, 1994.

Davies, J. G. *Dialogue with the World*. London: SCM, 1967.

Davies, W. D. *Paul and Rabbinic Judaism*. New York: Harper & Row, 1967.

———. *The Setting of the Sermon on the Mount*. Cambridge: Cambridge University Press, 1964.

De Boer, Esther A. *The Gospel of Mary: Listening to the Beloved Disciple*. London: Continuum, 2005.

Deissmann, Adolf. *St. Paul: A Study in Social and Religious History*. Translated by L. R. M. Strachan. London: Hodder & Stoughton, 1912.

Demandt, Alexander. *History That Never Happened*. Translated by C. D. Thomson. 3rd ed. Jefferson, NC: McFarland, 1993.

De Satge, John. *Mary and the Christian Gospel*. London: SPCK, 1976.

De Vries, Simon J. "Moses and David as Cult Founders in Chronicles." *Journal of Biblical Literature* 107 (1988): 619–39.

Dibelius, Martin. "The Apostolic Council." In *Studies in the Acts of the Apostles*, translated by M. Ling, 93–101. London: SCM, 1956.

Dibelius, Martin, and Hans Conzelmann. *The Pastoral Epistles*. Translated by Philip Buttolph and Adela Yarbro. Hermeneia. Philadelphia: Fortress, 1972.

Dillenberger, John, ed. *Martin Luther: Selections from His Writings*. Garden City, NY: Doubleday Anchor, 1962.

Dimont, Max. *Jews, God, and History*. New York: Simon & Schuster, 1962.

Ditchfield, Grayson. "Divine Right Theory and Its Critics in Eighteenth-Century England." In *Biblical Interpretation: The Meanings of Scripture—Past and Present*, edited by John M. Court, 156–67. London: T&T Clark, 2003.

Dodd, Brian J. *The Problem with Paul*. Downers Grove, IL: InterVarsity, 1996.

Doležel, Lubomír. *Possible Worlds of Fiction and History: The Postmodern Stage*. Baltimore: Johns Hopkins University Press, 2010.

Donahue, Paul J. "Jewish Christianity in the Letters of Ignatius of Antioch." *Vigiliae Christianae* 32 (1978): 81–93.

Doyle, Tom. *Dreams and Visions: Is Jesus Awakening the Muslim World?* Nashville: Nelson, 2012.

Drews, Arthur. *The Witnesses to the Historicity of Jesus*. Translated by J. McCabe. London: Watts, 1912.

Dudley, Donald R. *A History of Cynicism from Diogenes to the 6th Century*. Cambridge: Cambridge University Press, 1937.

Dunn, James D. G. *The Epistle to the Galatians*. Black's New Testament Commentaries. London: Black, 1993.

———. *The New Perspective on Paul*. Rev. ed. Grand Rapids: Eerdmans, 2008.

———. *The Parting of the Ways between Christianity and Judaism and Their Significance for the Character of Christianity*. London: SCM, 1991.

———. "Who Did Paul Think He Was? A Study of Jewish-Christian Identity." *New Testament Studies* 45 (1999): 174–93.

Durant, Will. *Caesar and Christ*. New York: Simon & Schuster, 1944.

Durrell, Lawrence. *Clea*. New York: Dutton, 1960.

Eagleton, Terry. *Why Marx Was Right*. New Haven: Yale University Press, 2011.

Ebied, Rifaat Y., and David Thomas, eds. *Muslim-Christian Polemics during the Crusades: The Letter from the People of Cyprus and Ibn Abī Ṭālib al-Dimashqī's Response*. Leiden: Brill, 2005.

Ehrensperger, Kathy. *That We May Be Mutually Encouraged: Feminism and the New Perspective in Pauline Studies*. New York: T&T Clark, 2004.

Ehrman, Bart D. "Christianity Turned on Its Head: The Alternative Vision of the Gospel of Judas." In *The Gospel of Judas*, edited by R. Kasser, M. Meyer, and G. Wurst, 77–120. Washington, DC: National Geographic, 2006.

———. *Forgery and Counterforgery: The Use of Literary Deceit in Early Christian Polemics*. Oxford: Oxford University Press, 2013.

———. *Peter, Paul, and Mary Magdalene: The Followers of Jesus in History and Legend*. Oxford: Oxford University Press, 2006.

Einhorn, Lena. *The Jesus Mystery: Astonishing Clues to the True Identities of Jesus and Paul*. Translated by R. Bradbury. Guilford, CT: Lyons, 2007.

Eire, Carlos M. N. "The Quest for a Counterfactual Jesus: Imagining the West without the Cross." In Tetlock, Lebow, and Parker, *Unmaking the West*, 119–42.

Eisenbaum, Pamela. "Following in the Footnotes of the Apostle Paul." In *Identity and the Politics of Scholarship in the Study of Religion*, edited by S. Davaney and J. Cabezon, 77–97. New York: Routledge, 2004.

———. *Paul Was Not a Christian: The Original Message of a Misunderstood Apostle*. San Francisco: HarperOne, 2009.

Eisenman, Robert. *James, the Brother of Jesus: The Key to Unlocking the Secrets of Early Christianity and the Dead Sea Scrolls*. New York: Viking, 1996.

Eliot, T. S. *Four Quartets*. Orlando: Harcourt, 1971.

Elliott, J. H. "Jesus the Israelite Was Neither a 'Jew' nor a 'Christian': On Correcting Misleading Nomenclature." *Journal for the Study of the Historical Jesus* 5 (2007): 119–54.

Elliott, James Keith. *The Apocryphal New Testament*. Oxford: Clarendon, 1993.

Elliott, Neil. *Liberating Paul: The Justice of God and the Politics of the Apostle*. 2nd ed. Minneapolis: Fortress, 2006.

Ellis, E. E. "Paul and His Opponents: Trends in Research." In *Christianity, Judaism and Other Greco-Roman Cults: Studies for Morton Smith at Sixty*, edited by Jacob Neusner, 1:264–98. Leiden: Brill, 1975.

———. *Paul and His Recent Interpreters*. Grand Rapids: Eerdmans, 1961.

Ellul, Jacques. *The Subversion of Christianity*. Translated by Geoffrey W. Bromiley. Grand Rapids: Eerdmans, 1986.

Emerson, Ralph Waldo. *Emerson's Complete Works*. Vol. 11, *Miscellanies*. Boston: Houghton, Mifflin, 1888.

Enelow, H. G. *A Jewish View of Jesus*. New York: Macmillan, 1920.

Engels, F. "The Book of Revelation." In Marx and Engels, *On Religion*, 205–12.

———. "Bruno Bauer and Early Christianity." In Marx and Engels, *On Religion*, 194–204.

Epstein, Isidore. *The Babylonian Talmud*. London: Soncino, 1935–59.

Ernst, Carl W. *Following Muhammad: Rethinking Islam in the Contemporary World*. Chapel Hill: University of North Carolina Press, 2004.

Exum, J. Cheryl, ed. *Virtual History and the Bible*. Leiden: Brill, 2000.

Farrar, Frederic W. *History of Interpretation*. London: Macmillan, 1886.

Ferguson, Niall. "Virtual History: Towards a 'Chaotic' Theory of the Past." In *Virtual History: Alternatives and Counterfactuals*, edited by N. Ferguson, 1–90. New York: Picador, 1997.

Fichte, Johann Gottlieb. *Characteristics of the Present Age*. Translated by W. Smith. London: John Chapman, 1847.

———. *The Way towards the Blessed Life; or, The Doctrine of Religion*. Translated by W. Smith. London: John Chapman, 1849.

Fischer, David Hackett. *Historians' Fallacies: Toward a Logic of Historical Thought*. New York: Harper & Row, 1970.

Fischer, Hermann. *Gespaltener christlicher Glaube: Eine psychoanalytisch orientierte Religionskritik*. Hamburg: Reich, 1974.

Fisher, Eugene J. "Typical Jewish Misunderstandings of Christ, Christianity, and Jewish-Christian Relations over the Centuries." In Garber, *Jewish Jesus*, 228–48.

Fitzmyer, Joseph A. *The Acts of the Apostles*. Anchor Bible 31. New York: Doubleday, 1998.

Fletcher, J. E. "The Spanish Gospel of Barnabas." *Novum Testamentum* 18 (1976): 314–20.

Fletcher, William. *The Works of Lactantius*. Ante-Nicene Christian Library 21–22. Edinburgh: T&T Clark, 1886.

Flood, Gavin. *An Introduction to Hinduism*. Cambridge: Cambridge University Press, 1996.

Foakes-Jackson, F. J. *Peter: Prince of Apostles*. New York: Doran, 1927.

Forbes, Christopher. "Comparison, Self-Praise and Irony: Paul's Boasting and the Conventions of Hellenistic Rhetoric." *New Testament Studies* 32 (1986): 1–30.

Forkman, Göran. *The Limits of the Religious Community: Expulsion from the Religious Community within the Qumran Sect, within Rabbinic Judaism, and within Primitive Christianity*. Lund: Gleerup, 1972.

Friedlander, Gerald. *The Jewish Sources of the Sermon on the Mount*. London: Routledge and Sons, 1911.

Fritsch, Erdmann. *Islam und Christentum im Mittelalter: Beiträge zur Geschichte der muslimischen Polemik gegen das Christentum in arabischer Sprache*. Breslau: Müller & Seifert, 1930.

Fromm, Erich. *The Dogma of Christ and Other Essays on Religion, Psychology and Culture*. New York: Holt, Rinehart and Winston, 1963.

Frost, Robert. *A Masque of Mercy*. New York: Holt, 1947.

Fuller, Robert C. *Spiritual, but Not Religious: Understanding Unchurched America*. New York: Oxford University Press, 2001.

Furnish, Victor Paul. "The Jesus-Paul Debate: From Baur to Bultmann." In Wedderburn, *Paul and Jesus: Collected Essays*, 17–50.

———. "Pauline Studies." In *The New Testament and Its Modern Interpreters*, edited by E. J. Epp and G. W. MacRae, 321–50. Atlanta: Society of Biblical Literature, 1989.

Gager, John G. *Moses in Greco-Roman Paganism*. Nashville: Abingdon, 1972.

———. "The Rehabilitation of Paul in Jewish Tradition." In *"The One Who Sows Bountifully": Essays in Honor of Stanley K. Stowers*, edited by Caroline Johnson Hodge, Saul M. Olyan, Daniel Ullucci, and Emma Wasserman, 29–41. Brown Judaic Studies 356. Providence: Brown University Press, 2013.

———. *Reinventing Paul*. New York: Oxford University Press, 2000.

———. "Simon Peter, Founder of Christianity or Saviour of Israel?" In *Toledot Yeshu ("The Life Story of Jesus") Revisited: A Princeton Conference*, edited by P. Schäfer, M. Meerson, and Y. Deutsch, 221–45. Texts and Studies in Ancient Judaism 143. Tübingen: Mohr Siebeck, 2011.

Galambush, Julie. *The Reluctant Parting: How the New Testament's Jewish Writers Created a Christian Book*. San Francisco: HarperCollins, 2005.

Gandhi, M. K. "Discussion on Fellowship." In *The Collected Works of Mahatma Gandhi*, 35:461–64. Ahmedabad: Navajivan Trust, 1958.

———. *The Message of Jesus Christ*. Bombay: Bharatiya Vidya Bhavan, 1963.

Garber, Zev, ed. *The Jewish Jesus: Revelation, Reflection, Reclamation*. West Lafayette, IN: Purdue University Press, 2011.

Gaston, Lloyd. *Paul and the Torah*. Vancouver: University of British Columbia Press, 1987.

Gaventa, Beverly Roberts. *From Darkness to Light: Aspects of Conversion in the New Testament*. Philadelphia: Fortress, 1986.

Gay, Peter. *Deism: An Anthology*. Princeton: Princeton University Press, 1968.

Geiger, Abraham. *Judaism and Its History, in Two Parts*. Translated by Charles Newburgh. New York: Bloch, 1911.

George, Lyman F. *The Naked Truth of Jesusism from Oriental Manuscripts*. Pittsburgh: George Publishing, 1914.

Georgi, Dieter. "The Early Church: Internal Jewish Migration or New Religion?" *Harvard Theological Review* 88 (1995): 35–68.

Gibran, Kahlil. *Jesus the Son of Man*. New York: Knopf, 1966.

Gillies, John. "A Sending Parable." *Christian Century* 58, no. 8 (February 24, 1971): 253–56.

Gilmore, David D. *Misogyny: The Male Malady*. Philadelphia: University of Pennsylvania Press, 2001.

Goddard, Hugh. *Muslim Perceptions of Christianity*. London: Grey Seal, 1996.

Goldstein, Jan. "Enthusiasm or Imagination? Eighteenth-Century Smear Words in Comparative National Context." *Huntington Library Quarterly* 60 (1997): 29–49.

Goldstein, Morris. *Jesus in the Jewish Tradition*. New York: Macmillan, 1950.

Goodman, Nelson. *Fact, Fiction, and Forecast*. Cambridge, MA: Harvard University Press, 1955.

Gortner, David T. *Varieties of Personal Theology: Charting the Beliefs and Values of American Young Adults*. Burlington, VT: Ashgate, 2013.

Graetz, Heinrich. *History of the Jews*. Translated by B. Löwy. Vol. 2. Philadelphia: Jewish Publication Society of America, 1902.

Graham, A. C. "The Origins of the Legend of Lao Tan." In *Lao-tzu and the Tao-te-ching*, edited by L. Kohn and M. LaFargue, 23–40. Albany: State University of New York Press, 1998.

Grant, Robert M. *Greek Apologists of the Second Century*. Philadelphia: Westminster, 1988.

———. "Porphyry among the Early Christians." In *Romanitas et Christianitas*, edited by W. den Boer, P. G. van der Nat, C. M. J. Sicking, and J. C. M. van Winden, 181–87. Amsterdam: North-Holland, 1973.

Greenfield, Jeff. *Then Everything Changed: Stunning Alternate Histories of American Politics*. New York: Putnam's, 2011.

Grimsley, Jim. *The Lizard of Tarsus*. In *Mr. Universe and Other Plays*, 67–128. Chapel Hill, NC: Algonquin, 1998.

Gross, Miriam, ed. *The World of George Orwell*. New York: Simon & Schuster, 1972.

Hafemann, S. J. "Paul and His Interpreters." In *Dictionary of Paul and His Letters*, edited by G. F. Hawthorne, R. P. Martin, and D. G. Reid, 666–79. Downers Grove, IL: InterVarsity, 1993.

Hagner, Donald A. "Paul in Modern Jewish Thought." In *Pauline Studies: Essays Presented to F. F. Bruce*, edited by D. A. Hagner and M. J. Harris, 143–65. Exeter, UK: Paternoster, 1980.

Hall, Sidney, III. *Christian Anti-Semitism and Paul's Theology*. Minneapolis: Fortress, 1993.

Hammond, Geordan. *John Wesley in America: Restoring Primitive Christianity*. Oxford: Oxford University Press, 2014.

Hanegraaff, Wouter J. *New Age Religion and Western Culture: Esotericism in the Mirror of Secular Thought*. Albany, NY: SUNY Press, 1998.

Hanges, James Constantine. *Paul, Founder of Churches: A Study in Light of the Evidence for the Role of "Founder-Figures" in the Hellenistic-Roman Period.* Wissenschaftliche Untersuchungen zum Neuen Testament 292. Tübingen: Mohr Siebeck, 2012.

Harnack, Adolf von. *Outlines of the History of Dogma.* Translated by E. K. Mitchell. Vol. 1. Boston: Beacon, 1957.

————. *What Is Christianity?* Translated by T. B. Saunders. New York: Putnam's Sons, 1901.

Harries, Richard, Norman Solomon, and Timothy Winter, eds. *Abraham's Children: Jews, Christians and Muslims in Conversation.* London: T&T Clark, 2006.

Harris, Frank. *My Life and Loves.* Paris: n.p., 1922.

Harris, Horton. *The Tübingen School: A Historical and Theological Investigation of the School of F. C. Baur.* Grand Rapids: Eerdmans, 1990.

Harris, Sam. "Killing the Buddha." *Shambhala Sun* (March 2006): 73–75.

Hassett, Miranda K. *Anglican Communion in Crisis: How Episcopal Dissidents and Their African Allies Are Reshaping Anglicanism.* Princeton: Princeton University Press, 2007.

Havemann, Daniel. *Der "Apostel der Rache": Nietzsches Paulusdeutung.* Berlin: de Gruyter, 2002.

Heitmüller, Wilhelm. "Zum Problem Paulus und Jesus." *Zeitschrift für die neutestamentliche Wissenschaft* 13 (1912): 320–37.

Hellekson, Karen. "Toward a Taxonomy of the Alternate History." *Extrapolation* 41 (2000): 248–56.

Hemingway, Ernest. *A Farewell to Arms.* New York: Charles Scribner's Sons, 1929.

Hendricks, Obery. *The Politics of Jesus: Rediscovering the True Revolutionary Nature of Jesus's Teachings and How They Have Been Corrupted.* New York: Doubleday, 2006.

Hengel, Martin. *Acts and the History of Earliest Christianity.* Philadelphia: Fortress, 1986.

————. "Der Jakobusbrief als antipaulinische Polemik." In *Tradition and Interpretation in the New Testament,* edited by Gerald F. Hawthorne and Otto Betz, 248–78. Grand Rapids: Eerdmans, 1987.

————. "Jakobus der Herrenbruder—der erste 'Papst'?" In *Glaube und Eschatologie,* edited by E. Grässer and O. Merk, 71–104. Tübingen: Mohr Siebeck, 1985.

————. *Judaism and Hellenism.* Translated by J. Bowden. 2 vols. Philadelphia: Fortress, 1974.

Herrick, James A. *The Radical Rhetoric of the English Deists: The Discourse of Skepticism, 1680–1750.* Columbia: University of South Carolina Press, 1997.

Heschel, Susannah. *Abraham Geiger and the Jewish Jesus.* Chicago: University of Chicago Press, 1998.

―――. *The Aryan Jesus: Christian Theologians and the Bible in Nazi Germany*. Princeton: Princeton University Press, 2008.

Heyd, Michael. "The Reaction to Enthusiasm in the Seventeenth Century: Towards an Integrative Approach." *Journal of Modern History* 53 (1981): 258–80.

Hirsch, William. *Religion and Civilization: The Conclusions of a Psychiatrist*. New York: Truth Seeker, 1912.

Hirschberg, Harris H. "Allusions to the Apostle Paul in the Talmud." *Journal of Biblical Literature* 62 (1943): 73–86.

Hisey, Alan, and J. S. P. Beck. "Paul's 'Thorn in the Flesh': A Paragnosis." *Journal of Bible and Religion* 29 (1961): 125–29.

Hoffmann, R. Joseph. *Porphyry's "Against the Christians": The Literary Remains*. Amherst, NY: Prometheus, 1994.

Holmen, R. W. *A Wretched Man: A Novel of the Apostle Paul*. Minneapolis: Bascom Hill, 2009.

Hong, Howard V., and E. H. Hong, eds. *Søren Kierkegaard's Journals and Papers*. Vol. 3. Bloomington: Indiana University Press, 1975.

Horsley, Richard A. "Unearthing a People's History." In *Christian Origins: A People's History of Christianity*, edited by R. A. Horsley, 1:1–20. Minneapolis: Fortress, 2005.

Horst, Pieter W. van der. "The Birkat ha-minim in Recent Research." *Expository Times* 105 (1994): 363–68.

Hughes, Aaron W. *Abrahamic Religions: On the Uses and Abuses of History*. Oxford: Oxford University Press, 2012.

Hughes, Julian C. "If Only the Ancients Had Had the DSM, All Would Have Been Crystal Clear: Reflections on Diagnosis." In *Mental Disorders in the Classical World*, edited by W. V. Harris, 41–58. Columbia Studies in the Classical Tradition 38. Leiden: Brill, 2013.

Hughes, Richard T., ed. *The American Quest for the Primitive Church*. Urbana: University of Illinois Press, 1988.

Hughes, Richard T., and C. Leonard Allen. *Illusions of Innocence: Protestant Primitivism in America, 1630–1875*. Chicago: University of Chicago Press, 1988.

Hume, David. "Of Superstition and Enthusiasm." In *Essays: Moral, Political, and Literary*, edited by Eugene F. Miller, 73–86. Indianapolis: Liberty Fund, 1985.

Hurth, Elisabeth. *Between Faith and Unbelief: American Transcendentalists and the Challenge of Atheism*. Studies in the History of Christian Traditions 136. Leiden: Brill, 2007.

Impey, Chris. *How It Began: A Time-Traveler's Guide to the Universe*. New York: Norton, 2012.

Issac of Troki. *Faith Strengthened: The Jewish Answer to Christianity*. Translated by Moses Mocatta. London: Wertheimer, 1851.

Jackson-McCabe, Matt. "The Invention of Jewish Christianity in John Toland's *Nazarenus*." In F. S. Jones, *Rediscovery of Jewish Christianity*, 67–90.

———, ed. *Jewish Christianity Reconsidered: Rethinking Ancient Groups and Texts.* Minneapolis: Fortress, 2007.

———. "What's in a Name? The Problem of 'Jewish Christianity.'" In Jackson-McCabe, *Jewish Christianity Reconsidered*, 7–38.

James, William. *The Varieties of Religious Experience.* London: Longmans, Green, 1902. Reprint, Rockville, MD: Arc Manor, 2008.

Janssen, L. F. "'Superstitio' and the Persecution of the Christians." *Vigiliae Christianae* 33 (1979): 131–59.

Jefferson, Thomas. "Syllabus." In vol. 3 of *Memoirs, Correspondence, and Miscellanies, from the Papers of Thomas Jefferson.* Edited by Thomas Jefferson Randolph. Boston: Gray & Bowen, 1830.

Jegher-Bucher, Verena. "Der Pfahl im Fleisch: Überlegungen zu II Kor 12,7–10 im Zusammenhang von 12,1–13." *Theologische Zeitschrift* 52 (1996): 32–41.

Jensen, Lionel M. *Manufacturing Confucianism: Chinese Traditions and Universal Civilization.* Durham, NC: Duke University Press, 1977.

Jensen, Peter. *Moses, Jesus, Paulus: Drei Varianten des babylonischen Gottmenschen Gilgamesh.* 3rd ed. Frankfurt am Main: Neuer Frankfurter Verlag, 1906.

Jewett, Robert. "The Agitators and the Galatian Congregation." *New Testament Studies* 17 (1971): 198–212.

———. *Paul the Apostle to America: Cultural Trends and Pauline Scholarship.* Louisville: Westminster John Knox, 1994.

Johnson, L. T. *The First and Second Letters to Timothy.* Anchor Bible 35A. New York: Doubleday, 2001.

———. "The New Testament's Anti-Jewish Slander and the Conventions of Ancient Polemic." *Journal of Biblical Literature* 108 (1989): 419–41.

Johnson, Matthew V., James A. Noel, and Demetrius K. Williams, eds. *Onesimus Our Brother: Reading Religion, Race, and Culture in Philemon.* Minneapolis: Fortress, 2012.

Jones, Christopher P. *Between Pagan and Christian.* Cambridge, MA: Harvard University Press, 2014.

Jones, F. Stanley. "The Genesis, Purpose, and Significance of John Toland's *Nazarenus*." In Jones, *Rediscovery of Jewish Christianity*, 91–103.

———, ed. *The Rediscovery of Jewish Christianity: From Toland to Baur.* Society of Biblical Literature History of Biblical Studies 5. Atlanta: Society of Biblical Literature, 2012.

Jónsson, Jakob. *Humour and Irony in the New Testament.* Leiden: Brill, 1985.

Jowett, Benjamin. "On the Interpretation of Scripture." In *Essays and Reviews*, 330–433. 7th ed. London: Longman, Green, Longman and Roberts, 1861.

Jung, C. G. "A Psychological Approach to the Dogma of the Trinity." In *The Collected Works of C. G. Jung*, translated by G. Adler and R. F. C. Hull, 11:107–200. Princeton: Princeton University Press, 1969.

———. "The Psychological Foundations of Belief in Spirits." In *The Collected Works of C. G. Jung*, translated by G. Adler and R. F. C. Hull, 8:301–18. Princeton: Princeton University Press, 1969.

Jüngel, Eberhard. *Justification: The Heart of the Christian Faith*. Translated by J. F. Cayzer. London: T&T Clark, 2001.

Just, Arthur A., Jr. "The Apostolic Councils of Galatians and Acts: How First-Century Christians Walked Together." *Concordia Theological Quarterly* 74 (2010): 261–88.

Juynboll, G. H. A. *The Authenticity of the Tradition Literature: Discussions in Modern Egypt*. Leiden: Brill, 1969.

Karris, Robert K. "The Background and Significance of the Polemic of the Pastoral Epistles." *Journal of Biblical Literature* 92 (1973): 549–64.

Käsemann, Ernst. "Paul and Early Catholicism." In *New Testament Questions of Today*, translated by W. J. Montague, 236–51. Philadelphia: Fortress, 1969.

Kaufmann, Walter. *Nietzsche: Philosopher, Psychologist, Antichrist*. 4th ed. Princeton: Princeton University Press, 1974.

———, ed. and trans. *The Portable Nietzsche*. New York: Viking, 1954.

Kazantzakis, Nikos. *The Last Temptation of Christ*. Translated by P. A. Bien. New York: Simon & Schuster, 1960.

Keck, Leander E. "The Poor among the Saints in Jewish Christianity and Qumran." *Zeitschrift für die neutestamentliche Wissenschaft* 57 (1966): 54–78.

Kennedy, D. James, and Jerry Newcombe. *What If Jesus Had Never Been Born? The Positive Impact of Christianity in History*. Nashville: Nelson, 1994.

Kersten, Holger, and Elmar Gruber. *The Jesus Conspiracy: The Turin Shroud and the Truth about the Resurrection*. Dorset: Element, 1994.

Kirk, J. R. D. *Jesus Have I Loved, but Paul? A Narrative Approach to the Problem of Pauline Christianity*. Grand Rapids: Baker Academic, 2011.

Klausner, Joseph. *From Jesus to Paul*. Translated by W. F. Stinespring. New York: Beacon, 1944.

Kling, David W. *The Bible in History: How the Texts Have Shaped the Times*. New York: Oxford University Press, 2004.

Klinghoffer, David. *Why the Jews Rejected Jesus: The Turning Point of Western History*. New York: Doubleday, 2005.

Knox, John. *Chapters in the Life of Paul*. Rev. ed. Macon, GA: Mercer University Press, 1987.

———. *Marcion and the New Testament: An Essay in the Early History of the Canon*. Chicago: University of Chicago Press, 1942.

Koch, Adrienne. *The Philosophy of Thomas Jefferson*. New York: Columbia University Press, 1943.

Kogan, Michael S. *Opening the Covenant: A Jewish Theology of Christianity*. Oxford: Oxford University Press, 2008.

Kohler, Kaufmann. *Christianity vs. Judaism: A Rejoinder to the Rev. Dr. R. Heber Newton*. New York: Stettiner, Lambert, 1890.

———. *Jesus of Nazareth from a Jewish Point of View*. New York: Funk & Wagnalls, 1899.

———. *Jewish Theology, Systematically and Historically Considered*. New York: Macmillan, 1918.

———. *The Origins of the Synagogue and Church*. New York: Macmillan, 1929.

———. "Saul of Tarsus." In *The Jewish Encyclopedia*, edited by I. Singer, 11:79–87. New York: Funk & Wagnalls, 1905.

Koningsveld, P. S. van. "The Islamic Image of Paul and the Origin of the Gospel of Barnabas." *Jerusalem Studies in Arabic and Islam* 20 (1996): 200–228.

Koningsveld, P. S. van, and G. A. Wiegers. "The Polemical Works of Muhammad al-Qaysī (fl. 1309) and Their Circulation in Arabic and Aljamiado among the Mudejars in the Fourteenth Century." *Al-Qanṭara* 15 (1994): 163–75.

Koskenniemi, Erkki. "Apollonius of Tyana: A Typical ΘΕΙΟΣ ΑΝΗΡ?" *Journal of Biblical Literature* 117 (1998): 455–67.

Kratz, Reinhard G. "Ezra—Priest and Scribe." In *Scribes, Sages, and Seers: The Sage in the Eastern Mediterranean World*, edited by L. G. Perdue, 163–88. Göttingen: Vandenhoeck & Ruprecht, 2008.

Krause, Deborah. "Paul and Women: Telling Women to Shut Up Is More Complicated Than You Might Think." In *Paul Unbound: Other Perspectives on the Apostle*, edited by Mark D. Given, 161–73. Peabody, MA: Hendrickson, 2010.

Kritzeck, James. *Sons of Abraham: Jews, Christians and Moslems*. Baltimore: Helicon, 1965.

Kümmel, W. G. *The New Testament: The History of the Investigation of Its Problems*. Translated by S. McLean Gilmour and H. C. Kee. Nashville: Abingdon, 1972.

Lagarde, Paul de. "Über das Verhältnis des deutschen Staates zu Theologie, Kirche und Religion: Ein Versuch, Nicht-Theologen zu orientieren." In *Deutsche Schriften*, 29–31. Göttingen: Dieterichsche Verlagsbuchhandlung, 1878.

Lambdin, Thomas O. "The Gospel of Thomas." In *The Nag Hammadi Library in English*, edited by James M. Robinson, 124–38. 4th rev. ed. Leiden: Brill, 1996.

Landman, Janet. "Through a Glass Darkly: Worldviews, Counterfactual Thought, and Emotion." In *What Might Have Been: The Social Psychology of Counterfactual Thinking*, edited by Neal J. Roese and James M. Olsen, 233–58. Mahwah, NJ: Erlbaum, 1995.

Langton, Daniel R. *The Apostle Paul in the Jewish Imagination: A Study in Modern Jewish-Christian Relations*. New York: Cambridge University Press, 2010.

Lapide, Pinchas, and Peter Stuhlmacher. *Paul: Rabbi and Apostle*. Translated by L. W. Denef. Minneapolis: Augsburg, 1984.

Lasker, Daniel J. "Anti-Paulinism, Judaism." In *Encyclopedia of the Bible and Its Reception*, edited by H.-J. Klauck et al., 2:284–86. Berlin: de Gruyter, 2009.

———. "The Jewish-Christian Debate in Transition: From the Lands of Ishmael to the Lands of Edom." In *Judaism and Islam: Boundaries, Communications, and Inter-action*, edited by B. H. Hary, J. L. Hayes, and F. Astren, 53–65. Leiden: Brill, 2000.

———. "*Qissat Mujadalat al-Usquf* and *Sefer Nestor Ha-Komer*: The Earliest Arabic and Hebrew Jewish Anti-Christian Polemics." In *Genizah Research after Ninety Years, the Case of Judaeo-Arabic: Papers Read at the Third Congress of the Society for Judaeo-Arabic Studies*, edited by Joshua Blau and S. C. Reif, 112–18. Cambridge: Cambridge University Press, 1992.

Lawson, Kenneth E. "Who Founded Methodism? Wesley's Dependence upon White-field in the Eighteenth-Century English Revival." *Reformation and Revival* 4, no. 3 (Summer 1995): 39–57.

Leary, T. J. "'A Thorn in the Flesh'—2 Corinthians 12:7." *Journal of Theological Studies* 43 (1992): 520–22.

Lebow, Richard Ned. *Forbidden Fruit: Counterfactuals and International Relations*. Princeton: Princeton University Press, 2010.

Legaspi, Michael C. *The Death of Scripture and the Rise of Biblical Studies*. Oxford: Oxford University Press, 2010.

Légasse, Simon. *L'antipaulinisme sectaire au temps des Pères de l'Eglise*. Cahiers de la Revue biblique 47. Paris: Gabalda, 2000.

———. "La légende juive des Apôtres et les rapports judéo-chrétiens dans le haut Moyen Age." *Bulletin de literature écclésiastique* 75 (1974): 99–132.

Leibig, Janis E. "John and 'the Jews': Antisemitism and the Fourth Gospel." *Journal of Ecumenical Studies* 20 (1983): 209–34.

Leirvik, Oddbjørn. "History as a Literary Weapon: The Gospel of Barnabas in Muslim-Christian Polemics." *Studia Theologica* 54 (2001): 4–26.

———. *Images of Jesus Christ in Islam*. 2nd ed. London: Continuum, 2010.

Leopold, David. "The Hegelian Antisemitism of Bruno Bauer." *History of European Ideas* 25 (1999): 179–206.

Lessing, Gotthold Ephraim. "The Religion of Christ." In *Philosophical and Theological Writings*, edited and translated by H. B. Nisbet, 178–79. Cambridge: Cambridge University Press, 2005.

Levenson, Jon D. *Inheriting Abraham: The Legacy of the Patriarch in Judaism, Christianity, and Islam*. Princeton: Princeton University Press, 2012.

Levy, David M. "Malthusianism or Christianity: The Invisibility of Successful Radicalism." *Historical Reflections* 25 (1999): 61–93.

Lewis, David. *Counterfactuals*. Oxford: Blackwell, 1973.

Licona, Michael R. *Paul Meets Muhammad: A Christian-Muslim Debate on the Resurrection*. Grand Rapids: Baker Books, 2006.

Lincicum, David. "F. C. Baur's Place in the Study of Jewish Christianity." In F. S. Jones, *Rediscovery of Jewish Christianity*, 137–66.

Lindemann, Andreas. *Paulus im ältesten Christentum: Das Bild des Apostels und die Rezeption der paulinischen Theologie in der frühchristlichen Literatur bis Marcion*. Beiträge zur historischen Theologie 58. Tübingen: Mohr Siebeck, 1979.

Lindlof, Thomas R. *Hollywood under Siege: Martin Scorsese, the Religious Right, and the Culture Wars*. Lexington: University Press of Kentucky, 2008.

Locke, John. *The Reasonableness of Christianity as Delivered in the Scriptures*. Edited by John C. Higgins-Biddle. Oxford: Clarendon, 1999.

Lopez, Davina C. *The Apostle to the Conquered: Reimagining Paul's Mission*. Minneapolis: Fortress, 2010.

Lopez, Donald S., Jr. *The Scientific Buddha: His Short and Happy Life*. New Haven: Yale University Press, 2012.

Lucci, Diego. "Judaism and the Jews in the British Deists' Attacks on Revealed Religion." *Hebraic Political Studies* 3 (2008): 177–214.

Lüdemann, Gerd. *Opposition to Paul in Jewish Christianity*. Translated by M. Eugene Boring. Minneapolis: Fortress, 1989.

———. *Paul: The Founder of Christianity*. Amherst, NY: Prometheus, 2002.

Lull, David J. "Paul and Empire." *Religious Studies Review* 36 (2010): 251–62.

Luomanen, Petri. "Ebionites and Nazarenes." In Jackson-McCabe, *Jewish Christianity Reconsidered*, 81–118.

Lurbe, Pierre. "John Toland's *Nazarenus* and the Original Plan of Christianity." In F. S. Jones, *Rediscovery of Jewish Christianity*, 45–66.

Maccoby, Hyam. *The Mythmaker: Paul and the Invention of Christianity*. New York: Harper & Row, 1986.

MacDonald, Margaret Y. *The Pauline Churches: A Socio-Historical Study of Institutionalization in the Pauline and Deutero-Pauline Writings*. Society for New Testament Studies Monograph Series 60. Cambridge: Cambridge University Press, 1988.

Machen, J. Gresham. "Jesus and Paul." In *Biblical and Theological Studies*, 547–78. New York: Scribner's Sons, 1912.

———. *The Origin of Paul's Religion*. New York: Macmillan, 1929.

Maggi, Armando. *The Resurrection of the Body: Pier Paolo Pasolini from Saint Paul to Sade*. Chicago: University of Chicago Press, 2009.

Malherbe, Abraham J. *The Letters to the Thessalonians*. Anchor Bible 32B. New York: Doubleday, 2000.

Manning, David. "'That Is Best, Which Was First': Christian Primitivism and the Reformation Church of England, 1548–1722." *Reformation & Renaissance Review* 13 (2011): 153–93.

Marler, Penny Long, and C. Kirk Hadaway. "'Being Religious' or 'Being Spiritual' in America: A Zero-Sum Proposition?" *Journal for the Scientific Study of Religion* 41 (2002): 289–300.

Martin, Clarice J. "The *Haustafeln* (Household Codes) in African American Biblical Interpretation: 'Free Slaves' and 'Subordinate Women.'" In *Stony the Road We Trod: African American Biblical Interpretation*, edited by C. H. Felder, 206–31. Minneapolis: Augsburg Fortress, 1991.

Marx, Karl, and Friedrich Engels. *On Religion*. Moscow: Foreign Languages, 1957.

Mason, David Vaughn. *Brigham Young: Sovereign in America*. London: Routledge, 2015.

Mason, Steve. "Jews, Judeans, Judaizing, Judaism: Problems of Categorization in Ancient History." *Journal for the Study of Judaism* 38 (2007): 457–512.

Masuzawa, Tomoko. *The Invention of World Religions: Or, How European Universalism Was Preserved in the Language of Pluralism*. Chicago: University of Chicago Press, 2005.

Mattingly, Harold B. "The Origin of the Name '*Christiani*.'" *Journal of Theological Studies*, n.s., 9 (1958): 26–37.

Mattox, Mickey L. "Martin Luther's Reception of Paul." In *A Companion to Paul in the Reformation*, edited by R. Ward Holder, 93–128. Brill's Companions to the Christian Tradition 15. Leiden: Brill, 2009.

Maude, Aylmer. *The Life of Tolstoy*. Vol. 2. Oxford: Oxford University Press, 1930.

McClelland, Peter D. *Causal Explanation and Model Building in History, Economics, and the New Economic History*. Ithaca, NY: Cornell University Press, 1975.

McCloskey, D. N. "Counterfactuals." In *The New Palgrave: A Dictionary of Economics*, edited by J. Eatwell, M. Milgate, and P. Newman, 1:701–3. London: Macmillan, 1987.

McDonough, Sheila. "The Muslims in South Asia (1857–1947)." In *Muslim Perceptions of Other Religions: A Historical Survey*, edited by Jacques Waardenburg, 250–62. Oxford: Oxford University Press, 1999.

McKnight, Scot. "Was Paul a Convert?" *Ex Auditu* 25 (2009): 110–32.

McKown, Delos Banning. *Behold the Antichrist: Bentham on Religion*. Amherst, NY: Prometheus, 2004.

McLellan, David. *The Young Hegelians and Karl Marx*. London: Macmillan, 1969.

Medzhibovskaya, Inessa. *Tolstoy and the Religious Culture of His Time: A Biography of a Long Conversion, 1845–1887*. Lanham, MD: Lexington, 2008.

Meeks, Wayne A. "The Christian Proteus." In Meeks and Fitzgerald, *Writings of St. Paul*, 689–94.

Meeks, Wayne A., and John T. Fitzgerald, eds. *The Writings of St. Paul.* 2nd ed. New York: Norton, 2007.

Meissner, Stefan. *Die Heimholung des Ketzers: Studien zur jüdischen Auseinandersetzung mit Paulus.* Wissenschaftliche Untersuchungen zum Neuen Testament 2/87. Tübingen: Mohr Siebeck, 1996.

Mencken, H. L. *Notes on Democracy.* New York: Knopf, 1926.

Merk, O. "Paulus-Forschung, 1936–1985." *Theologische Rundschau* 53 (1988): 1–81.

Meyers, Robin R. *Saving Jesus from the Church: How to Stop Worshipping Christ and Start Following Jesus.* San Francisco: HarperOne, 2009.

Michaels, J. Ramsey. "Paul and John the Baptist: An Odd Couple?" *Tyndale Bulletin* 42, no. 2 (November 1991): 245–60.

Michel, Oskar. *Vorwärts zu Christus! Fort mit Paulus! Deutsche Religion!* 3rd ed. Berlin: Seeman, 1906.

Michener, James. *Legacy.* New York: Random House, 1987.

Middleton, Christopher, ed. and trans. *Selected Letters of Friedrich Nietzsche.* Indianapolis: Hackett, 1996.

Miller, David M. "Ethnicity Comes of Age: An Overview of Twentieth-Century Terms for *Ioudaios.*" *Currents in Biblical Research* 10 (2012): 293–311.

Mitchell, Margaret M. "The Letter of James as a Document of Paulinism?" In *Reading James with New Eyes: Methodological Reassessments of the Letter of James,* edited by Robert L. Webb and John S. Kloppenborg, 75–98. London: Continuum, 2007.

———. *Paul, the Corinthians and the Birth of Christian Hermeneutics.* Cambridge: Cambridge University Press, 2010.

———. "'A Variable and Many-Sorted Man': John Chrysostom's Treatment of Pauline Inconsistency." *Journal of Early Christian Studies* 6, no. 1 (1998): 93–111.

Mitchell, Matthew W. "Reexamining the 'Aborted Apostle': An Exploration of Paul's Self-Description in 1 Corinthians 15.8." *Journal for the Study of the New Testament* 25 (2003): 469–85.

Mitchell, Stephen. *The Gospel according to Jesus: A New Translation and Guide to His Essential Teachings for Believers and Unbelievers.* New York: Harper, 1991.

Monk, Ray. *Ludwig Wittgenstein: The Duty of Genius.* London: Jonathan Cape, 1990.

Montefiore, C. G. *Judaism and St. Paul: Two Essays.* London: Max Goschen, 1914.

Morgan, Robert. "*Sachkritik* in Reception History." *Journal for the Study of the New Testament* 33 (2010): 175–90.

Morgan, Thomas. *The Moral Philosopher.* Vol. 1. London: n.p., 1738.

Muller, Herbert J. *The Uses of the Past: Profiles of Former Societies.* New York: Oxford University Press, 1952.

Müller, Mogens. "Kierkegaard and Eighteenth- and Nineteenth-Century Biblical Scholarship: A Case of Incongruity." In *Kierkegaard and the Bible,* edited by Lee C. Barrett and Jon Stewart, 285–324. Aldershot, UK: Ashgate, 2010.

Mullins, Terrence Y. "Paul's Thorn in the Flesh." *Journal of Biblical Literature* 76 (1957): 299–303.

Mulsow, Martin. "Socinianism, Islam and the Radical Uses of Arabic Scholarship." *Al-Qanṭara* 31 (2010): 549–86.

Murphy, George. "On Counterfactual Propositions." *History and Theory* 9 (1969): 14–38.

Murphy-O'Connor, Jerome. *Jesus and Paul: Parallel Lives*. Collegeville, MN: Liturgical Press, 2007.

Myers, Jason A. "Law, Lies and Letter Writing: An Analysis of Jerome and Augustine on the Antioch Incident (Gal. 2:11–14)." *Scottish Journal of Theology* 66, no. 2 (2013): 127–39.

Nattier, Jan. *Once upon a Future Time: Studies in a Buddhist Prophecy of Decline*. Berkeley: Asian Humanities, 1991.

Nelson-Pallmeyer, Jack. *Jesus against Christianity: Reclaiming the Missing Jesus*. Harrisburg, PA: Trinity, 2001.

Neufeld, K. H. "'Frühkatholizismus'—Idee und Begriff." *Zeitschrift für katholische Theologie* 94 (1972):1–28.

Newman, John Henry. *An Essay on the Development of Christian Doctrine*. London: W. Blanchard and Sons, 1845.

Nickelsburg, George W. E. "An Ἔκτρωμα, Though Appointed from the Womb: Paul's Apostolic Self-Description in 1 Corinthians 15 and Galatians 1." *Harvard Theological Review* 79 (1986): 198–205.

Niebuhr, H. Richard. *The Kingdom of God in America*. New York: Harper, 1937.

Nietzsche, Friedrich. *The Antichrist*. In Kaufmann, *Portable Nietzsche*, 565–656.

———. *The Dawn of Day*. Translated by J. M. Kennedy. London: Allen & Unwin, 1911.

———. *The Will to Power*. Edited by W. Kaufmann. Translated by W. Kaufmann and R. J. Hollingdale. New York: Random House, 1967.

Niose, David. *Nonbeliever Nation: The Rise of Secular Americans*. New York: Palgrave Macmillan, 2012.

Nock, A. D. *Conversion: The Old and the New in Religion from Alexander the Great to Augustine of Hippo*. Oxford: Clarendon, 1933.

Nolan, Daniel. "Why Historians (and Everyone Else) Should Care about Counterfactuals." *Philosophical Studies* 163 (2013): 317–35.

Norich, Anita. *Discovering Exile: Yiddish and Jewish American Culture during the Holocaust*. Stanford, CA: Stanford University Press, 2007.

Novenson, Matthew V. *Christ among the Messiahs: Christ Language in Paul and Messiah Language in Ancient Judaism*. Oxford: Oxford University Press, 2012.

Oakeshott, Michael. *Experience and Its Modes*. Cambridge: Cambridge University Press, 1933.

Ochs, Christoph. *Matthaeus adversus Christianos: The Use of the Gospel of Matthew in Jewish Polemics against the Divinity of Jesus*. Wissenschaftliche Untersuchungen zum Neuen Testament 2/350. Tübingen: Mohr Siebeck, 2013.

O'Collins, Gerald. *Philip Pullman's Jesus*. London: Darton, Longman & Todd, 2010.

O'Connor, Flannery. *Wise Blood*. New York: Harcourt, Brace, 1952.

Omerzu, Heike. "The Portrayal of Paul's Outer Appearance in the *Acts of Paul and Thecla*: Re-Considering the Correspondence between Body and Personality in Ancient Literature." *Religion and Theology* 15 (2008): 252–79.

Onfray, Michel. *Atheist Manifesto: The Case against Christianity, Judaism, and Islam*. Translated by J. Leggatt. New York: Arcade, 2007.

Oppenheimer, Mark. "For Episcopal Church's Leader, a Sermon Leads to More Dissent." *New York Times*, June 22, 2013, A16.

Padover, Saul K., ed. *Thomas Jefferson on Democracy*. New York: New American Library, 1967.

Padovese, Luigi. "L'antipaulinisme chrétien au IIe siècle." *Recherches de science religieuse* 90 (2002–3): 399–422.

Paine, Thomas. *The Age of Reason: Being an Investigation of True and Fabulous Theology*. Paris: Barrois, 1794.

———. *The Age of Reason: Part the Second; Being an Investigation of True and of Fabulous Theology*. London: H. D. Symonds, 1795.

———. "Of the Books of the New Testament." In *The Theological Works of Thomas Paine*, 342–46. London: R. Carlisle, 1824.

Paradkar, Balwant A. M. "Hindu Interpretation of Christ from Vivekananda to Radhakrishnan." *India Journal of Theology* 18 (1969): 65–80.

Parsons, Ernest William. "The Significance of John the Baptist for the Beginnings of Christianity." In *Environmental Factors in Christian History*, edited by J. T. McNeill, M. Spinka, and H. R. Willoughby, 1–17. Chicago: University of Chicago Press, 1939.

Pascal, Blaise. *Pensées and Other Writings*. Translated by Honor Levi. Introduction and Notes by Anthony Levi. Oxford: Oxford University Press, 1995.

Patsch, Hermann. "The Fear of Deutero-Paulinism: The Reception of Friedrich Schleiermacher's 'Critical Open Letter' concerning 1 Timothy." *Journal of Higher Criticism* 6 (1999): 3–31.

Pelikan, Jaroslav. *Mary through the Centuries: Her Place in the History of Culture*. New Haven: Yale University Press, 1996.

Penner, Todd. "The Epistle of James in Current Research." *Currents in Research: Biblical Studies* 7 (1999): 257–308.

Perlmann, Moshe. *Ibn Kammūna's Examination of the Three Faiths: A Thirteenth-Century Essay in the Comparative Study of Religion*. Berkeley: University of California Press, 1971.

Pervo, Richard I. *The Making of Paul: Constructions of the Apostle in Early Christianity*. Minneapolis: Fortress, 2010.

Peters, F. E. *The Children of Abraham: Judaism, Christianity, and Islam*. Princeton: Princeton University Press, 2004.

Peters, Sally. *Bernard Shaw: The Ascent of the Superman*. New Haven: Yale University Press, 1996.

Pfister, Oskar. *Christianity and Fear: A Study in History and in the Psychology and Hygiene of Religion*. Translated by W. H. Johnson. London: Allen & Unwin, 1948.

———. "Die Entwicklung des Apostels Paulus: Eine religionsgeschichtliche und psychologische Skizze." *Imago* 6 (1920): 243–90.

Pfleiderer, Otto. *The Development of Theology in Germany since Kant and Its Progress in Great Britain since 1825*. Translated by J. F. Smith. 2nd ed. London: Swan Sonnenschein, 1893.

Piovanelli, Pierluigi. "Exploring the Ethiopic *Book of the Cock*, An Apocryphal Passion Gospel from Late Antiquity." *Harvard Theological Review* 96 (2003): 427–54.

Popper, Karl R. *The Open Society and Its Enemies*. Vol. 1, *The Spell of Plato*. London: Routledge, 1945.

Pulcini, Theodore. *Exegesis as Polemical Discourse: Ibn Ḥazm on Jewish and Christian Scriptures*. Atlanta: American Academy of Religion, 1998.

Pullman, Philip. "The Dark Side of Narnia." *The Guardian*, October 1, 1998.

———. *The Good Man Jesus and the Scoundrel Christ*. Edinburgh: Canongate, 2010.

Punt, Jeremy. "Postcolonial Approaches: Negotiating Empires, Then and Now." In *Studying Paul's Letters: Contemporary Perspectives and Methods*, edited by Joseph A. Marchal, 191–208. Minneapolis: Fortress, 2012.

Quintilian. *The Institutio Oratoria of Quintilian*. Translated by H. E. Butler. Loeb Classical Library. London: Heinemann; New York: Putnam, 1921–22.

Qutb, Sayyid. *Islam: Religion of the Future*. Kuwait: Holy Koran Publishing House, 1984.

Raboteau, Albert J. *Slave Religion: The "Invisible Institution" in the Antebellum South*. Oxford: Oxford University Press, 1978.

Radhakrishnan, Sarvepalli. *East and West in Religion*. 2nd ed. London: Allen & Unwin, 1949.

———. *East and West: Some Reflections*. London: Allen & Unwin, 1955.

Ragg, Lonsdale, and Laura Ragg. *The Gospel of Barnabas*. Oxford: Clarendon, 1907.

Räisänen, Heikki. *Paul and the Law*. Philadelphia: Fortress, 1983.

Raz, Gil. *The Emergence of Daoism: Creation of Tradition*. London: Routledge, 2012.

Reinach, Salomon. *A Short History of Christianity*. Translated by F. Simmonds. New York: Putnam's, 1922.

Reis, David. "Flip-Flop? John Chrysostom's Polytropic Paul." *Journal of Greco-Roman Christianity and Judaism* 4 (2007): 9–31.

Renan, Ernest. *The Apostles.* New York: G. W. Carleton, 1869.

———. *The Life of Jesus.* Translated by C. E. Wilbour. London: Trübner, 1864.

———. *Saint Paul.* Translated by Ingersoll Lockwood. New York: G. W. Carleton, 1869.

Reventlow, Henning Graf. *The Authority of the Bible and the Rise of the Modern World.* Translated by John Bowden. Philadelphia: Fortress, 1985.

Reynolds, Gabriel Said. *A Muslim Theologian in the Sectarian Milieu: 'Abd al-Jabbār and the "Critique of Christian Origins."* Islamic History and Civilization: Studies and Texts 56. Leiden: Brill, 2004.

Reynolds, Gabriel Said, and Samir Khalil Samir, trans. and eds. *'Abd al-Jabbār, "Critique of Christian Origins": A Parallel English-Arabic Text.* Provo, UT: Brigham Young University Press, 2010.

Richards, Richard A. *The Species Problem: A Philosophical Analysis.* Cambridge: Cambridge University Press, 2010.

Richardson, Peter, and John C. Hurd, eds. *From Jesus to Paul: Studies in Honour of Francis Wright Beare.* Waterloo, ON: Wilfrid Laurier University Press, 1984.

Rivkin, Ellis. "Paul's Jewish Odyssey." *Judaism* 38 (1989): 225–34.

Roberson, Susan L. *Emerson in His Sermons: A Man-Made Self.* Columbia: University of Missouri Press, 1995.

Robertson, Archibald, and Alfred Plummer. *A Critical and Exegetical Commentary on the First Epistle of St. Paul to the Corinthians.* 2nd ed. International Critical Commentary. Edinburgh: T&T Clark, 1914.

Robinson, James M., ed. *The Nag Hammadi Library in English.* 4th rev. ed. Leiden: Brill, 1996.

Rohde, Peter, ed. *The Diary of Søren Kierkegaard.* New York: Citadel, 1960.

Rollmann, Hans. "*Paulus Alienus*: William Wrede on Comparing Jesus and Paul." In Richardson and Hurd, *From Jesus to Paul*, 23–45.

Ronning, Halvor. "Some Jewish Views of Paul." *Judaica* 24 (1968): 82–97.

Roof, Wade Clark. *Spiritual Marketplace: Baby Boomers and the Remaking of American Religion.* Princeton: Princeton University Press, 1999.

Rose, Herbert J., and Antony J. S. Spawforth. "Apollonius of Tyana." In *The Oxford Classical Dictionary*, edited by Simon Hornblower and Antony Spawforth, 128. 3rd ed. Oxford: Oxford University Press, 1999.

Rosenberg, Alfred. *The Myth of the Twentieth Century.* Translated by James Whisker. Sussex: Historical Review, 2004.

Rosenfeld, Gavriel. "Why Do We Ask 'What If?': Reflections on the Function of Alternate History." *History and Theory* 41, no. 4 (2002): 90–103.

Rubenstein, Richard L. *My Brother Paul.* New York: Harper & Row, 1972.

Ruether, Rosemary Radford. *Faith and Fratricide: The Theological Roots of Anti-Semitism.* New York: Seabury, 1974.

———. *Sexism and God-Talk: Toward a Feminist Theology.* Boston: Beacon, 1993.

Ruprecht, Louis A., Jr. *This Tragic Gospel: How John Corrupted the Heart of Christianity.* San Francisco: Jossey-Bass, 2008.

Russell, Norman. *Cyril of Alexandria.* London: Routledge, 2000.

Russell, Walt. "Who Were Paul's Opponents in Galatia?" *Bibliotheca Sacra* 147 (1990): 329–50.

Sade, [Marquis] Donatien-Alphonse-François de. *Dialogue between a Priest and a Dying Man.* Translated by S. Putnam. Chicago: P. Covici, 1927.

Sanders, E. P. *Paul and Palestinian Judaism.* Minneapolis: Fortress, 1977.

———. "Paul's Attitude toward the Jewish People." *Union Seminary Quarterly Review* 33 (1978): 175–87.

Sandys-Wunsch, John, and Laurence Eldredge. "J. P. Gabler and the Distinction between Biblical and Dogmatic Theology: Translation, Commentary, and Discussion of His Originality." *Scottish Journal of Theology* 33 (1980): 133–58.

Sanford, Charles B. *The Religious Life of Thomas Jefferson.* Charlottesville, VA: University Press of Virginia, 1984.

Santaniello, Weaver. *Nietzsche, God, and the Jews: His Critique of Judeo-Christianity in Relation to the Nazi Myth.* Albany: State University of New York Press, 1994.

Sawyer, John F. A. *The Fifth Gospel: Isaiah in the History of Christianity.* Cambridge: Cambridge University Press, 1996.

Schaberg, Jane. *The Resurrection of Mary Magdalene: Legends, Apocrypha, and the Christian Testament.* New York: Continuum, 2002.

Schaberg, Jane, and Melanie Johnson-DeBaufre. *Mary Magdalene Understood.* New York: Continuum, 2006.

Schaefer, Markus. "Paulus, 'Fehlgeburt' oder 'unvernünftiges Kind'? Ein Interpretationsvorschlag zu 1 Kor 15,8." *Zeitschrift für die neutestamentliche Wissenschaft* 85 (1994): 207–17.

Schäfer, Peter, Michael Meerson, and Yaacov Deutsch, eds. *Toledot Yeshu ("The Life Story of Jesus") Revisited: A Princeton Conference.* Texte und Studie zum antiken Judentum 143. Tübingen: Mohr Siebeck, 2011.

Schimmel, Annemarie. *And Muhammad Is His Messenger: The Veneration of the Prophet in Islamic Piety.* Chapel Hill: University of North Carolina Press, 1985.

Schleiermacher, Friedrich D. E. *On Religion: Speeches to Its Cultured Despisers.* Translated by R. Crouter. Cambridge: Cambridge University Press, 1996.

———. *Über den sogenannten ersten Brief des Paulus an den Timotheus: Ein kritisches Sendschreiben an J. C. Gass.* Berlin: Realbuchhandlung, 1807.

Schnackenburg, Rudolf. "Apostles before and during Paul's Times." In *Apostolic History and the Gospel*, edited by W. W. Gasque and R. P. Martin, 287–303. Exeter, UK: Paternoster, 1970.

Schoeps, Hans-Joachim. *Paul: The Theology of the Apostle in the Light of Jewish Religious History*. Translated by H. Knight. London: Lutterworth, 1961.

Schofield, Philip. "Jeremy Bentham: Prophet of Secularism." *Philosophy and Public Issues* 1 (2011): 50–74.

Scholder, Klaus. *The Churches and the Third Reich*. Vol. 1, *Preliminary History and the Time of Illusions, 1918–1934*. Translated by J. Bowden. Philadelphia: Fortress, 1988.

Schüssler Fiorenza, Elisabeth. *In Memory of Her: A Feminist Theological Reconstruction of Christian Origins*. New York: Crossroad, 1983.

———. "Paul and the Politics of Interpretation." in *Paul and Politics: Ekklesia, Israel, Imperium, Interpretation. Essays in Honor of Krister Stendahl*, edited by Richard A. Horsley, 40–57. Harrisburg, PA: Trinity, 2000.

———. *Rhetoric and Ethic: The Politics of Biblical Studies*. Minneapolis: Fortress, 1999.

Schweitzer, Albert. *The Mysticism of Paul the Apostle*. Translated by W. Montgomery. 2nd ed. London: Black, 1931.

———. *Paul and His Interpreters: A Critical History*. Translated by W. Montgomery. London: Black, 1912.

———. *The Quest of the Historical Jesus: A Critical Study of Its Progress from Reimarus to Wrede*. Translated by W. Montgomery. New York: Macmillan, 1961.

Schweizer, Eduard R. *Church Order in the New Testament*. London: SCM, 1961.

Scroggs, Robin. "Paul and the Eschatological Woman." *Journal of the American Academy of Religion* 40 (1972): 283–303.

Seesengood, Robert Paul. *Paul: A Brief History*. Chichester, UK: Wiley-Blackwell, 2010.

Segal, Alan F. *Paul the Convert: The Apostolate and Apostasy of Saul the Pharisee*. New Haven: Yale University Press, 1990.

Sellin, Gerhard. "Die Häretiker des Judasbriefes." *Zeitschrift für die neutestamentliche Wissenschaft* 77 (1986): 206–25.

Seltman, Charles. *Women in Antiquity*. London: Thames & Hudson, 1956.

Shapiro, Gary. "Nietzsche contra Renan." *History and Theory* 21 (1982): 193–222.

Shaw, G. B. "Preface on the Prospects of Christianity." In *Androcles and the Lion*, xiii–cxxvii. New York: Brentano's, 1914.

———. "Preface to *Major Barbara*." In *"John Bull's Other Island" and "Major Barbara,"* 157–200. New York: Brentano's, 1907.

Shaw, Graham. *The Cost of Authority: Manipulation and Freedom in the New Testament*. London: SCM, 1982.

Shedinger, Robert F. *Radically Open: Transcending Religious Identity in an Age of Anxiety*. Eugene, OR: Wipf & Stock, 2012.

———. *Was Jesus a Muslim? Questioning Categories in the Study of Religion*. Minneapolis: Fortress, 2009.

Shoemaker, Stephen J. *The Death of a Prophet: The End of Muhammad's Life and the Beginnings of Islam*. Philadelphia: University of Pennsylvania Press, 2012.

Sider, Ronald J. *Andreas Bodenstein von Karlstadt: The Development of His Thought, 1517–1525*. Studies in Medieval and Reformation Thought 11. Leiden: Brill, 1974.

Sim, David C. "Matthew, Paul and the Origin and Nature of the Gentile Mission: The Great Commission in Matthew 28:16–20 as an Anti-Pauline Tradition." *Hervormde Teologiese Studies* 64 (2008): 377–92.

———. "Matthew's Anti-Paulinism: A Neglected Feature of Matthean Studies." *Hervormde Teologiese Studies* 58 (2002): 767–83.

Simmons, Michael B. "Porphyry of Tyre's Biblical Criticism: A Historical and Theological Appraisal." In *Reading in Christian Communities: Essays on Interpretation in the Early Church*, edited by Charles A. Bobertz and D. Brakke, 90–105. South Bend, IN: University of Notre Dame Press, 2002.

Singer, Peter. *Animal Liberation: A New Ethics for Our Treatment of Animals*. New York: Random House, 1975.

Skinner, Christopher W. "The *Gospel of Thomas*'s Rejection of Paul's Theological Ideas." In *Paul and the Gospels: Christologies, Conflicts, and Convergences*, edited by M. F. Bird and J. Willitts, 220–41. London: T&T Clark, 2011.

Slomp, Jan. "The 'Gospel of Barnabas' in Recent Research." *Islamochristiana* 23 (1997): 81–109.

Smith, Jonathan Z. *Drudgery Divine: On the Comparison of Early Christianities and the Religions of Late Antiquity*. Chicago: University of Chicago Press, 1990.

Smith, Morton. "Palestinian Judaism in the First Century." In *Israel: Its Role in Civilization*, edited by M. Davis, 67–81. New York: Harper, 1956.

Sommerville, C. John. *Religion in the National Agenda: What We Mean by Religious, Spiritual, Secular*. Waco: Baylor University Press, 2009.

Speer, Albert. *Inside the Third Reich*. Translated by Richard and Clara Winston. New York: Simon & Schuster, 1970.

Spong, John Shelby. *Rescuing the Bible from Fundamentalism: A Bishop Rethinks the Meaning of Scripture*. San Francisco: HarperSanFrancisco, 1991.

———. *The Sins of Scripture: Exposing the Bible's Texts of Hate to Reveal the God of Love*. New York: HarperCollins, 2005.

Stambaugh, John E., and David L. Balch. *The New Testament in Its Social Environment*. Library of Early Christianity 2. Philadelphia: Westminster, 1986.

Stanley, Christopher D., ed. *The Colonized Apostle: Paul through Postcolonial Eyes*. Minneapolis: Fortress, 2011.

Stanley, David. "Imitation in Paul's Letters: Its Significance for His Relationship to Jesus and to His Own Christian Foundations." In Richardson and Hurd, *From Jesus to Paul*, 127–41.

Stanton, Elizabeth Cady. *The Women's Bible*. New York: European Publishing, 1895–98. Reprint, Boston: Northeastern University Press, 1993.

Stauffer, Ethelbert. "Zum Kalifat des Jakobus." *Zeitschrift für Religions- und Geistesgeschichte* 4 (1952): 193–214.

Stendahl, Krister. *Paul among Jews and Gentiles, and Other Essays*. Philadelphia: Fortress, 1976.

Stern, Fritz Richard. *The Politics of Cultural Despair: A Study in the Rise of the Germanic Ideology*. Berkeley: University of California Press, 1961.

Stern, S. M. "Abd al-Jabbār's Account of How Christ's Religion Was Falsified by the Adoption of Roman Customs." *Journal of Theological Studies*, n.s., 19 (1968): 128–85.

Still, Todd D. "Did Paul Loathe Manual Labor? Revisiting the Work of Ronald F. Hock on the Apostle's Tentmaking and Social Class." *Journal of Biblical Literature* 125 (2006): 781–95.

Sullivan, Robert E. *John Toland and the Deist Controversy: A Study in Adaptations*. Harvard Historical Studies 101. Cambridge, MA: Harvard University Press, 1982.

Sumney, Jerry L. "Studying Paul's Opponents: Advances and Challenges." In *Paul and His Opponents*, edited by Stanley E. Porter, 7–58. Leiden: Brill, 2005.

Sun, Anna. *Confucianism as a World Religion: Contested Histories and Contemporary Realities*. Princeton: Princeton University Press, 2013.

Swidler, Leonard, Lewis Eron, Gerard S. Sloyan, and Lester Dean. *Bursting the Bonds? A Jewish-Christian Dialogue on Jesus and Paul*. Maryknoll, NY: Orbis, 1990.

Tabor, James D. *The Jesus Dynasty: The Hidden History of Jesus, His Royal Family, and the Birth of Christianity*. New York: Simon & Schuster, 2006.

———. *Paul and Jesus: How the Apostle Transformed Christianity*. New York: Simon & Schuster, 2012.

Talbert, Charles H., ed. *Reimarus: Fragments*. Philadelphia: Fortress, 1970.

Talmage, Frank E. "The Polemical Writings of Profiat Duran." *Immanuel* 13 (1981): 679–84.

Taubes, Jacob. *The Political Theology of Paul*. Translated by D. Hollander. Stanford, CA: Stanford University Press, 2004.

Tetlock, Philip E., and Aaron Belkin, eds. *Counterfactual Thought Experiments in World Politics: Logical, Methodological, and Psychological Perspectives*. Princeton: Princeton University Press, 1996.

Tetlock, Philip E., Richard Ned Lebow, and Geoffrey Parker, eds. *Unmaking the West: "What-If?" Scenarios That Rewrite World History*. Ann Arbor: University of Michigan Press, 2006.

Tetlock, Philip E., and Geoffrey Parker. "Counterfactual Thought Experiments: Why We Can't Live without Them & How We Must Learn to Live with Them." In Tetlock, Lebow, and Parker, *Unmaking the West*, 14–44.

Theissen, Gerd. *Psychological Aspects of Pauline Theology*. Translated by J. P. Galvin. Philadelphia: Fortress, 1987.

Thielman, Frank. *Theology of the New Testament: A Canonical and Synthetic Approach*. Grand Rapids: Zondervan, 2005.

Thomas, David. "The Bible in Early Muslim Anti-Christian Polemic." *Islam and Christian-Muslim Relations* 7 (1996): 29–38.

Thurian, Max. *Mary, Mother of the Lord, Figure of the Church*. Translated by N. B. Cryer. London: Faith, 1963.

Thurman, Howard. *Jesus and the Disinherited*. Nashville: Abingdon, 1949.

Tingay, Kevin. "Madame Blavatsky's Children: Theosophy and Its Heirs." In *Beyond New Age: Exploring Alternative Spiritualities*, edited by S. Sutcliffe and M. Bowman, 37–50. Edinburgh: Edinburgh University Press, 2000.

Tinsley, Barbara Sher. *Pierre Bayle's Reformation: Conscience and Criticism on the Eve of the Enlightenment*. Cranbury, NJ: Susquehanna University Press, 2001.

Toland, John. *Amyntor*. London: n.p., 1699.

———. *Nazarenus; or, Jewish, Gentile, and Mahometan Christianity*. London: J. Brown, J. Roberts, and J. Brotherton, 1718.

Tolstoy, Leo. *Church and State, and Other Essays*. Translated by Victor Yarros. Boston: Benjamin R. Tucker, 1891.

———. *My Religion*. Translated by H. Smith. New York: Thomas Y. Crowell, 1885.

———. *War and Peace*. Translated by L. Maude and A. Maude. New York: Simon & Schuster, 1942.

Toynbee, Arnold. *Some Problems in Greek History*. London: Oxford University Press, 1969.

Trebilco, Paul R. *Self-Designations and Group Identity in the New Testament*. Cambridge: Cambridge University Press, 2012.

Trevor-Roper, Hugh, ed. *Hitler's Secret Conversations, 1941–1944*. New York: Octagon, 1981.

Tuchman, Barbara. *A Distant Mirror: The Calamitous 14th Century*. New York: Ballantine, 1978.

Twain, Mark. *The Bible according to Mark Twain*. Edited by H. G. Baetzhold and J. B. McCullough. New York: Simon & Schuster, 1995.

Tyent, Nōni. "Miriam." In Bishop, *Cross of Centuries*, 29–34.

Urantia Book, The. Chicago: Urantia Foundation, 1955.

Vedder, Henry C. *Socialism and the Ethics of Jesus*. New York: Macmillan, 1912.

Vidal, Gore. *Julian*. New York: Ballantine, 1986.

————. *Live from Golgotha*. New York: Random House, 1992.

Volf, Miroslav. *Allah: A Christian Response*. New York: HarperOne, 2011.

————, ed. *Do We Worship the Same God? Jews, Christians, and Muslims in Dialogue*. Grand Rapids: Eerdmans, 2012.

Volf, Miroslav, Ghazi bin Muhammad, and Melissa Yarrington, eds. *A Common Word: Muslims and Christians on Loving God and Neighbor*. Grand Rapids: Eerdmans, 2010.

Voltaire. *A Philosophical Dictionary*. London: John and Henry L. Hunt, 1824.

Wainwright, Arthur W., ed. *John Locke: A Paraphrase and Notes on the Epistles of St. Paul to the Galatians, Corinthians, Romans, Ephesians*. 2 vols. Oxford: Clarendon, 1987.

Wall, Robert. "Israel and the Gentile Mission in Acts and Paul." In *Witness to the Gospel: The Theology of Acts*, edited by I. H. Marshall and D. Peterson, 437–57. Grand Rapids: Eerdmans, 1998.

Walters, Kerry S. *Revolutionary Deists: Early America's Rational Infidels*. Amherst, NY: Prometheus, 2010.

Wand, J. W. C. *What St. Paul Really Said*. London: Macdonald, 1968.

————. *What St. Paul Said*. London: Oxford University Press, 1952.

Watt, W. Montgomery. *Muslim-Christian Encounters: Perceptions and Misperceptions*. New York: Routledge, 1991.

Webster, David. *Dispirited: How Contemporary Spirituality Makes Us Stupid, Selfish and Unhappy*. Alresford, UK: Zero, 2012.

Wedderburn, A. J. M., ed. *Paul and Jesus: Collected Essays*. Journal for the Study of the New Testament Supplement Series 37. Sheffield: JSOT Press, 1989.

————. "Paul and Jesus: The Problem of Continuity." In Wedderburn, *Paul and Jesus: Collected Essays*, 99–115.

Wehnert, Jürgen. "Antipaulinismus in den Pseudoklementinen." In *Ancient Perspectives on Paul*, edited by Tobias Nicklas, Andreas Merkt, and Joseph Verheyden, 170–90. Göttingen: Vandenhoeck & Ruprecht, 2013.

Wells, H. G. *The Outline of History*. 3rd ed. New York: Macmillan, 1921.

Wenham, David. *Did St. Paul Get Jesus Right? The Gospel according to Paul*. Oxford: Lion, 2010.

————. *Paul: Follower of Jesus or Founder of Christianity?* Grand Rapids: Eerdmans, 1995.

Westerholm, Stephen, ed. *The Blackwell Companion to Paul*. Chichester, UK: Wiley-Blackwell, 2011.

————. *Perspectives Old and New on Paul: The "Lutheran" Paul and His Critics*. Grand Rapids: Eerdmans, 2004.

Westerink, Herman. "The Great Man from Tarsus: Freud on the Apostle Paul." *Psychoanalytic Quarterly* 76 (2007): 217–35.

White, Bouck. *The Call of the Carpenter*. Garden City, NY: Doubleday, Page, 1914.

———. *Letters from Prison*. Boston: Richard G. Badger, 1915.

Whitehead, Alfred North. *Dialogues of Alfred North Whitehead as Recorded by Lucien Price*. Edited by Lucien Price. Boston: Little, Brown and Co., 1954.

———. *Religion in the Making*. Cambridge: Cambridge University Press, 1926.

Wiefel, Wolfgang. "Paulus in jüdischer Sicht." *Judaica* 31 (1975): 109–15, 151–72.

Wiener, Joel H. *Radicalism and Freethought in Nineteenth-Century Britain: The Life of Richard Carlile*. Westport, CT: Greenwood, 1983.

Wiese, Christian. *Challenging Colonial Discourse: Jewish Studies and Protestant Theology in Wilhelmine Germany*. Translated by B. Harshav and C. Wiese. Studies in European Judaism 10. Leiden: Brill, 2005.

Wilcox, Miranda, and John D. Young. *Standing Apart: Mormon Historical Consciousness and the Concept of Apostasy*. New York: Oxford University Press, 2014.

Wilder, Alexander. "Paul, the Founder of Christianity." *The Evolution* 13 (September 1877): 250–53.

Wiles, Maurice F. *The Divine Apostle: The Interpretation of St. Paul's Epistles in the Early Church*. Cambridge: Cambridge University Press, 1967.

Wilken, Robert Louis. *The Christians as the Romans Saw Them*. New Haven: Yale University Press, 1984.

Williams, Delores S. *Sisters in the Wilderness: The Challenge of Womanist God-Talk*. Maryknoll, NY: Orbis, 1993.

Wills, Gary. *What Paul Meant*. New York: Viking, 2006.

———. *Why Priests? A Failed Tradition*. New York: Viking, 2013.

Wilson, A. N. *Paul: The Mind of the Apostle*. New York: Norton, 1997.

Wilson, Barrie. *How Jesus Became a Christian*. New York: St. Martin's, 2008.

Wilson, Colin. *The Occult: A History*. New York: Random House, 1971.

Wilson, S. G. "From Jesus to Paul: The Contours and Consequences of a Debate." In Richardson and Hurd, *From Jesus to Paul*, 1–21.

Wink, Walter. *John the Baptist in the Gospel Tradition*. Society for New Testament Studies Monograph Series 7. Cambridge: Cambridge University Press, 1968.

Winston, Alice. *Apollonius of Tyana, Founder of Christianity*. New York: Vantage, 1954.

Winthrop-Young, Geoffrey. "Fallacies and Thresholds: Notes on the Early Evolution of Alternate History." *Historical Social Research* 34 (2009): 99–117.

Wise, Isaac Mayer. "Paul and the Mystics." In *Three Lectures on the Origin of Christianity*, 53–75. Cincinnati: Bloch, 1883.

Wittgenstein, Ludwig. *Culture and Value*. Translated by P. Winch. Edited by G. H. von Wright. Chicago: University of Chicago Press, 1980.

Wrede, William. *Paul*. Translated by E. Lummis. London: Philip Green, 1907.

Wright, N. T. *What Saint Paul Really Said: Was Paul of Tarsus the Real Founder of Christianity?* Grand Rapids: Eerdmans, 1997.

Wright, Robert. *The Evolution of God.* New York: Little, Brown, 2009.

Wright, Wilmer Cave. *Julian.* Loeb Classical Library. Cambridge, MA: Harvard University Press, 2014.

Yao, Xinzhong. *An Introduction to Confucianism.* Cambridge: Cambridge University Press, 2000.

Yerushalmi, Yosef Hayim. *Freud's Moses: Judaism Terminable and Interminable.* New Haven: Yale University Press, 1991.

Zastoupil, Lynn. "'Notorious and Convicted Mutilators': Rammohun Roy, Thomas Jefferson, and the Bible." *Journal of World History* 20 (2009): 399–434.

Zerbe, Gordon. "The Politics of Paul." In *The Colonized Apostle: Paul through Postcolonial Eyes*, edited by Christopher D. Stanley, 62–73. Minneapolis: Fortress, 2011.

Zetterholm, Magnus. *Approaches to Paul: A Student's Guide to Recent Scholarship.* Minneapolis: Fortress, 2009.

———. *The Formation of Christianity in Antioch: A Social-Scientific Approach to the Separation between Judaism and Christianity.* London: Routledge, 2003.

Zinnbauer, Brian J., Kenneth I. Pargament, Brenda Cole, Mark S. Rye, Eric M. Butter, Timothy G. Belavich, Kathleen M. Hipp, Allie B. Scott, and Jill L. Kadar. "Religion and Spirituality: Unfuzzying the Fuzzy." *Journal for the Scientific Study of Religion* 36 (1997): 549–64.

Zufferey, Nicolas. *To the Origins of Confucianism: The Ru in Pre-Qin Times and during the Early Han Dynasty.* New York: Peter Lang, 2003.

SCRIPTURE AND ANCIENT WRITINGS INDEX

AUTHOR INDEX

Subject Index